PHILADELPHIA FIGHTERS

The Golden Era of Greatness

LEW FREEDMAN

Camino Books, Inc.
Philadelphia

Manufactured in the United States of America

1   2   3   4   17   16   15

Library of Congress Cataloging-in-Publication Data

Freedman, Lew.
  Philadelphia fighters: the golden era of greatness / Lew Freedman.
     pages cm
  ISBN 978-1-933822-65-5 (alk. paper)
  1. Boxing—Pennsylvania—Philadelphia—History. 2. Boxing—New Jersey—Atlantic City—History. 3. Boxers (Sports)—United States—Biography. I. Title.
  GV1125.F74 2014
  796.830974811—dc23   2014026788

ISBN 978-1-933822-65-5
ISBN 978-1-933822-66-2 (ebook)

Cover and interior design: Jerilyn Bockorick
Joe Frazier cover photo courtesy of Joe Hand Sr.

This book is available at a special discount on bulk purchases for promotional, business, and educational use.

Publisher
Camino Books, Inc
P.O. Box 59026
Philadelphia, PA 19102
www.caminobooks.com

CONTENTS

INTRODUCTION

Warriors. That is the word that best describes Philadelphia fighters. They are men with fast fists, hard heads, long reaches and a sense of pride in place. They are boxers with toughness, savvy and dedication to being the best.

Philadelphia was a place where top boxers settled and where great fighters grew up. It was always one of the hotbeds of the sport, and over the decades that reputation solidified. Being a Philadelphia fighter encompassed both geography and a state of mind. Boxing was part of the local culture, and it was part of the local heritage.

Sylvester Stallone's *Rocky* was set in Philadelphia because it made sense. "Yo, Adrian" would never have been a line of dialogue spoken in a film set in any other location. In Philadelphia, boxers grew up dreaming of world titles, but it also meant something to be king of the neighborhood.

Throughout the first half of the 20th century, boxing was one of the most popular sports in the United States, as big as anything in the public mind except baseball. The biggest personalities and the best fighters remained important in the sports world into the 1980s, before society's interests changed and a drop-off in support began.

During those decades, boxers came from everywhere in the country, but always most of the best fighters had their roots in the larger cities. New York staged the big title bouts at Yankee Stadium and Madison Square Garden. It was like an actor performing on Broadway. Fighting for a title in New York meant you had hit the big time.

Always, always, though, Philadelphia helped prepare men for those big nights under the bright lights. Philadelphia had gyms where a beginner could learn his craft. Philadelphia had venues like the Blue Horizon, where a newcomer could gain seasoning. Philadelphia had arenas like the Spectrum, where a more seasoned veteran could headline a few blocks from where he grew up.

More importantly, Philadelphia always had someone willing to organize, plan and promote matches, arrange cards, provide opportunities to feed the fans and guide the boxers. Over the past several decades—a period of great expansion in the boxing game and then a period of great contraction—one man has remained rock steady there in promoting the sport he loves.

J. Russell Peltz, a member of the International Boxing Hall of Fame in Canastota, New York, has been a passionate advocate for Philadelphia boxing, and through times of plenty and times of drought, he has continued to promote fight cards.

Peltz grew up in the Philadelphia suburbs watching TV fights with his father, and while other youths imagined careers as doctors or lawyers, his sole ambition was to become the boxing writer for the Philadelphia *Bulletin*. It was just as well that he didn't, since the *Bulletin* folded in 1980. Instead he turned to promoting and made that his life's work. The first live card Peltz attended was in December 1960, when he saw lightweight Len Matthews fight in Philadelphia. Seeing the sport up close and personal rather than filtered through a television set was even more exciting to the 14-year-old.

"I fell more in love with boxing," Peltz recalled.

Records show that Matthews lost a 10-round decision to Doug Valliant at Convention Hall on December 6th of that year, and it so happened that those were the kinds of evenly matched fights Peltz relished in the coming years.

Len Matthews, who died in 2005, retired from the ring with a record of 42-10-3. As a tribute to Philadelphia boxing, there is an Internet site devoted solely to its history. Matthews is quoted describing himself with these words: "As a child I was quiet, obedient and shy. But I suppose deep inside there was always a lust for battle."

Those two simple sentences probably apply to more than a few fighters who slowly came to discover an inner flame burning that defined their lives and livelihoods more than an innate shyness. Perhaps they were picked on or bullied when young. Perhaps they naturally gravitated to fisticuffs. But over time they learned something essential about themselves and only expressed it fully in a man-to-man sporting encounter.

I grew up in the Boston area, not Philadelphia, and when I was eight or nine, a friend and I were surrounded by a group of bullies outside a semi-pro football game. We were taunted and hit a few times, not badly beaten, but that led to my taking boxing lessons. I was the youngest and the smallest boy in the group, and the lessons didn't last long because my family moved to another city, but I picked up some of the basics.

In 1964, I was on a family trip to Washington, D.C. when I listened on the radio as Muhammad Ali won the heavyweight championship from Sonny Liston. By then I was also subscribing to *The Ring* magazine and learning about Cleveland Williams, Willie Pastrano and Dick Tiger, too.

I was in college when Muhammad Ali was banned from boxing because of his resistance to a different kind of fight, the Vietnam War, and I met him for the first time when he fought an exhibition—he needed the money. It would not be the last time that I crossed paths with the man who is probably the greatest boxer of all time, although never in Philadelphia.

For a time, Ali did live in the Philadelphia area. He had a house in Cherry Hill, New Jersey. In his 61 professional fights, the former heavyweight champion never fought closer to Philadelphia than New York City, nearly 100 miles away. Ali was not a Philadelphia fighter. He was born in Louisville, Kentucky, but he belonged to the world.

The adopted son of Philadelphia was Joe Frazier, the slugger from South Carolina who escaped his boyhood poverty on a farm in Beaufort and won an Olympic gold medal. When he turned pro, Frazier's start was financed by a group of Philadelphia businessmen that formed an association called Cloverlay. Later, when he became successful, Joe Frazier's gym opened on North Broad Street.

In 1979, I was hired by the *Philadelphia Inquirer* as a sportswriter, and part of my job was to take over the boxing beat. One of the first things I thought I should do was to meet Joe Frazier, the biggest name in the sport in town. Although Frazier was retired from the ring, his gym was an important gathering place for fight figures. But I was warned that Frazier might not greet me very warmly as a representative of the *Inquirer*.

Here's why. A sports feature writer, departed by this time, had written somewhat scandalously about Joe's up-and-coming heavyweight son, Marvis. He suggested that an amateur fight featuring Marvis might have been fixed, or that he had won it only because he was Joe's son and the judges wore tinted glasses. This rather reckless statement had eluded the fact-checking eyes of the copy desk, and Joe was making noise about suing the paper.

Just be-bopping up Broad Street and dropping in on Frazier might not be the way to go for me. Some kind of peace offering might be necessary. So I wrote Joe Frazier a letter, introduced myself as the new *Inquirer* boxing writer, and let him know that I considered him to be an icon of the sport, an important fellow on the local boxing landscape, and that I would like to start fresh.

We arranged an appointment at the gym for one late afternoon, and I drove the couple of miles north. I was aware that I had parked in a time-limit space that became illegal at rush hour, but didn't sweat it because I would be gone by then. Only Joe kept me waiting and waiting. I didn't dare go out to move the car for fear of being absent when he was ready to see me.

Eventually, we had a friendly chat, established diplomatic relations, and I exited the gym well into rush hour. Sure enough, my car was gone, towed no doubt to some municipal garage where it was being held hostage for $100. While pondering my next move, someone sidled up and informed me that yes, my car had been towed, but only to a vacant lot a block or so up the street. If you were parked right in front of Joe Frazier's gym, it was assumed that you might be somebody, and apparently as a courtesy to the champ the police didn't automatically whisk your car away to be impounded.

That was the start of my adventures on the boxing beat. I was now tight with Joe Frazier, one of the greatest heavyweight champions of all time. And there were fights scheduled all around me—from the Spectrum downtown to New Jersey and New York—that I could reach in anywhere from minutes to an hour and a half.

It was a grand time to write about boxing. Larry Holmes of Easton, Pennsylvania, ruled the heavyweight ranks. For my purposes, he was a local. South Philadelphia's Jeff Chandler was about to become the bantamweight champion. There was, as always, a tough, wily group of middleweight contenders, from Bennie Briscoe to Cyclone Hart to Bobby Watts to Willie Monroe and Curtis Parker—all of them Philadelphians. Then Frank Fletcher came along.

Matthew Saad Muhammad of Philadelphia, a man whose matches always seemed to carry the dramatic punch of a Eugene O'Neill play, owned a piece of the light-heavyweight crown. So did New Jersey's Mike Rossman. Then Michael Spinks, the Olympic gold-medal winner from St. Louis, won a piece of the title and practically became a fixture at the casinos in Atlantic City. And Dwight Braxton (soon to be Dwight Muhammad Qawi) rose up from South Jersey and captured the light-heavy bauble. That may have been the greatest crop of light-heavyweights to battle at the same time.

We also had Sugar Ray Leonard, Thomas Hearns, Marvin Hagler and Roberto Duran overlapping in the middle divisions with their star power and intense one-on-one competitions, although they rarely appeared in the neighborhood. Hagler was the exception. As the middleweight contender, to establish his legitimacy, he had to plow through the Philadelphia 160-pounders.

The timing of my arrival on the boxing beat for the *Philadelphia Inquirer* also dovetailed with the near-concurrent rise of the sport in Atlantic City. About 60 miles from Philadelphia, Atlantic City had long been the backyard beach for the City of Brotherly Love, the weekend escape hatch for families seeking the surf.

In the late 1970s, Atlantic City borrowed the model for putting on successful boxing cards from Las Vegas. The formula of casinos, high rollers and television bankrolling the shows meant that promoters did not have to rely on a heavy gate from the ticket-buying public. The economics changed. Even Russell Peltz abandoned the Spectrum for the shore. Suddenly, almost all Philadelphia fights and Philadelphia fighters called Atlantic City home. There was no other way to describe it. It was almost as if Atlantic City had been annexed geographically to make it an official part of William Penn's community.

Although the gyms all remained in Philadelphia, boxers, promoters, trainers, cut men and managers made the trek to the shore via the Atlantic City Expressway so often that they wore grooves into the highway. It was almost as if the Philadelphia Eagles or the Philadelphia Phillies were playing their home games overlooking the ocean instead of in South Philadelphia.

Between press conferences announcing future fights, interviews with fighters completing their last-minute training, and the fights themselves, there might be some boxing-related activity of importance to the Philadelphia fight fan going on in Atlantic City five or six times a week. New casinos were opening and they plunged right into the fight business, too. It was as if someone in the marketing department decreed that the front line in the battle for customers was going to be drawn in the ring, the temporary ring set up in a showroom.

Many of the biggest-name fighters in the world came to Atlantic City in the late 1970s and early 1980s on my watch, and most of the undercards were bursting with Philadelphia or South Jersey fighters as well. These were home fights for these boxers. Sometimes there were two homegrown guys in the same bout.

I was fortunate. Many times the best boxers in the world came to me in my home territory. And many of the best boxers in the world were already there because it was their home territory, too. The time period was one of the great golden eras of boxing and I was right in the middle of it.

For a few years, I got to see some of the greats of the sport, Hall of Famers in their prime. I got to see many classic fights. And I got to know many of the men at the peak of their powers and fame. It was a glorious time for Philadelphia and Atlantic City boxing and boxers.

More than 30 years have gone by, and re-connecting with many of those fighters has been special for me. Visiting with them has been like traveling back in time. But several sadnesses were revealed as well. Some have passed away. Some have fallen on hard times. Boxing, as we know, can be a cruel game. Yet many of the former contenders and champs made great memories and while they have gone on with life, they still savor the glory years.

THE PHILADELPHIA FIGHTER

I f they ever build a statue symbolizing the ultimate Philadelphia fighter instead of the fictional Rocky Balboa, the model should be Bennie Briscoe.

Briscoe is gone now. He passed away at the end of 2010 at age 67, and while I saw him fight, I missed his prime by a couple of years. Briscoe was born in Augusta, Georgia in 1943, but he became "Bad Bennie" while growing up and living in Philadelphia.

A five-foot-nine middleweight, Briscoe was a terror of the 160-pound class during an exceptionally long boxing career. He accomplished everything he wanted to except winning the world title. Before boxing cheapened itself with the proliferation of weight classes and with the bizarre expansion of governing authorities, there was only one titleholder for each of eight weight classes.

As a result, many worthy fighters with exceptional skills never held a world crown, when in later years, many who could not have carried their spit buckets did have that distinction. Briscoe was one of the talented fighters who lost out, at least on big paydays, because of the timing of his birth, though he did have his chances.

Bennie Briscoe was an active fighter for parts of 21 years, between 1962 and 1982, and he fought 96 times. His record was 66-24-5 with one no-contest, and he fought for the title three times, but couldn't bring the belt home.

Briscoe refused to shake hands with opposing fighters before the opening bell—maybe because he saw the incongruity of it since seconds later, he was going to be trying to knock the guy's block off. Perhaps it was also to play with his foe's head. There was something about Briscoe that always stood out,

"Bad Bennie" Briscoe (*right*), who wasn't bad at all, but was the ultimate Philadelphia fighter, never won the middleweight crown, but he was one of the most popular of the city's boxers. Here Briscoe takes on Jean Mateo in a 1977 fight. (Photo courtesy of J. Russell Peltz)

whether it was his tenacity or fearlessness, intangibles like that. Plus, he eschewed sitting down on a stool between rounds, seemingly making a statement by forsaking that one minute of rest. It was a good psych-out maneuver. Essentially, Briscoe was telling his opponent that he must be throwing marshmallows since nothing he could do was even tiring him. Another signature when Briscoe fought was wearing a Star of David as an emblem on his shorts as an homage to men of the Jewish faith who helped manage his career and finances.

An outstanding amateur career with a 70-3 mark heralded Bennie Briscoe's glittering pro career. Briscoe's trademarks included a shaved head (making it difficult to tell how old he was), devastating body punching, patience in picking his spots, and a peek-a-boo defense that made him hard to hit. At the same time he hit hard, carrying thunder in his fists that produced 53 knockouts. Briscoe had a fearsome glower that could make an inexperienced opponent shake in his shoes, and he also understood his own punching capabilities. He once explained some of that power: "Anybody I hit has got to go, and if they don't, they'll be fouled up for the rest of their career."

Briscoe harbored a legendary toughness, and it was not only physical. That also applied to his mental state. Unlike many other boxers, he was always willing to fight the best around, and he would go on the road to do so as well. Bennie didn't take matches to pad his record, but to keep his eyes on the prize, always seeking to advance himself in the ratings so that a champion could not ignore or avoid him.

The list of the top fighters on Briscoe's lifetime résumé was astounding. It is a "who's who" of the middleweight division, including champions and those that passed through the class on their way to higher weights.

Bennie Briscoe met Marvin Hagler, Carlos Monzon, Emile Griffith, Vito Antuofermo, Rodrigo Valdez, Eddie Mustafa Muhammad, Billy "Dynamite" Douglas, George Benton, Eugene "Cyclone" Hart, Charley Scott, Richie Bennett, Vinnie Curto, Willie Warren and Tom Bethea. He went to Argentina to face Monzon, and came home with a draw. When they fought again, Monzon took a 15-round decision in defense of the middleweight crown. Briscoe did everything in the sport but win the title.

Those who knew Briscoe considered him both a courageous role model and a stand-up guy. Hall of Fame Philadelphia promoter J. Russell Peltz said he was the most important fighter in his own career, and Nigel Collins, the longtime editor of *The Ring* magazine from Philadelphia, said Briscoe was his favorite fighter. Having those guys testify to your ability and character meant something.

"I wouldn't be where I am without him," Russell Peltz said about Briscoe in 2012, some 40 years into his promoting career. "He was never in a bad fight. He never talked trash. He was durable in the ring and he was a nice guy." So nice, said Collins, that "he gave away everything he had. He was very generous."

To excel as a fighter, a man must have guts and *cojones*, and Briscoe had both. One doesn't have to be a showman who blabs a lot about opponents, and he did not bother with such ancillary activity. "Bennie could still fight all of the young middleweights," Nigel Collins remembered. "Bennie struck a chord with the people of Philadelphia. He was the perfect guy for Philadelphia. He never went Hollywood. You knew when he was fighting it was going to be a real fight."

Stylistically, Briscoe did not dance and run away from his foes in the ring. He was a stalker, the one who made the fight. "Bennie was a naturally rough guy," Collins added. "He'd throw a left hook to the head and slip in an uppercut to the cup. Before and after the fight, he'd never say a bad word about them."

During the 1970s in particular, it was a truism in the fight game that if a middleweight, especially an American middleweight, aspired to hold the 160-pound division title, he had to come through Philadelphia to prove his mettle. If you were going to become the number-one ranked contender, you had to show your worth against the best that Philly offered.

In his prime there was no doubt that Bennie Briscoe was the best of those Philadelphia middleweights. One had to wonder how Briscoe might have fared if his two title bouts with Carlos Monzon took place in the United States, Philadelphia, or really anywhere except Buenos Aires.

Briscoe met Tony Mundine of Australia in February 1974 in a showdown that was important to Bennie's future. At stake was a shot at the world championship against Rodrigo Valdez. Mundine, born in New South Wales in 1951, was much younger than Briscoe and is still regarded as one of the greatest of all Australian fighters.

During his 96-fight career, Mundine won his country's championship as a middleweight, light-heavyweight, cruiserweight and heavyweight, and finished 80-15-1. The Briscoe fight took place in Paris, and Bennie knocked Mundine out in the fifth round. "The highlight of my career was when Briscoe knocked out Tony Mundine in France," Peltz recalled.

He was thrilled for Briscoe and what it meant. In his next bout, Briscoe took on Rodrigo Valdez for the second time. In January 1973, Bennie was out-pointed in 12 rounds by Valdez in New Caledonia. This time he was certain the result would be different, but it wasn't. Valdez scored a technical knockout in the seventh round.

Three years later, Briscoe got a third crack at Valdez and the title, but lost a 15-round decision in Italy. He tried to rebuild his résumé, but although Briscoe fought five more years, until he was 39, he did not get another chance to win the middleweight crown.

Russell Peltz said that Briscoe never made more than $50,000 for a fight during the 13 years he promoted him, but if he had been just a little bit younger when boxing was all over TV during that halcyon Atlantic City era, he would surely have had million-dollar paydays.

Bennie Briscoe added a few more stamps to his passport, fighting in such locales as Belgium and Halifax, Nova Scotia, but most of his fights over the last half-decade of his career took place in Philadelphia, with a smattering of appearances in Atlantic City, New York and Boston.

In the final years of his career, Briscoe was still willing and able to take on up-and-coming fighters who felt ready to meet a big name. When he was matched against "Irish" Teddy Mann, then 18-1, in the fall of 1979, Bennie half-jokingly said the setup was just part of the old boxing trick of mixing ethnic groups to rev up partisan juices. In this case it was black versus white: "Bennie and the white kid. It's got a ring. Sounds like a record. It'll sell. Don't make it sound like I'm being obnoxious or nothin', but a black boy and a white boy sells tickets." More tellingly, Briscoe added that he hardly knew a thing about Mann, but it didn't make any difference in his fight preparation: "Don't know nothin' about him and don't have to. I just do my thing with whoever they put in there." That was about the size of it.

I missed out on young Bennie, but he was still active, still the touchstone for Philadelphia middleweights that hoped to go somewhere with their careers. One by one, he had deflected them over the years, and he was still a formidable challenge for a young man stepping out into the world. It was usually a thankless task going up against a still-dangerous Briscoe with his lifetime of experience, even with the bald wonder past his prime.

On January 24, 1980, Briscoe, then 36, was pitted against an up-and-coming Richie Bennett Jr., who was nicknamed "The Bandit." Bennett did not acquire the nickname by doing John Dillinger imitations or anything shady either. He said that when he was starting out in the career he began at 14, a ring announcer mispronounced his name so that it sounded more like bandit than Bennett.

Bennett was 21. He owned a 21-2-2 record. The fight was the headliner on a local card in Upper Darby, a Philadelphia suburb, and the arena held 1,500 people. This was Richie's hometown, but it wasn't as if Briscoe hadn't played tougher venues in other guys' hometowns like Buenos Aires.

A Bennett victory could do special things for his career. "This is real important to me," he said. "This could be the start of big money. It feels good to be here finally." Bennett's manager, Marty Feldman, believed that his charge would be internationally known if he defeated Briscoe.

Which Bennett did. He won what was announced as a 10-round, unanimous decision by sticking and moving, staying away from Briscoe's power, and piling up points without getting caught by big blows. The judges' point spreads were pretty big: three points, three points, and seven points.

"I thought it could have been judged a little closer," Briscoe recalled. "He's a good, young boy. He's coming up. He beat me fair. I thought I'd win it with the jab." Bennie was smarter than the ring announcer that night. It was learned about a week later that the result was actually a split decision favoring Bennett. The numbers were announced incorrectly, although the decision itself did not change. In the dressing room, Briscoe's head glistened with sweat and he seemed weary. He admitted that he had had an off night.

Bennett was jubilant but respectful of Briscoe's status as a local star: "He's an old Bennie, but he's still good. He's seasoned. He's got wit and brains."

The end of Briscoe's career beckoned. There were many cries for him to retire, and one of those who urged him to do so was Russell Peltz. That was a hard message to deliver, and Briscoe didn't like it one bit. Still, fight fans had to wonder if Briscoe would call it quits after this loss. But he didn't. Instead, there was a rematch, also scheduled for 10 rounds, this time at Martin Luther King Arena in Philadelphia.

During his long career, middleweight Bennie Briscoe (*left*) fought everyone around, including George Benton, the Philadelphia contender who later became a Hall of Fame trainer. (Photo courtesy of J. Russell Peltz)

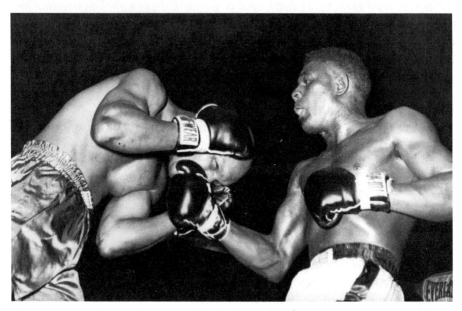

Upbeat after besting Briscoe, Richie Bennett's career took a surprise turn a few months later when he lost to a lesser competitor, Skipper Jones, and then had to be hospitalized with a hairline fracture of his jaw. Bennett was not even sure when he incurred the injury, but he was set back by the combination of the fracture and the fight loss. So he had to rebuild, and he accepted a $5,000 purse to meet Briscoe again.

The rematch went off on the night of August 24, 1980. By then Bennie Briscoe had celebrated another birthday and was 37. Proving that he was still popular with the fans, attendance was 3,500. And proving that he still had the know-how to deal with a young fighter, Briscoe scored a split decision. The foes completed 20 rounds of boxing with no knockdowns and few seriously telling blows, but this time Bennie drew blood from Bennett's nose twice, in the second and sixth rounds.

It was Bennett who appeared sluggish and slower, not the older man, and Briscoe out-boxed him: "There were times I felt frustrated and tired. I'm glad I got the win."

As it so happened, it was one of the last wins of Briscoe's career. He maintained that he was in much better shape than his age indicated because he ran 10 miles a day, and the December 1980 issue of *Boxing Illustrated* printed a feature on him, marveling that Briscoe was still a top gun in the middleweight division. "I ain't through yet," he declared.

Briscoe fought six more times, against the wishes of Russell Peltz, at whom he became angry for trying to talk him into retirement. His last victory was recorded on March 23, 1982 in Atlantic City when Briscoe topped Norberto Sabater, 24, of Brooklyn. Referee Frank Cappuccino would not let Sabater out of his corner to start the sixth round in the scheduled 10-rounder because of an eye injury.

I was at ringside for Briscoe's final triumph, and he dominated the bout. He pressured Sabater, knocked him into the ropes, landed the better punches, and his contact created red marks on his foe's face and began closing his left eye. Sabater's lack of maneuverability played into Briscoe's game plan.

Once again after notching still another win in his long career, Briscoe took issue with critics who had suggested he retire. "I knew I wasn't through," he commented.

And he wasn't for the time being, but even Bennie was starting to form the belief that retirement was on the horizon. After the Sabater win, Briscoe fought twice more, losing both 10-round bouts by decision. He hung up his gloves after losing a 10-round unanimous decision to Jimmie Sykes on December 15, 1982.

The location of Briscoe's last fight was appropriate. The bout took place at the Blue Horizon, the legendary fight club in Philadelphia that was the scene of so many special local bouts.

And what became of Richie Bennett? He did not fight much longer, retiring with a 25-6-2 record, and he was only 32 when he died. In March 1991, the Philadelphia Medical Examiner said that Bennett died of "an adverse reaction to drugs." It was a tragic ending to a career and a life that held great promise.

Bennie Briscoe retired from boxing in 1982, but in 2007, Philadelphia boxing historian John DiSanto revived interest in his name in conjunction with the local chapter of the Ring One Veterans Boxing Association. Each year the group presents the Briscoe Award, a sculpture of Bennie, to the best Philadelphia fighter and to the two combatants who competed in the best fight of the year.

DiSanto said he chose Briscoe as the symbol of the awards because other great Philadelphia fighters had won championships or were inducted into the Hall of Fame, while he felt Briscoe's legacy was being neglected and he deserved more attention. He created the Philadelphia Boxing History website and acts more or less as a consultant to Ring One. In addition, DiSanto is active in recommending candidates for the Pennsylvania Boxing Hall of Fame. He likes to think that he serves as a link between the underappreciated fighter and those who should honor him. To many, Briscoe is one of the best fighters of all time who never won a title. DiSanto believes strongly that it is important to keep Bennie Briscoe's name alive, and his image on the award helps in that effort.

When Briscoe died on December 28, 2010, leaving a wife and three children, Nigel Collins wrote a glowing tribute to the fighter he so admired in *The Ring* magazine's April 2011 issue.

"I can still see him in my mind's eye," Collins' story began, "his trademark shaven head shining in the lights as he jogged down the aisle to the ring, the crowd cheering him every step of the way. The anticipation was palpable. You knew if Bennie Briscoe was on the card you were going to see a real fight. Somebody was going to get hurt."

Philadelphia is known as a demanding sports town. Nationwide it is remembered as the town that booed Santa Claus and that is always hard on its football team. Bennie Briscoe might have lost fights as he aged, but he was never booed. His effort never shorted the paying customer.

"Briscoe's utter lack of pretension juxtaposed against his fearsome ring persona were a perfect match for a shot-and-beer city like Philadelphia," Collins wrote. "Briscoe was a genuine badass, but a badass with a generous heart for everybody except the guy in the other corner."

Briscoe's funeral brought out the names of the Philadelphia boxing world on a cold January day about two weeks after his death following a long illness. Joe Frazier, Bobby Watts, Cyclone Hart, Willie Monroe, Stanley "Kitten" Hayward, Eddie Mustafa Muhammad and others came to pay their respects. Many of those men were middleweights who felt the sting of Briscoe's blows, but they came nonetheless to honor the man.

At the funeral, Briscoe's brother, Archie Glenn, said that Bennie was as generous a man as they came, sensitive to those less fortunate than he was: "If Briscoe had a million dollars he wouldn't have a dime. He would give it all away. He knew what it was like to be hungry."

More than a year had passed since the funeral when I had lunch with Collins, and he told me about sitting down to tackle the Bennie Briscoe farewell story.

"I was crying as I wrote it," he confided.

SMOKIN' JOE FRAZIER

Boxing is sport as war, without the determination to kill, maim or capture territory. It is a challenging, brutal and demanding sport, but when two great practitioners of the "sweet science" are matched, they can steal the breath from a crowd and make memories that endure for lifetimes.

It is said that the true measure of greatness is the confrontation with an equal, not simply dominance over the weaker. And while Muhammad Ali and Joe Frazier would have been regarded as all-time greats whenever they inhabited the heavyweight division, their time was the same time and their head-to-head battles defined an age of boxing.

They also became a metaphor for great sporting clashes, as in saying that a football game was an Ali-Frazier fight. Ali-Frazier became a synonym for classic meetings in sport. The men were each other's foil, and their incredible skill and will to win on display three times can without hyperbole be termed the greatest individual rivalry in the history of sport.

Circumstances allowed both men to become heavyweight champions, both after representing the United States and winning gold in the Olympics. Ali won the title first, but then was suspended from the game because he declared himself a conscientious objector and refused to accept induction into the Army. He was the champion of the young fans who loved his braggadocio, jokes, poetry and swift fists.

When Muhammad Ali was tossed out of the sport temporarily as he took his case against military service to the Supreme Court, Joe Frazier stepped in and won the title. A good man with a big heart, Frazier brought a deep-seated ferocity to the ring, and his fists were sledgehammers capable of beating down anything in his way. The Frazier trademark was a left hook that gave opponents indigestion when it struck their stomachs. It was as important to Frazier's arsenal as the hook shot was to Kareem Abdul-Jabbar. When he was at his best, Joe was very difficult to hit. His defensive style, bobbing and weaving, protected him from opponents' biggest shots.

Ali had movement and style in his favor. Frazier had power and pride in his when they first fought on March 8, 1971 in New York City. Frazier, proving his fill-in as champion was far more than that, won a 15-round decision. He walked out of the ring still in possession of the heavyweight crown, one of the most valuable properties in sport. The two met a second time in January 1974 when neither was champion. George Foreman had lifted Frazier's title. Ali won this time in a 12-round decision. Their third fight, "The Thrilla in Manila," came in 1975 after Ali improbably regained the crown from Foreman.

In the 14th round, with Ali pouring it on, Frazier's trainer, Eddie Futch, refused to let his man go out and take more punishment for the sake of going the 15-round distance. The fight propelled the series into boxing lore and also sent both men to the hospital because their equality in the ring was almost too much for their bodies to take. The three-fight series ensured that when Ali and Frazier retired, they both departed the sport as legends.

He may have been born in South Carolina, but Joe Frazier built his legend in Philadelphia, raised his children in Philadelphia, and opened his gym in Philadelphia. Frazier was 32-3 after losing to Ali the second time and did not believe he was through as a contender. He was just shy of his 31st birthday.

Joe Frazier lost his title to young George Foreman in Jamaica and was knocked down six times. Foreman was much bigger, with a longer reach, and the comparatively stationary Frazier could not cope with Foreman's explosive punches. After recovering from the last title bout with Ali, Frazier engaged in a rematch with Foreman in June 1976, but that didn't go well, either.

By the time I had my car towed from in front of Joe's gym, he was nurturing son Marvis' impending move from amateur to the pro ranks. He also kept busy playing nightclub dates as the front-man singer for a group billed as "Joe Frazier and The Knockouts." People came to listen, but not many critics were kind. Frazier had other businesses going, including a limousine service and a barbeque restaurant, and he acted in beer commercials.

Thus I was startled when an interview session back at the gym (this time legally parked) in January 1981 turned into an announcement of an impending Joe Frazier comeback to the ring. It was a couple of days before Frazier's 37th birthday, and although four and a half years had passed since he last threw a punch in anger (or better put, for pay), Joe thought he was in fine shape, needing to lose just 10 pounds from the 235 he weighed. Also, studious attention to the top-10 heavyweight rankings convinced him that there was no one around who could prevent him from earning a title shot against World Boxing Council champ Larry Holmes or World Boxing Association champ Mike Weaver.

"Who out there can beat me?" Frazier declared, a firm look of confidence on his face. "Nobody. I am the best in the business. There ain't nobody out there who can hold their head up and say, 'I'm the champion.' There's nobody walking proud."

Larry Holmes, for one, would have disputed that. Only a couple of months earlier, he had put the same foolish intentions of a comeback for Muhammad Ali to rest with a thorough beating in Las Vegas. Ali looked as if he was in shape, but Holmes was younger and stronger and simply overwhelmed him. Mike Weaver was less dangerous, but at Frazier's age, after all that layoff time, anybody would be dangerous.

It takes phenomenally single-minded focus to whip a body into top, firm shape for a high-level boxing match. Running long distances, sparring many rounds, belting that heavy bag for long periods of time, all are required. Almost all boxing comebacks end badly, fueled by too much bravado and too little training. Frazier insisted he had never been out of shape: "I ain't never left. I've been in the gym from the time I retired. I've run on the road with my music group."

Being in the gym training other fighters is not the same as being in the gym training oneself. This appeared to be an ill-advised quest, but it was the job of his wife, Florence, his children and his close personal friends to get that message across to Frazier, not the sporting media.

Joe had a simple game plan in mind. Clearly, he would be trading upon his good name to get a bout with someone in the top 10. It didn't matter much to him who it was, though he kind of liked the notion of fighting Leon Spinks, who for an eye-blink of six months in 1978 had borrowed the heavyweight crown from Ali in one of boxing's greatest upsets before returning it to him in a rematch defeat.

The way Frazier saw it, he would beat one guy in the top 10 and then get a title shot against either Holmes or Weaver, beat one of them, remind the world of his greatness and then retire again—two fights and out.

"There are too many champions," Frazier stated. "I want to show them I can beat them and I'm still the best."

Frazier was never a theoretical philosopher. When he said something, he meant it. So despite the caveat that he needed his five daughters' permission to go ahead with this plan, he sounded serious.

At some point during these public ruminations about his comeback, an 8-by-10 folder that appeared to be the beginning of the campaign to promote Frazier's return came into my hands. More than 30 years later, I still have it. The

A fight poster advertising Smokin' Joe Frazier's bout with Jerry Quarry.
(Photo by Lew Freedman)

front cover of the four-page foldout featured a nice sketch of Frazier's head, as if he was modeling for a bust, and a glove-encased fist. It was accompanied by the words: "The Fire Is Back in the Heavyweight Division Now...watch out for the smoke. Smokin' Joe Frazier, Comeback '81." The other three pages of the handout were blank, waiting to be filled in with information about Frazier's comeback fight.

Just six weeks later, I was back in Frazier's office in his gym, listening to him say that he had shelved the entire comeback idea. His family had given him the OK. That wasn't the problem. He didn't really need the money (although he would have liked to get more). That wasn't the issue. But Marvis was 2-0 and back in action after an injury layoff, and he needed his father's help with training. Likewise, the other raw boxers working out in the gym also needed him. He couldn't abandon them: "My boys, I can't leave them alone. I don't know nobody in the world who can do my job. I've got a gym full of guys and they need me."

Eddie Futch, Frazier's longtime trainer, was credited in the third Ali-Frazier bout for having the resolve to stop the fight because he worried about Joe's overall health if it continued even for one more round. He did not wish to see an older and slower Frazier come out of retirement and risk his well-being. "Joe was a great fighter," Futch admitted. "He left a legacy to the boxing world of fine performance. I would hate to see him go in there as a shadow of himself and destroy that image."

That was the end of that—we thought. Likely the right decision—we thought. Let Joe teach his son and a younger generation the finer points of the fight game.

Some months later, I was given a tip that seemed almost too stunning to believe. There had been a plan afoot for a fourth Ali-Frazier fight, the two old-timers meeting for another fight in their epic series in Atlantic City during the summer of 1981. The talks had gone beyond the loose discussion stage and a venue was selected—the Playboy Hotel & Casino. Ali had fought in Las Vegas in October 1980, and although he went into the ring at Caesars Palace at a trim 218 pounds, he was easily dispatched by Larry Holmes in a title fight. Frazier had been talking comeback since January. Presumably, those two circumstances had sparked in someone's brain the idea that they should get together one more time for something beyond coffee and cake.

An Ali legal representative approached the New Jersey State Athletic Commission and chairman Jersey Joe Walcott, a former heavyweight champ, and his deputy, Robert W. Lee, discussed the matter. They wrote a letter to Ali in care of his associates and listed pre-fight conditions that had to be fulfilled because both men were more than 35 years of age.

The letter laid out a plan for a New Jersey license. Both Ali and Frazier were required to journey to Trenton and pass a detailed physical examination. Then they would have to engage in an exhibition of at least six rounds while wearing heavier-than-usual 12-ounce gloves. Then it would be up to Walcott to determine if they should be licensed. The back-and-forth communication took place in the spring, but there was no follow-up and the plan evaporated.

Such a match-up between the two old adversaries would have been a shocking development. By the time I heard about these discussions and reported them in the *Philadelphia Inquirer*, the idea was dead. Muhammad Ali had not officially gone back into retirement, however, and did fight one more time in December 1981, losing to Trevor Berbick in the Bahamas. That was his last hurrah.

Despite Joe Frazier's February proclamation, the itch to fight again had wormed itself under his skin, and while he pretended he had no need to scratch it, before the year was out, Frazier escalated his comeback from talk to reality. He too would fight in December, although not against Ali and not in the Bahamas. Once again the two protagonists were on parallel trails, but I never again heard a whisper that any additional talks took place to arrange that fourth fight.

Frazier dug up an opponent, found a venue and three weeks before Christmas 1981, my Philadelphia colleagues and I were in Chicago to witness the boxing comeback of one of the legends of the sport. Joe Frazier, now only a month shy of his 38th birthday, couldn't talk himself out of finding what he had left.

Frazier was the youngest of 13 children on the 50-acre farm in Beaufort, South Carolina tilled by his father, Rubin. For some reason, when he was born, his dad declared that "this will be my famous son." Rubin died in 1965 without knowing just how true his words would prove. Joe Frazier still had the fame, and he did not need this notoriety at a comparatively advanced boxing age—at least that's what everyone said out loud. But apparently he did or he wouldn't have committed to this highly suspect errand of a scheduled 10-round fight at the Chicago International Amphitheatre.

If Frazier had expected the boxing world to welcome him back after almost five years of inactivity by throwing big money at him, he guessed wrong. There were millions of dollars to be had in the fight game at that time, but his share of the purse for the comeback bout was $85,000, plus $15,000 in training expenses. That was recompense for his name because other fighters not competing for championships were being paid much less, even if they headlined a card.

Frazier was not going up against Leon Spinks, as he had hoped some months earlier, and he was not going up against any ranked fighter. His opponent was Floyd "Jumbo" Cummings, a heavyweight with a 17-1 record who was originally from Mississippi, but whose home address in recent years had been a variety of Illinois institutions specializing in incarceration.

A couple of days before the fight, Frazier met the press on a cold Chicago afternoon, and his give-and-take was lighthearted. Inevitably, he was asked if he was fighting because he needed the money, often the root cause of boxing comebacks. He didn't say yes and he didn't really say no, although his old connection to Cloverlay, his original backers, meant that he was paid $70,000 a year out of a trust fund.

"I always need money," Frazier remarked as he toweled sweat from his brow. "I love money. I love to spend money, to party." It was not clear just what to take from that comment, but spending any time talking to Joe about this adventure made it seem too simplistic to conclude that it was only about the money.

Maybe Frazier believed he had retired too early. Maybe he truly believed he could whip any man in the house, or in the rankings themselves. "I found out I had something left," Joe reflected at one point. He had to learn that piece of information in the gym, when he was working with the boys. "I've been training, running, going to bed early, staying away from the partying. Believe me, that's a hard job."

There was plenty of skepticism about just what kind of shape Frazier kept himself in while training others in the gym, but Marvis spoke up for him, announcing that not only did the family support his dad, but that his dad still packed a pretty good wallop. "He's taking it and dishing it out," the younger Frazier said of the action at his father's gym.

Joe Frazier's comment about resisting the party life drew laughs from the assembled crowd. Everyone wished him well. They doubted that his comeback would go very far. He was never a big heavyweight, though very muscular and sturdily built, standing five-feet-eleven. For Frazier's first fight against Muhammad Ali, he weighed 205 pounds. But heavyweights were not only younger, they were getting bigger.

Floyd Cummings was nearly six-feet-three and weighed in at 228 pounds. His biceps bulged, mostly from weightlifting during 12 years at the Joliet penitentiary, not from picking cotton as a youth in Getback, Mississippi. Cummings was 30, but at age 16, he drove the getaway car in a robbery which left one person killed, and he was originally sentenced to at least 50 years in prison. Floyd pumped so much iron behind bars that he bulked up to 275 pounds and gained the nickname "Jumbo the Elephant." Losing pounds reduced the nickname to just Jumbo.

Cummings was a surprise attendee at one of Joe Frazier's workouts, and he looked dashing in a cowboy hat and a red-and-white jacket that had the words "Believe It" scrolled on the sleeves. Cummings tapped Frazier in the mid-section and told him he was soft. Frazier just chuckled and thanked him for fighting an old man when other boxers wouldn't sign to face him. "I'll remember you in my will," Joe promised.

Frazier weighed in at 229 pounds, the most of his career, and that number may have served as confirmation that he was a bit soft around the mid-section. Indeed, once the contest began, the once-firm belly of Frazier did some jiggling as he boxed.

Neither man moved around the ring very quickly. Both plodding heavy-weights, the fighters actually resembled elephants, not merely the aptly named Jumbo. There was little speed in their movement, but there was sting in their punches. It was not surprising to see Frazier unload his favorite left hook with abandon and stagger the larger Cummings with it on occasion. It was more surprising to see Cummings draw blood from Frazier's mouth and for the for-mer champ's left eye to be nearly closed by punches.

What both men lacked was the precision timing they needed to take control of the fight. It was more alarming in Frazier's case, though it should not have caught too many of the 6,500 observers in attendance off-guard. He was rusty after being away from the ring so long, despite his protestations of maintaining his crispness in the gym. And as the eighth round passed, it appeared as if age had caught up to Frazier, too. He was definitely slowing.

The bout went the distance and ended in a draw. The judges' scores were very close, and each man believed he should have been declared the winner. "I thought I won the decision," Frazier recalled.

Joe was ahead early on, for sure, but he probably lost that edge in the eighth. Still, there were times when he was smiling in the ring and seemed to enjoy him-self. He was back in his element. Frazier began almost every round by trying to land a roundhouse hook on Cummings' head. He got some of them in, but didn't score much with the big swings. When they went toe-to-toe, however, the old hook did some damage to the body, and the short shots connected to Cum-mings' head.

But the eighth round changed the picture. It certainly had to seem like more than three minutes long to Frazier. That was the dominant round for Cummings, who backed Joe up along the ropes with several shots to the head and then trapped him in a neutral corner and unleashed 15 straight blows. The fight was close enough that any result would have been hard to protest. On my unofficial scorecard, I had Cummings ahead by one point, a direct result of a generous two-point spread in the eighth. If not for that, I too would have called it a draw.

In my heart, I wanted to see Joe Frazier win. I knew him and I didn't know Floyd Cummings. I knew of his legend and place in boxing history, and although I didn't think the smart move was to return to the ring after such a long layoff, I didn't want him to be defeated or embarrassed.

Somehow the draw seemed an appropriate result. Cummings could always say that he went the distance with the great Joe Frazier. He later lost to such well-known heavyweights as Frank Bruno, Mitch Green, Renaldo Snipes and Tim Witherspoon. Although Floyd Cummings' record was said to be 17-1 when he met Frazier, other sources give his lifetime boxing mark as 15-6-1. Worse for him, in 2002, he went back to prison. He was sentenced to serve a life term for armed robbery.

In the immediate aftermath of the fight, Frazier seemed reasonably content with the draw. He felt he had shown something by withstanding Cummings' pressure in the eighth round without being knocked down, and he could see losing some weight and taking another fight over the coming months. In his mind, the comeback was still on.

A day after the bout, Frazier's face was not an advertisement for skin cream. He had facial lumps and wore dark glasses to cover the swelling. But he dismissed his aches, saying, "I didn't get hurt. Bumps and bruises, so what? Everything I wanted to do, I did out there." Maybe, maybe not, since he didn't win and he didn't stop Cummings.

There were plenty of critics around who seemed likely to have a private moment or two with Frazier and tell him to give it up. Florence, his wife, only ventured a "No comment" on his showing, which was not a strong endorsement.

Butch Lewis, a boxing promoter and a close friend of Frazier's, offered a wise assessment: "I came because I love him. He has been a special individual to a lot of people in the world. But if everyone saw with their own eyes what I saw, we could say, 'Joe, you proved your point. Now let's quit while we're ahead.'"

It was Lewis who said that the one person Joe Frazier might listen to with advice about terminating his comeback was Marvis. I don't know if such a conversation ever took place, but the months came and went and there was no more discussion about another Joe Frazier fight; there were no summonses to the gym to talk about Joe's next opponent or about a fourth fight with Ali. The topic faded away, and the Frazier who increased the pace of his fight schedule was Marvis.

Joe Frazier had too much pride to say that he was over the hill. He was too proud to admit that he was too old to wage a fresh campaign to regain the heavyweight championship. He did not possess the kind of self-deprecating humor that would allow him to call a press conference, make fun of the erosion of the skills that made him world-famous, and pull off a retirement show.

Instead, he just stopped talking about fighting again. Months passed. Years passed. The official Joe Frazier boxing slate remained stagnant, the final bout on his record a 10-round draw against "Jumbo" Cummings in 1981.

I was glad that I had seen Frazier fight in person, although I knew I was not seeing the genuine model. But it was fun to be around him when he was thinking those grand thoughts all over again. And Joe Frazier remained on the scene, front and center with Marvis at all of his fights as a cornerman, so it wasn't as if he went into seclusion.

We could still visit Joe at his gym, still see him at ringside. The Philadelphia legend was still in the game.

THE PROMOTER

J. Russell Peltz was driving back to Philadelphia with his wife, Linda, from the Foxwoods Casino in Connecticut the morning after a fight card when the phone call came. Peltz was on the ballot for the International Boxing Hall of Fame in Canastota, New York for the third year, and he was aware that nominees for the June 2004 induction ceremony were scheduled to be notified soon.

Peltz was driving along the highway between 10 and 11 a.m. when his cell phone buzzed: "I knew this was the week we were going to find out whether or not we made it. My heart started pumping and I thought, 'Here we go.'" The caller, Hall of Fame director Ed Brophy, began by saying that he was sorry to bother Peltz on a Sunday morning, but it was his job to notify him of the IBHF's decision.

"You have been chosen for the International Boxing Hall of Fame," Brophy announced. "I started shaking," Peltz recalled. "I was crying." He held the phone in the air and his wife looked at him in alarm and asked, "What's wrong?"

Nothing was wrong, of course. Things were just great. But Peltz was so overcome that he lost the thread of the conversation as Brophy kept talking. He passed the phone to Linda.

That call was one of the greatest moments of his life: "You have been handed the Holy Grail. It doesn't get any better than that. It was the right time. And when you go there that weekend, they treat you like a rock star."

Russell Peltz had every reason to be overjoyed and grateful. In many ways, his selection was a blow struck for the little guy. Although he was the king of Philadelphia boxing promoters and had been for ages, at the same time he was the king of the small boxing show, the club fight and the grassroots fights.

Promoter J. Russell Peltz has invested more than 40 years in promoting Philadelphia boxing and earned a spot in the International Boxing Hall of Fame in Canastota, New York. (Photo courtesy of J. Russell Peltz)

It is true that Peltz promoted at big houses like the Spectrum, where the Philadelphia 76ers and the Philadelphia Flyers played their games. And he also promoted world title fights. But in an era when Don King and Bob Arum were the majordomos of the fight game, the promotional royalty that amassed fabulous wealth and fame by handling the biggest-name fighters and promoting their bouts in Las Vegas and around the world, Russell Peltz held fast to his corner of the boxing universe—Philadelphia, Atlantic City and the surrounding area. That was his territory. He didn't try to slug it out with the deep-pocket players, although at various times others did.

Maybe Peltz would have become a big name on the international scene, and maybe he would have been crushed by the ruthlessness inherent in the game. Instead, he outlasted everyone else by plying his home area and by sticking to a philosophy of providing good, even bouts to the public. Certainly, there were going to be favored fighters who were groomed for great things. But Russell started his love affair with boxing as a fan, and he never lost that outlook. He organized matches that he wanted to see, not matches that were really mismatches to protect one fighter's career.

It was Peltz's good fortune that he was born and grew up in and around a city that revered boxing, one of the best fight communities in the world. He could make a living there, carving out a career through Peltz Boxing Productions, Inc. He may have made deals with the devil to survive because boxing is like that, and something always happens to alter the view through rose-colored glasses. I can't speak to that because I don't know anything about it.

Certainly, some fighter might be found who doesn't believe Russell Peltz gave him a fair shake, but who knows how such an allegation would be handled by a court of arbitration? Boxing is a hard game and there are treacherous trails that lead to dead ends and disappointments. Often compromises are made. To me, it looks as if Peltz is the last man standing, someone who rode the up-and-down waves of the sport over the last 40 years and is still promoting his cards for the masses, trying to give them a good show.

Russell was quite young when he was introduced to the glamour and excitement of big-time boxing, and he was not someone who wanted to grow up and be a policeman, a fireman, or even a doctor or a lawyer. He decided that he wanted to be a fighter. He signed up for boxing lessons, even though it was tricky to schedule them around Hebrew school, and he decided that it was his destiny to become the lightweight champion of the world. Given that Peltz grew to be six feet tall and his walking-around weight far exceeded the division's 135-pound threshold, it was just as well that he let go of that aspiration. However, as a 13-year-old, he did fight an opponent to a draw that earned him a medal, even though his long-term prospects seemed limited.

"It wasn't a good profession for kids from the suburbs," Peltz admitted with a light laugh. "I came to the realization it wasn't going to happen."

Now past 65, Russell Peltz began watching boxing on television with his father, Bernard, in their home in the Philadelphia suburb of Bala Cynwood around 1960. He said that his dad (who must have been hard to please) referred to every fighter he watched as "a ham-and-egger." He meant the guy was a bum. Peltz was more readily impressed by some of the notable fighters of the day and remembers watching fabled heavyweight Cleveland Williams and Gene Fullmer, a onetime world champion middleweight, and becoming fans of theirs. Harold Johnson, who was from nearby Manayunk and had the nickname "Hercules" even before becoming the light-heavyweight champion of the world, was Peltz's real boyhood idol.

Once it became obvious that his future did not revolve around the lightweight class, Russell modified his ambition. He aimed for the job of boxing writer for the Philadelphia *Bulletin*. It was a very specific aspiration, and one would have to say a very narrow one. Even in boxing's glory days, there were a finite number of full-time boxing writers, but definitely no more than one per newspaper. Of course, the world has changed dramatically for boxing and newspapers since Peltz was in his early teens, but even if it had not, he could have endured a lengthy wait. Prince Charles is still waiting to become King of England since that's the only job for him.

By the end of 1960, Peltz saw his first live fight in Philadelphia, a card featuring local lightweight Len Matthews. Witnessing up close what he had only previously seen on television left Russell even more enamored of the fight game.

Peltz attended Temple University and majored in journalism. In 1967, he took the first step toward his dream job when he was awarded a summer internship in the sports department of the *Bulletin*, the city's longtime afternoon newspaper, and he worked for the paper into 1969.

It seemed that Peltz was on the cusp of achieving his goal. There was only one problem. He wasn't covering boxing, but other sports. While the boxing writer, Jack Fried, was a much older man, there was every indication he planned to hang onto his position until he celebrated his 100th birthday or died trying. "I left because the boxing writer wouldn't retire," Peltz recalled.

Instead, he crossed the Rubicon from news reporter to newsmaker and began giving the boxing writer something to do. The new kid on the block began promoting fight cards regularly at the age of 22. His first card, on September 30, 1969, featured (wouldn't you know it) Bennie Briscoe against Tito Marshall, and to top it off the fight was at the Blue Horizon, the purist's boxing venue that became Peltz's home away from home.

Peltz raided his piggy bank to fund the show, but it was standing room only, more than 1,600 people in attendance. He made $1,500 on his first card, which was better than starvation hourly wages (or his annual newspaper salary of $7,500), and he promoted 15 shows in eight months. He also hedged his bets by working one night a week at the *Bulletin* just in case his new operation failed and he had to beg for his old job back. It was not necessary.

"I was having more fun," Peltz reflected, meaning more than he had as a sportswriter. "I was doing what I loved. It was 100 percent boxing. I was just immersed in it."

He had tried fighting, took a turn at writing, but found his niche as the matchmaker and promoter who put together the cards and sold them to the public. "Thank god he didn't retire," Peltz said of the boxing writer whose shoes he had hoped to fill. "I never said that before."

Peltz's office is situated a short distance from the Philadelphia Museum of Art, where the fictional fighter Rocky Balboa ran up the steps during his workouts. The office is in a four-story building that is a magnificent shrine to the sport Russell has made his life. There are framed fight posters from numerous great events of the past and if the observer doesn't figure it out on his own, Peltz may point out that they all represent Philadelphia fighters. They are nice personal mementoes from more than 40 years (and counting) of boxing promotions.

Old enough to slow down, Russell Peltz has done so to a certain degree. He spends a good chunk of the year in Florida, but he keeps promoting in Philadelphia or Atlantic City, and that brings him back to town regularly. Boxing still has a hold on him, even if he finds the outside-the-ring stuff less enjoyable than it used to be. There were times when boxing was openly referred to as a racket.

Partially fueled by movies with hard-edged plots like *On the Waterfront*, tragic stories of boxers who squandered all of their money, and others who donated too many brain cells to the sport and died from dementia, boxing has often suffered from an unsavory image.

"I still love boxing," Peltz admitted recently. "But I don't love the business of boxing. You can't trust people anymore. The negotiations don't start until you sign the contracts. In the last 10 or 15 years, society has changed." By that he meant people always wanted to change the deal they made.

From 1946 to 1960, boxing was a prime-time home television show, first on Monday nights and then on Friday nights under the auspices of *The Gillette Cavalcade of Sports*. The shows created fans like Peltz, and they made names out of up-and-coming fighters. No one was too big to box on Friday night fights, not Sugar Ray Robinson, Rocky Marciano or Archie Moore.

The demise of those popular cards marked the end of an era in boxing. But the sport stayed alive in gyms and theaters and small arenas. The soul of the game was the local show where the promoter had a venue holding 1,500 to 6,000 people and had to hustle to sell tickets. Fans knew that they were going to see quality action and usually the headliner was a local boy on the way up, trying to bridge the gap from 10-0 to contender status.

That's what the Blue Horizon was all about. It was to Philadelphia fight patrons what the Olympic Auditorium was to Los Angeles fight fans or the Savoy was to Chicago boxing believers. On a good night, and almost all of them were, 1,200 fans crammed into the Blue Horizon, a building located on North Broad Street that was built about 145 years ago and was originally a mansion.

The Blue Horizon was converted to a boxing arena in 1961 after its central building was merged with others and had served different purposes for decades. Unexpectedly, it became a Philadelphia institution, particularly from the 1970s on when Russell Peltz promoted there. Tickets were reasonably priced, fans bought hot dogs and beer, and then watched as many as eight fights of comparably talented boxers going at it. Often there was standing room only, but the absolute best seats in the house were in the front row of the balcony. The balcony tilted so far forward that viewers really did feel as if they were on top of the action.

Local fighters on the come wanted to show their stuff at the Blue Horizon. It was an aficionado's world, almost like a smoky jazz club off the beaten path where on a given night some maestro of the trumpet might stop by and play for a bit. For the most part, the fights weren't on TV and the ticket buyers were from the neighborhood, not high rollers on vacation at a casino, taking time out for amusement.

Over recent decades, the Blue Horizon had its return, if not to full glory, then at least to prominence, only to suffer through periodic closings, complaints from building inspectors and demands for renovation. Peltz almost bought it once, but someone beat him to it. You don't have to talk to him long before intuition tells you that he will always have a soft spot in his heart for the old venue.

In a perfect Peltz world, the Blue Horizon would be thriving and weekly cards would sell out as a fresh crop of young fighters with fast fists and big dreams rotated through year after year. Maybe Blue Horizon fighters on the undercard were equivalents of Class A or Class AA baseball players, but the shows let them be seen and make a few bucks instead of being closed out of fancier, more sterile venues.

While Peltz was a beneficiary when the casinos came to Atlantic City, beginning in the late 1970s, and he chose to invade the boxing business by making deals with TV to pay bigger purses to fighters and then paper the house with high-roller comps, the dynamic of how to promote a fight had changed. He had to adapt or be ruined, but the purist inside him was disenchanted.

"Casinos made people lazy," Peltz believed. "Fight cards became packages. The fans were high rollers. There was no affiliation with the fighters. All of the great boxing promoters throughout history had their own territory—Miami, Chicago, Detroit. TV traveled from town to town. That's the way it was. Those were pretty good times."

All of a sudden, Atlantic City became a huge boxing Mecca. Only a few of the very biggest stars in the sport stayed away. If heavyweight champ Larry Holmes, Sugar Ray Leonard or Thomas Hearns were going to fight at a casino, that casino was in Las Vegas. But over time, almost everyone else stopped on the boardwalk, from Michael Spinks to Aaron Pryor to Marvin Hagler, and the kings of the lesser-weight classes.

"Guys who couldn't promote a kid from second grade to third grade suddenly were promoters because they knew people in the casinos or in TV," Peltz commented memorably.

The approval of casino gambling came about in 1976 as an effort to save the city from crime and decay. Resorts International Casino Hotel opened on the Atlantic City boardwalk in May 1978. It was the first casino to open under the legislation designed to refurbish and rebuild the fading beach community that had once been one of America's favorite playgrounds, but had become dilapidated and worn out.

Atlantic City was a beach destination, via train, as early as 1854. Its streets inspired the board game Monopoly. Saltwater taffy was invented there. Diving horses jumped off the Steel Pier into the water starting in the 1880s and for many years after.

In 1973, Russell Peltz began promoting monthly shows at the Philadelphia Spectrum, an arena that held about 18,000 people and was a major step up from the Blue Horizon in size and amenities. Today Peltz, who wears glasses and has fairly closely cropped hair, looks little changed from that era except for some gray. In the 1970s, he was already wearing glasses, but had dark hair that was a bit bushier.

During the halcyon days of the '70s, Peltz helped build the fortunes of top-caliber Philadelphia fighters, but he also opened the doors to some of the biggest names in the sport. The Spectrum was big enough to attract Marvin Hagler, Thomas Hearns, Roberto Duran and Bobby Chacon.

In 1978, business was booming at Philadelphia fight cards in the Spectrum. A year later, business was plummeting. I attended some of the last Spectrum shows, and I still have the programs. The September show featured rising middleweight Curtis Parker against Elisha Obed in the featured bout. Parker was 13-0 and attempting to burrow a path into the ranks of esteemed Philadelphia middleweights. Obed, from the Bahamas, was 76-8-5 and had previously been World Boxing Council junior middleweight champ.

Also on the card was a match between Bennie Briscoe and Teddy Mann. Light-heavyweight Jerry "The Bull" Martin, originally from Antigua but transplanted to North Philadelphia, was scheduled to face Leo Rogers. That is a triple-header I would pay to see right now, provided we were all transported back into our primes.

By November, Martin was world-ranked and fighting the highly respected Jesse Burnett of Los Angeles, with the United States Boxing Association belt at stake. Parker was on the card again, too, going after Gary Guiden. Both Martin and Parker had won in September. The local fans were going to cheer for Parker, Briscoe and Martin, but they were not "gimme bouts." Those were the types of fights Peltz loved to make, crowd pleasers, what we might call honest fights, where the winner was in doubt and the local guys were not protected.

With fights like those and a venue like the Spectrum, things couldn't have been healthier on the Philadelphia fight scene, and Russell Peltz could not have been happier. But it took almost no time for the Spectrum fights to go into the tank, brushed aside by the wheeling and dealing in Atlantic City. Attendance dropped to 5,000 from 7,000 per show. After a February 1 card that featured Jeff Chandler, fast on his way to the bantamweight title, Peltz announced that Spectrum fights would be no more, and he also started promoting at the Shore.

"The casinos were calling you up and throwing money at you," Peltz remembered. "Probably 1979 was the worst year. Then Bob Arum offered me the chance to promote ESPN fights, and the early 1980s were boom years." Except the boom was 60 miles away in Atlantic City, overlooking the Atlantic Ocean, not in Philadelphia, overlooking Broad Street.

The announcement that Russell Peltz would promote many of the ESPN shows was made in late March 1980, just three weeks before the series made its debut. The event was packaged as a tournament, with paydays of about $1,000 a fight to start for contestants of limited experience, but those with good promise made their way to a championship round. Those who fought on Peltz's ESPN cards were not so dissimilar from those who would have been part of the undercard highlights at the Blue Horizon.

During its peak, Atlantic City hosted about 150 boxing shows in a year. The casinos were a juggernaut with TV money backing them, and the economics were all on their side. When the network shows that had built weekend afternoon programming around Atlantic City fights backed off due to the rise of cable TV, Peltz renewed his love affair with the Blue Horizon.

"Russell brought it alive," said Nigel Collins, the longtime editor of *The Ring* magazine. "It was an incredible venue. They would sell out before the main event was announced. There were great fights, and that reputation built and built. It built as a phenomenon. Before that it was a Philadelphia secret. For some shows, they packed 2,000 people [into the Blue Horizon]. It was insane. It would take you a half hour to get from your seat to the bathroom.

"The first row of the balcony was the best seat," Collins continued, "and the crowd would gather in the lobby, waiting for the doors to open. A hundred people would charge up the stairs. It was kind of surreal to see these people break their necks, trying for the best seats. It was the last of the old-fashioned fight clubs. It was like a throwback. You could have jumped into the ring if you wanted to because of the proximity of the audience to the fighters. That made the fighters fight harder. The noise, the screaming, the building would shake. Sometimes I thought the balcony would collapse."

In the 1990s, Russell Peltz masterminded such popular cards that he never had to worry about selling out the show. That meant he had the freedom to put on competitive matches rather than worry about finding easy opponents for selected boxers. A fighter had to be prepared if he was going to fight at the Blue, as it was sometimes called. That portion of Blue Horizon history ended after the USA Network pulled the plug on its backing of the shows.

In 2005, *The Ring* magazine called the Blue Horizon "the best place to watch a boxing match in the world," and by the time its mission was changed to host banquets and functions and an attempt was made to turn it into a North Philadelphia cultural center, an estimated 50 fighters who had graced that ring went on to win world championships. The Blue Horizon was put up for sale in 2007, and tax problems shut the doors altogether in 2010. In 2011, the famed battleground was purchased for six million dollars, and was accompanied by an announcement that it would be turned into a hotel and restaurant serving the nearby Temple University community.

In early 2012, I dropped by the Blue Horizon one last time. The front doors were padlocked. An enduring mural of fighters was still splashed upon an outside wall. An official government marker had been placed in front of the building, noting that it was a civic institution.

No construction had begun that would have transformed the Blue Horizon into an unrecognizable hotel, but it seemed certain that one day the only thing left of the onetime fight palace where so many memories were made would be that curbside sign. And maybe that's the way it should be. Deep inside the truest of Blue Horizon and Philadelphia boxing fans there is a burning desire to see the old lady restored one more time in an attempt to recapture past glory. But maybe it is better that it never happen. Times have changed in the boxing world, and Nigel Collins doesn't think the good old days are ever coming back, or should: "I am a firm believer you can't go back again. It's like visiting an old girlfriend that doesn't look as good anymore."

In the summer of 2004, on a June weekend filled with lunches, dinners and meet-the-public events, J. Russell Peltz was inducted into the International Boxing Hall of Fame. The day was a scorcher in upstate New York. I was one of those in attendance, and I think Peltz walked around with a smile on his face the entire weekend, as was appropriate. He had reached the pinnacle of his field.

The class of 2004 in Canastota, in addition to Peltz, included fighters Carlos Palomino, Azumah Nelson, Daniel Zaragoa, Dwight Muhammad Qawi, referee Stanley Christodoulou and writer W.C. Heinz, as well as a handful of old-timers and pioneers. It was good company.

Whenever Russell Peltz reflects on his long career as a promoter, he always circles around to one fact: he could not have made it big in Philadelphia when he broke in if he had not had a promotional agreement with Bennie Briscoe. It was Bad Bennie's talent and reputation that brought the best around to him, and the most popular fighter in town was the headliner who helped Peltz build a following. Bennie Briscoe made his career. Russell knows it and he is grateful.

4

CURTIS PARKER

H e was a Philadelphia middleweight with potential, and that made him a prized property in the early 1980s when the sky was the limit and a good break might propel him into a title shot. Curtis Parker was home-grown, a local warrior from Frankford with speed in his fists and courage in his heart.

But in some ways Parker was an uncommon fighter. He thought a lot about things. He wanted to have a family. He thought boxers might need a union to protect their rights, to give them health coverage and a pension. For a 21-year-old guy, sometimes he sounded as if he was going on 40.

That can be a pretty good thing in the wide world, but at times the raw, young boxer who dreams of a world title needs to be single-minded, to focus. Rewards in the fight game come to the hungry and talented who set their minds on the great goal and are taskmasters for their muscular bodies.

To become the champ, a boxer must think of himself as invulnerable; he must believe that he is a perfect fighting machine that cannot be beaten. The trainer will repeat the theme so often that it will settle into the mind as a truism impossible to doubt. Curtis Parker understood all of this, and he followed the advice and the train of thought religiously—until one day a tiny sliver of worry seeped into his brain and expanded like a disease.

That can happen when those fists of fury that are supposed to carry you to a life of glory and financial ease do something so terrible you call into question all that you knew. On March 21, 1978, Parker had just turned 19. He was just a beginner in the ring, chasing his fourth professional victory. It sounded good to hear people say he was undefeated.

Parker was scheduled on the card at the Blue Horizon, the North Philadelphia institution that was the proving ground for up-and-coming Philly fighters, where a young player could get noticed. He fought Jody White, 27, of Trenton, New Jersey, who as an amateur had been a Golden Gloves champ. It was Parker's night and four rounds into the evening, he knocked White out.

That was a good win for someone as inexperienced as Parker, and he earned the right to celebrate. He did a little of that, but he went home early because he already had a day job working as a cook at the University of Pennsylvania. Young Curtis still lived with his mother, Johnni Mae. The next day he went to work as usual, but while reading the paper, he was shocked to learn that his opponent had been taken to the hospital and then died.

Died? Parker was aghast that he had killed a man with his fists. He was distraught and had to leave work. His mom picked him up and drove him home. Curtis went into seclusion, hiding in his bedroom at home, tearful all day. How could this have happened? It was a sporting event, not a street fight. Parker was no thug. He was not a mean man. He was a good guy. And yet, Jody White, whom he knew nothing about, was dead because he beat him up.

The first time Parker told me the story, I thought he was going to burst into tears. He was visibly moved, and it was already a few years in the past. The magnitude of what he did stayed with him, and he brought up the Jody White incident on his own again some 30 years after it happened.

The weight of the guilt was like a Mack truck resting on his shoulders. "Man, I was so confused," he recalled. Curtis couldn't think clearly, and didn't want to think clearly. He wanted to obscure the memory, to wipe it out. "I daydreamed. I went to the movies. I passed out money to the people in the streets." That was a form of atonement. "My friends told me I was crazy, but it made me feel better." Not much could make him feel better at that time. Those were dark days. "It was steady on my mind—constant, constant, constant," he remembered.

When Parker couldn't duck the issue, he confronted it. He was a boy in a man's body, and now he was a man because only a man could be mature enough to deal with such a situation. He had to act grown-up. Things happen in this world that accelerate the process, and you can't take them back or take them over.

Parker could repress his thoughts and pretend. He could walk away from boxing, quit the fight game, the thing he was best suited for, but where would he be then? What he did instead of taking either path was set out to learn about Jody White, about what kind of man he was. He listened when people told him that White was a good guy, that he was nice to people. It took a little while, but Curtis concluded, "I feel I know him now."

He did something harder still. When they held a service for Jody White and buried him, Parker went to the funeral. He could not know if he would be welcome, or if he belonged, but he felt it was the right thing to do: "That was hard, man. I was trying to get myself together in the car." He tried, but that didn't work, and he probably cried as hard as anyone else at the funeral, releasing emotions that he barely comprehended.

Parker did return to the ring. His next fight was three months later. The opponent was a guy named Sam Long, and inside of two rounds, Parker was dominating. He was hitting Long the way a fighter is supposed to, with an eye toward a knockout. Then suddenly, a vision of Jody White interfered. He looked at Long but saw White: "I stopped right there and looked at him," Parker remembered. "I pictured Jody White."

Then he knocked his foe out and went about building the career he knew he was destined for as one of the best middleweights in the world. However, Parker kept White in his thoughts. There was an especially harsh reminder when he was scheduled to fight Wilford Scypion, another contender out of New York. Scypion, too, had killed a man in the ring, a boxer named Willie Classen. He also had retreated to his family home, and was unlucky enough to fight Classen in a higher-profile environment, so the newspaper people kept pressuring him to talk about it.

By the time the Scypion bout came around for Parker, three years had passed since his knockout of White: "I remember him. He's dead physically, but I think of him a lot, not in terms of the darkness, but in the light."

Such tragedy is not easily forgotten and for a man with a conscience, it would be easy to remain haunted. Parker overcame the incident that can only be described as fate, and went on to fight better opponents for more money, seeking to maneuver his way into and then up the world rankings.

The victories mounted up. In Parker's pro debut on December 6, 1979, he beat Frank Williams. Then he defeated Harry Fryar and Kid Sampson before taking on White. In order he bested Sam Long, Dan Snyder, Jerome Goodman, Larry Davis, Ray Smith, Charles Carey, Arnell Thomas and Willie Warren. All but the Long fight took place in Philadelphia.

Parker was 12-0, but if you are a Philadelphia middleweight with ambition, you can't hide. You don't have to leave town to find the best—the best will find you. There is no such thing as ducking the good ones in Philadelphia. On July 16, 1979, Parker made a calculated move up in class. He got it on with Willie "The Worm" Monroe.

Monroe was nearing the end of an excellent career—40-10-1—and owned a decision over Marvin Hagler. Monroe had just celebrated his 30th birthday, but for a next-generation fighter like Parker, he was a very dangerous foe. They headlined a card at the Spectrum and gave fans their money's worth. Parker won a 10-round decision and that launched him to the next level of the middleweight division. The victory transformed him from an undercard boxer to a main event fighter at a big house like the Spectrum.

The program cover from the classic middleweight fight between
Curtis Parker and Willie Monroe in 1979. (Photo courtesy of J. Russell Peltz)

Parker had a chiseled body with broad shoulders and no difficulty making
the 160-pound weight limit. His biggest physical disadvantage compared to
some other rugged middleweights was a lack of height. He stood just five-feet-
eight. It wasn't a hopeless problem, but was worrisome against certain of the
taller men in the division. Not yet, though.

Promoter J. Russell Peltz was guiding Curtis Parker's career. His job was to
ensure that Parker kept improving. He needed to face ever-bigger-name fighters,

but with luck they would be on the downside of their careers, so Parker would have a chance to win and build his reputation. In September 1979, Peltz put Parker into another feature: a 10-round event against a former World Boxing Council junior middleweight champ, the 154-pound Elisha Obed.

It was a nearly perfect showing by Parker. He pounced on Obed early, knocked him to the canvas four times, and finished him in the seventh round. It was an impressive showing against a fighter with tremendous experience. "I was just waiting for him to tire out a bit," Parker recalled. "It was a survival game for him, not a fighting game."

It was intriguing that another 10-round bout on the card featured Bennie Briscoe, who while 13 years older than his opponent, Irish Teddy Mann, polished him off by technical knockout. Sometimes promoters showcase fighters of the same weight class like this with the notion that they will meet next. That is exactly what Parker wanted, but his trainer, the wiser Willie Reddish, said no way. Briscoe, Reddish contended, may have been old, but he still packed the goods, and Parker wasn't ready for Bennie's best. While the fan demand would have been high for tickets to such a bout, no Parker-Briscoe fight ever took place.

Despite his demolition of Obed, Curtis Parker was still a pup in the boxing game. His record was 14-0, and each step that he took had to be carefully planned to maximize exposure, but minimize risk. He was still building the kind of record that he needed to gain national and worldwide supporters, not just among the cognoscenti from Philadelphia.

The plan was for Parker to take on David Love two months after disposing of Elisha Obed, again at the Spectrum. This indeed would be a step up in class. Only Love hurt his back and withdrew. Instead, Parker drew a last-minute replacement in Gary Guiden of Muncie, Indiana. Guiden looked pretty good on paper with a 28-4 record and 24 knockouts, so it wasn't as if meeting him was a waste of time.

At the time Parker was only 20, and like many young men of his age, he was impatient to get going in life. The Love fight had been portrayed as a fast-track to the world rankings. "I've been told I have a good future ahead of me," Parker stated, "and not to rush it. But I think I'm moving at a fast rate. The 10-rounders came up all of a sudden."

They did, but that didn't mean Parker, 15-0, was ready to take on the whole world. Gary Guiden proved to be no serious obstacle, though, with Parker walking away with a five-round TKO. For the moment, he was a big fish in his hometown, but he wanted more and he wanted it in a hurry. Parker looked at the Love fight as a lost opportunity, but he was wrong. It was back on the radar screen quickly, with David Love's manager, the famous Angelo Dundee, saying the bout would be made, and oh, by the way, the back injury was real. "He was like this," Dundee demonstrated, stooping halfway over in imitation of how Love looked when the fight was postponed.

The new date was March 9, 1980, and the new venue was not going to be the Spectrum after all. The new boxing hot spot was Atlantic City where casinos were going up faster than ocean-view condos. It may not have been apparent yet, but it soon would be—Atlantic City was the new Philadelphia in the local boxing world. The date was also Parker's 21st birthday. As a bonus, there was something tangible at stake. The bout was for 12 rounds because the prize was acquisition of the U.S. Boxing Association middleweight title. The crown was unclaimed.

"I'm not too concerned about David," Parker remarked, showing little love for his foe. "I definitely don't doubt myself. He's just another opponent, a little stronger and more effective, but I know his style is a lot of lateral move-ment. David Love is good. I'll say that up front. He's good enough to win the fight, but so am I. This is a big step for me, but it's just a step to better things."

Much of the commentary was level-headed. Every fighter will tell you that he is going to win. Every fighter believes in the infallibility of his own powers. There are turning points in every life, turning points in every career. The Love bout shaped up as one of those times for Curtis Parker.

There was every reason to believe that David Love could present Parker with the biggest challenge of his life. Love, from San Diego, stood six feet tall, and he had a superior reach. The scariest part of Love's résumé was the fact that he had victories over Bennie Briscoe, Willie Monroe and Bobby "Boogaloo" Watts, among the finest of the Philly middleweight crop, as well as some years earlier a Spectrum win over Perry Abney in a 10-rounder. Why wouldn't Love believe he could eliminate Parker from contention, too?

Parker had his difficulties. A Love punch opened a cut above his left eye and he bruised his right hand in the fifth round—the hand he most effectively employed to knock people out. But the bout did not go the distance. Curtis Parker stopped David Love 19 seconds into the ninth round for the most impor-tant triumph of his career. "This is truly a good day for me," Parker said of the title he won as a birthday present to himself. "I think I'm going towards the middleweight title."

There was every reason to think that way. Two months later, also in Atlantic City, Parker faced Mike Colbert in a scheduled 12-rounder, putting his new national title up for grabs. Colbert was a slick boxer from Portland, Oregon, a defensive artist with a talent for sticking and moving.

Parker was a pursuer. Emboldened by his previous results, the confident Curtis sought a knockout of the West Coast visitor. But these are the types of nights that come along in a young boxer's education, where a savvy, ring-wise veteran makes him look bad. Mike Colbert (26-5-1) did that to Parker on this night, and the Philadelphian was lucky he didn't absorb a loss along with the lesson.

It may be wrong, but it happens often—the out-of-towner has to score big, knock down the local favorite, or knock him out. Colbert did not put Parker on the canvas, but he thwarted his rushes and outmaneuvered him to avoid his biggest shots. Parker escaped with a decision, and it seemed as if the main reason the judges gave it to him was that Colbert spent the duration back-peddling. Officials do not look kindly upon a fighter who spends the entire night in retreat.

"I learned that there are fighters who can run for 12 rounds," Parker noted. "I have to be more patient and not let them do it. I have got to cut the ring off."

Colbert executed his game plan, but was not rewarded for it. He said he thought he had confused Parker and made Curtis fight his (Colbert's) fight, but to no avail. For the previous couple of years, Parker had been fighting on a fast-track pace. He fought eight times in 1978 and six times in 1979. He took on two 12-rounders in the first five months of 1980, and his record was 17-0. *The Ring* magazine was on his bandwagon, ranking him fifth in the world.

Curtis Parker needed to beat a highly ranked contender to move into real contention for a title shot. It was time to take a little breather and ponder the future—the right move against the right opponent. By besting Love and Colbert, Parker had also accomplished the enviable. He had inched into the world rankings without fighting a series of wars with other Philadelphia middleweights.

And while they were aging warhorses, they were still around. Most notably, Bennie Briscoe was the king of the town, but there was no reason to fight him at this stage. But neither Bobby "Boogaloo" Watts nor Eugene "Cyclone" Hart had given up on their dreams, either.

In early 1982, Hart was 31, and he had not had a fight in almost five years. He had turned pro in 1969, and never fought a fight outside of Philadelphia. He didn't lose a bout until 1974, when "Willie The Worm" got him in a 10-round decision. But then he was knocked out by Watts, and Eddie Gregory, who was on his way to eventually claiming the light-heavyweight title under the name Eddie Mustapha Muhammad. In 1975, Hart and Briscoe fought to a draw. However, in their 1976 rematch, Briscoe KO'd Hart in one round, and Hart also fell to Marvin Hagler. In 1977, Vito Antofermo, on his own path to the middleweight crown, felled Hart in five rounds.

And that was all. He was only 26, but Eugene Hart stopped fighting. He was 30-8-1 with a no-contest and after the long layoff, he decided he should make a comeback. Hart's life had many of the makings of an inspirational, made-for-TV movie. He had polio as a child, grew up fatherless in North Philadelphia, and concluded that in his first go-around he was immature, partying too much, not training hard enough, thinking too much about girls and not enough about his opponents' right hands whizzing at his head. "I wasn't ready," Hart confessed in February 1982. "I was inexperienced, unaware, doing a lot of foolish things."

Hart was also haunted by an incident earlier in his career. After going 21-0, he met Denny Moyer, a former junior middleweight world champion, at the Spectrum. Moyer was 33 in 1971, but still fit and a big name. In the sixth round, as Cyclone crunched a right against Moyer's head, the onetime champ grabbed him in a clinch and they somehow fell through the ropes onto the hard Spectrum floor. Hart hit his head and was knocked out. That was the no-decision on his record. He sued the Spectrum and years later was awarded $54,000. However, he was never the same fighter. He lost too often and quit, in his view, too early. In the interim, he married, had three children and let his weight balloon from 160 to 190. And now he was convinced that he could do it all over again, the right way this time.

"I had the chance to be the champ when I was much younger," Hart observed. "I'm coming back to be the champ now."

He certainly had refreshed his fighter talk. It was one of those cases of "if you don't believe in yourself, no one else will," and if you don't believe in yourself, you don't belong in the ring anyway.

Trainer Sam Solomon agreed with Eugene Hart's analysis that he always had a big punch and he still did, and that he never took much punishment in his career, so that shouldn't be a factor the second time around. Solomon did admit one thing: "He will be rusty. Regardless of how he looks in the gym, it takes actual combat."

The other combatant was Tony Suero, an Upper Darby tough guy with a 9-3-2 record and a refreshing propensity for candor. He informed the local media that his tattoo, the name "Tony" under a drawing of a boxer, was carved into his left arm when he was not quite sober by someone named Sailor Eddie in Camden, New Jersey. The image dated to about 1978, when tattoos were not yet all the rage.

Suero was 23, and it wasn't clear if his subsequent comment about Hart was to be taken as an insult or just another example of his ingenuous way of making chit-chat. "I've never seen him fight," Suero said of Hart. "But my father saw him [ooh, that had to hurt the Cyclone], and he thinks I'll knock him out."

As it so happened, daddy knew best. Suero knocked Hart down twice and stopped him in the fourth round at the Tropicana Hotel and Casino. It was the only fight of Hart's career outside the Philadelphia city limits, and while he walked away saying he would be back for more in this quixotic comeback try, Hart never fought again. Dreams almost always die hard for boxers. They literally take it on the chin, and the impact delivers hard reality.

However, Hart raised a son who took to the ring with the same flair as his father. Jesse Hart, 23, compiled an 85-11 amateur record in the weight regions of super-middleweight and light-heavyweight, won a national Golden Gloves title, and came very close to being a member of the United States Olympic team in 2012. The younger Hart signed a promotional agreement with Top Rank in the same year and swiftly won his first five bouts.

While Curtis Parker was on the rise, Bennie Briscoe was holding steady, and Eugene Hart was trying his one-and-done comeback, Bobby Watts entertained his own notions about who was the toughest middleweight in Philadelphia. Watts laid off from the ring from autumn 1978 until the fall of 1979, about 11 months. A few years earlier in the 1970s, *The Ring* magazine ranked Watts number two in the world. But he got frustrated, despite a win over Marvin Hagler. He started losing and took some time off. Bobby found work driving a forklift in a warehouse, but when he walked down the street in North Philadelphia, all of his friends asked if he was retired and what was going on with his boxing career.

So Boogaloo began training again at Joe Frazier's Gym and at age 30, he thought about easing back into the fray. One thing about Watts—he always put on a good show in the ring with his fists and his slippery movements, and he always dressed with some flash. When he fought Clifford Wills in October 1979 to end his self-imposed exile, Watts wore the long-style shorts that had not yet become popular in college basketball, and red tassles on his shoes.

Watts smashed Wills with some left hooks and before long, he was finished. It was a TKO for Watts, raising his record to 33-5-1, and a whole bunch of fresh confidence oozed forth in words of excitement and prediction: "It's time to go get a title. In two fights, I'll be real sharp again. Maybe the layoff was for the best. I'm a new man."

It certainly was positive thinking. For Bobby Watts, it was as if he had answered all of the questions in less than nine minutes of action. Bring 'em on. Watts won another fight and then took on Marvin Hagler again. That did not go so well. Hagler won on a second-round TKO in Portland, Maine. A win there would likely have given Watts the title shot he sought. Bobby kept going, though, winning four straight bouts. On May 3, 1983 in Wembley Arena in London, Watts took on unbeaten Mark Kaylor, but was stopped in the fourth round. That was his retirement fight. After he gave up boxing for good, Watts trained Charles Brewer and Buster Drayton, two solid fighters.

Although he looks much younger, Watts turned 63 in 2012. At times, he still shows himself in Philadelphia boxing circles and was an attendee at that year's Philadelphia Boxing Hall of Fame banquet. Like many retired athletes from a previous generation, he speaks up for the years of his prime over the athletes of today. Watts was a member of an exclusive club—world-ranked Philadelphia middleweights—and the likes of the group from his heyday may never be seen or matched again.

"During that time back then," Watts reminisced, "you had fighters who really liked to fight. If anybody wanted to get anywhere as a middleweight, they had to come into Philadelphia and beat one of us. It was kind of a tough road. Cyclone [Hart] was a tough fighter. We were friends, but it was a business."

Boogaloo got his nickname because he could dance in the ring, and he felt it did him no harm to have such a showy, memorable moniker. A ring announcer spat it out during a fight introduction in New Jersey "and then the name stuck," Bobby recalled.

Watts admits that he wishes he came along at another time when just surviving the other tough guys in Philadelphia was a chore, adding that if he knew then what he knows now, he probably would have become middleweight champ. "I wish I was in a different time. I could have been one of the greatest. You know, I don't really have a favorite fight or special memory. They were all my favorites when I won. All of my wins were important."

Watts is no longer training world-class fighters, but notes that he does go into the gym and offer pointers to young boxers. He is amazed that some of them work out wearing earplugs to listen to music, adding that never would have played well with the trainers of his era. "I train some kids," Watts states simply. "I just teach them old school. I teach them how I won. I teach them that they've got to be dedicated to what they are doing."

Boogaloo is not as light on his feet as he was when he was younger, so he can't show the young bucks his lightning speed or blind them with those red tassles. But he hopes that they will listen to the words of a man who has been in the ring with the best of them.

While the older generation of Philadelphia middleweights tried to rejuvenate itself, Curtis Parker was on hiatus. He fought Mike Colbert in May 1980 and then rested a bit. He had been keeping a frenetic pace, and it would do no harm to back off for a little while. Parker, however, was impatient at this stage of his life. He wanted promoter Russell Peltz and his handlers to hurry things along. He felt ready for that step up into the limelight, and so a deal was cut to pit Parker against Dwight Davison at Caesars Palace in Las Vegas on August 8. From the hindsight of 30 years later, Peltz remarked, "I never should have taken the Dwight Davison fight. I didn't think of styles."

The bout was nationally televised. Davison was 26-0 and Parker was 17-0. One of the commentators was retired multi-weight-class champ Sugar Ray Leonard. When asked who was going to emerge undefeated, Leonard replied, "It depends on who wakes up on the right side of the bed."

Dwight Davison, who was from Detroit, stood six-feet-one, which meant that he towered over Parker, and his size advantage meant that he was hard to reach for the shorter Philadelphian. He also had a big knockout punch. The men battled for 10 rounds, but Davison won on points. The upward curve of Parker's career had leveled off. "His career went nowhere after that," Peltz admitted. "After David Love, he was on fire. Even after Colbert."

The loss to Davison represented the train running off the tracks, but it didn't have to be fatal. Parker refused to take a step back in class, though. He could have returned to Philadelphia, piled up a few more wins and then challenged one of the other top middleweights. Instead, he forged on just if he had defeated Davison. He took another break and then met Mustafa Hamsho in Atlantic City on February 15, 1981.

Hamsho, a native of Syria, wore a khafeh head covering into the ring early in his career. He said he wore it for fun, but dropped the habit. "People started throwing beer cans at it," he recalled. He was 31-1-1 when matched with Parker, and very much a contender. When he wasn't fighting, Hamsho worked part-time in his uncle's bakery in Brooklyn, though he lived in Bayonne, New Jersey. Curly-haired with a somewhat Americanized sense of humor, Mustafa, a southpaw fighter, noted that he did not grow up in the desert, but in a seaport city. All people could think of when they heard of his home country was the movie *Lawrence of Arabia*: "People think I come from the desert and ride a camel," he commented.

Parker and Hamsho were classified as bombers and heavy punchers, each with the potential to score a knockout. That's how the experts saw the fight. "This is one of the greatest fights on paper," declared Hamsho's manager Paddy Flood. "The loser, Hagler, wouldn't want to box. They both walk in. They're slam-bang…quality fighters." Flood, who never saw a fight he didn't love if one of his guys was in it, compared Curtis Parker to "a small Joe Frazier."

The matchup made Parker think of a different movie: *Raging Bull*. He was not predicting bloodshed, but a war propagated by warriors: "There was only one raging bull in the movie, but there's going to be two in the ring. It's going to be a slugfest."

It was. Hamsho, who was ranked number two in the world at the time, had the early advantage in the 10-round fight at Bally's Park Place Hotel Casino. Although there were no knockdowns, in the fifth and sixth rounds, Parker landed big blows. In the seventh, he staggered Hamsho and nearly sent him to the canvas. The longer the fight went, the better Curtis looked. Yet when the judges' scores were tallied, a split decision went Hamsho's way. Many observers felt the scoring was backward and Parker was the loudest protester among them. "I thought I won the fight," he recalled, but instead he suffered a career-debilitating defeat. "It was a close fight. I thought I came on strong."

That made two straight, close, 10-round decision losses for Curtis Parker. His career cried out for regrouping, but once again he was presented with an opportunity he thought could not be passed up. It was another money fight against a highly regarded opponent. This was the Scypion fight. Wilford Scypion carried a 19-1 record, with only a loss to Mustafa Hamsho.

Before this bout, for the first time, Parker went into a sort of seclusion. It was mother Johnni Mae's idea and Willie Reddish concurred. He camped out at the Montgomery County Boys Club in the Philadelphia suburb of Eagleville, doing his road and gym work there, sleeping on a cot in a row of beds just like a military barracks, and eating closely supervised, highly nutritional meals. He had to win the fight. Parker was still ranked sixth in the world by *The Ring* magazine. Scypion was ranked seventh.

When Curtis Parker was right and at the peak of his game, he could bull through jabs and overpower foes with his strength. He worked his way inside where he could whomp them on the head. But Scypion neutralized these charges and pecked away at Parker's face. He opened cuts above both of Parkers' eyes, and the blood could not be contained for long in the latter rounds. At times the fight seemed more like a wrestling match with referee Tony Perez three times warning the boxers about holding. The unanimous decision went to Wilford Scypion.

Parker was demoralized. He had a falling out with trainer Willie Reddish. He blamed Reddish and Russell Peltz for the loss. He desperately sought change, making his mother his manager and subbing in Slim Robinson, another renowned Philly trainer, to guide his preparations. Robinson's advice was for Parker to change his spots, always a complicated request to make of a leopard. Instead of rushing to swarm a foe when the bell rang to begin the fight, he wanted Curtis to be more patient, to take his time a little bit. "Each fight is very important," Robinson stressed, well aware of the recent Parker 0-3 stretch potentially ruining a promising career.

By September 26, 1981, Parker had gone 16 months without a victory. He was fighting for his career. He fought Lancelot Innes of Guyana and knocked him out in the seventh round in Atlantic City. Parker was in command during the entire bout, but he demonstrated more patience and displayed brutal body work, pounding Innes' midsection until he weakened, then finishing him off with a major fusillade.

A couple of months later, Parker picked off another win, a five-round knockout of Jerry Holley of Orlando. Then opportunity knocked—quite loudly—at the front door. A rematch was made with Mustafa Hamsho for March 13, 1982: 10 rounds in Atlantic City at the Playboy Hotel & Casino. Just over a year had passed since their last fight, one that Parker believed with his heart and soul he had won. A victory in the rematch with still another trainer, the legendary George Benton, in his corner, might make everything well again. Benton, a brilliant defensive strategist, taught Parker a peek-a-boo defense, and Hamsho didn't come close to penetrating it.

Time after time, Parker unleashed big right hands that struck hard and either wobbled Hamsho or pushed him backward. When the fight was over, going the 10-round distance, Parker looked fresh, as if ready to go dancing, but Hamsho had bruises and welts all over his face. Yet once again, he was declared the victor, this time by majority decision. Parker was warned once by referee Joe Cortez for using his head, but it was Hamsho who had a point deducted by the ref for head-butting. Then Parker was penalized a point for a head butt and low blows.

Curtis nearly broke down and cried after attempting to deal with the shock of the verdict. "Why is it the referee always despises me?" he asked in a confused, sad comment on the proceedings, "I was constantly hitting him."

I felt bad for Parker that night; I felt that he had been the winner, and that his career would inevitably take a dive after the loss. Sadly, I was right.

The fourth 10-round decision loss for Curtis Parker knocked his career askew. He went back to fighting lesser boxers for a while, working his way back to a prime-time fighter. A first-round knockout loss to John Mugabi set him back in 1983. Many years later, Parker recalled, "I felt so light-headed. The air was thick. It felt like I was in a sauna that night." And he recorded only one other win over a major middleweight figure during the rest of his career. In 1985, Parker knocked out Frank Fletcher in two rounds.

Curtis Parker retired in 1988 with a record of 29-9, never having fought for the title, and graduated on to the rest of his life. It was hard not to wonder about just how things may have turned out if some of those close, sometimes controversial decisions went his way.

In March 2012, Parker was 53 years old. He had worked for the University of Pennsylvania Hospital for 25 years, constantly taking courses that qualified him for different jobs. As a teenager, he had been a cook. Now he was a building maintenance roofer. Curtis had studied carpentry. He took courses that made him an electrical expert. His short hair was black and white. He still had very powerful-looking forearms, and he lived in a South Philadelphia row house, not far from the waterside restaurant where he had lunch. "I always said I would get into other things," Parker noted. He always wanted to keep growing and changing and learning new things.

Curtis has four daughters and eight grandchildren—seven boys and one girl. He calls the little ones "my grands." The home he shares with his partner, Barbara, has some boxing mementos on display. His mom, Johnni Mae Parker, turned 70 in 2012.

Philadelphia is enough of a fighter's town that people still ask Parker for his autograph. He wonders why sometimes, but he signs. "Some people say, 'I enjoyed your fights.' My boxing career will live on in the minds of people who saw my fights or heard of me."

Three decades have passed, so those memories must be good ones. Once in a while, Parker will watch a tape of one of his best bouts and shake his head because he doesn't always remember his younger self fight by fight. "I am surprised to see what I've done. In some fights, I'm amazed that I looked so unstoppable."

And still he remembers that long-ago tragic fight and its victim: "The one that bothers me is Jody White. He died. I felt so low and sad, especially when I saw his wife and daughter. I had no intention of doing anything like that. That happens. Since I retired, I never talk about it."

Boxing was a tough way to make a living, but it made Curtis Parker as a person; it gave him direction and discipline. When he was 14, Parker ran the streets and got into trouble. He admitted to stealing cars. One of the friends of his youth was killed, and one went to jail. Parker went into the ring. He went before a judge, too, and was told to join a Police Athletic League football team. Curtis was a little, spunky guy who played guard and center, and he smiles when he says he was pretty good at that game. But upstairs there was a gym, and he got curious about what went on and checked it out.

That's where Curtis met Willie Reddish, who was 75 when he died in 1988. He asked the big man, "How can I join?" Parker was taken in, but he didn't know the first thing about the sweet science, only how to street-fight. For a fighter with form he was easy prey, and he didn't like getting hit in the face.

"I started running, 10 miles a day, and I started listening to Willie Reddish," Parker remembered. "I got better. It felt good because it was a challenge. My challenge was my height, five-eight, as a middleweight."

Parker's first payday in 1977 was $600. The most he made for a fight was $80,000—good money for the day, but not golden-parachute, nest-egg money. "I wasn't wasteful," he noted.

All these years later, Parker still can't believe how the Hamsho fights were ruled. "Oh yeah, I was shocked," he recalled. "Beating Hamsho, that would have led me to a fight for a championship. To fight for the championship, that's what I wanted the most."

No doubt those Philadelphia middleweights were a special breed. "They took Philadelphia and put it on the map," he remarked. "Boy, could he hit," he added about Bennie Briscoe. "When you came through Philadelphia, you knew you had been in a fight." Marvin Hagler fought his way through Philadelphia and became the middleweight of his generation and one for the ages. What would a Parker–Hagler fight have been like? "I don't know what would happen. He couldn't have backed off and I wouldn't have backed off."

Parker said he enjoyed all of his wins, and he enjoyed all of his losses in a way, too. He soaked up knowledge from prominent Philadelphia boxing men with smarts. When he looks back and thinks of Peltz, Reddish, Benton and Robinson, all of them, Curtis said they taught him a lot.

"I got to meet Joe Louis and I got to spar with Ali," Parker reflected. The sparring with Ali took place at Muhammad Ali's Deer Lake, Pennsylvania training camp. He has no illusions about how he rated compared to the boxer regarded by many as the best in history. "He was toying with me."

A few years ago, the Pennsylvania Boxing Hall of Fame inducted Curtis Parker, and he has a souvenir plaque of that honor in his living room. He tries to attend the induction events each year because that's where he sees the old fight crowd that he knew so well. "Sometimes I feel like I never did it," Curtis said of his distinguished boxing career, "it's so long ago."

Parker didn't travel as often as many world-ranked fighters did. He fought in Las Vegas, Florida and California; he was one of the boxers who pioneered the fights in Atlantic City and he's proud of that. "Boxing gave me a good living," Parker stated. "I do appreciate it. I met a lot of people. I had fun. I never had a bad experience with fans. Out of all my years in boxing, all of the opponents I met, I'm wishing them well."

There is no wistfulness in Parker's tone of voice, no expressions of regret. He is still a hard-working man who takes great pleasure in playing with his grandchildren these days. He tells those youngsters, and any other kids he might address, that education is the most important thing.

Maybe someday when he finishes taking classes and stops working, Parker thinks he just might spend a little time back in the gym, training the boys turning into men who are naïve and hungry just like he was in the 1970s. If he gets their attention, he will show them the art of self-defense, the way it was taught by Willie Reddish, Slim Robinson and George Benton. Those three wise men from the Philadelphia gyms are all gone now. The young men they talked wisdom to are going gray themselves, yet they can speak for them and help others to understand what it is to be a Philadelphia fighter.

That sounds pretty good to Curtis Parker—becoming an instructional channel for the knowledge to be passed on to another generation.

5

MATTHEW SAAD MUHAMMAD

B orn Maxwell Antonio Loach, known as Matthew Franklin as a young man, and attaining fame as Matthew Saad Muhammad, there are powerful overtones of tragedy wrapped around magnificent images of achievement in examining a complex life that even today mixes inspiration and sadness.

Even while becoming the best in the world in his specialty, there were always struggles in Matthew Saad Muhammad's life. He was an orphan who was abandoned as a child; he was homeless and dependent on charity, but he reached the top of his world, only to become homeless again. One of Philadelphia's greatest fighters and noteworthy champions lived a life that can be simultaneously admired and pitied.

The Matthew Saad Muhammad story began with his birth in Philadelphia on June 16, 1954. His memories are inconsistent and vague because his mother died when he was still a baby. He and his older brother went to live with an aunt. She was not wealthy, and the battle to house, feed and clothe the two boys was a perpetual challenge. The financial pinch peaked for her when Saad Muhammad was five years old, and his aunt told his brother to take him out and lose him in the streets.

The terrified youngster was picked up by the police and turned over to Philadelphia's Catholic Social Services. Since he had no identification with him and apparently could not relay his name, the nuns gave him a new one. They chose Matthew Franklin. The first name was bestowed in honor of the apostle and saint. The last name was chosen because the boy had been picked up on the Benjamin Franklin Parkway.

Matthew Saad Muhammad (*left*) became one of Philadelphia's most popular boxers on his way to winning the light-heavyweight title. His fight against another light-heavyweight champion, Marvin Johnson, was an epic battle at the Spectrum in 1977. (Photo courtesy of J. Russell Peltz)

An abandoned orphan, Matthew remained with Catholic Social Services until he was eight, when John and Bertha Santos adopted him. When he was a little older, he got into trouble, especially for fighting, and was sent to a youth center. Back with his adoptive parents, Matthew attended high school and developed a passion for carpentry. He also got a job as a loader on the docks and that built up his muscles. Although a counselor suggested that if he was going to fight so much, he should become a boxer, it was not until some time later that he did so.

Matthew Franklin got his start at the Juniper Street Gym in South Philadelphia, one of the many gyms that dotted the city in the 1970s. Nick Belfiore molded him into an accomplished amateur champion and by 1974, Franklin turned pro. His rise at the 175-pound weight class was steady, if not perfect. By 1976, he was meeting some of the best competition in the division, including Marvin Camel, Mate Parlov and Eddie Gregory.

He lost some of his bouts as he learned, but in July 1977, Franklin bested Marvin Johnson for the North American Boxing Federation title. It was a fight between little-known boxers who were still hungry and struggling for recognition, but they were later to become renowned fighters. The win put Franklin on a path to compete for a world championship. Philadelphia promoter J. Russell Peltz, who has seen more bouts than almost anyone else in his long career, still raves about the match: "Matthew Franklin–Marvin Johnson is the greatest fight I ever saw in person. It was toe-to-toe for 12 rounds."

Matthew's title opportunity came in April 1979 as a rematch. In the intervening time, Johnson had won the World Boxing Council title. His defense against Franklin took place in the champ's hometown of Indianapolis, but Matthew went home with the crown, a victor by an eighth-round technical knockout.

Around that time, Matthew Franklin became Matthew Saad Muhammad. He had had no choice in his earlier names, but now he put substance behind them. He explained that Matthew means "chosen one," Saad means "bright future" and Muhammad means "praiseworthy." For someone who came into the world with so little, the selection of those names signaled a new direction. Indeed, Matthew Saad Muhammad was a world boxing champion, and he commanded fees in the hundreds of thousands of dollars.

Just reaching that point represented a remarkable accomplishment for the orphan who did not know his own name in his early youth, and who had been a lost boy with little love and support for several years. It turned out that it was going to be no easy task to hang on to what he earned. Saad Muhammad was a fantastically trained athlete with a physique as impressive as a Charles Atlas ad. He had broad shoulders, powerful biceps and a midsection firm and trim. A handsome man with an earnest demeanor, he was confident but not cocky.

As a fighter, Saad Muhammad packed a big-time wallop in his right hand, and he seemed to have an iron chin. Defensively, though, he lacked the degree of side-to-side movement that was necessary to escape the blows of other world-class light heavyweights. Above all, Matthew showed heart in the ring. He was tremendously resilient and was able to take a foe's best punches and overcome them. He showed a relentless will, time and again shrugging off punches that would fell a lesser man. Matthew was the watch that kept on ticking. Again and again, he made mini-comebacks within the course of a single fight.

No matter who was the challenger and what was the obstacle, somehow, some way, Saad Muhammad prevailed to hang on to the title belt. It also should be noted that the period from the late 1970s to the early 1980s may be categorized as the high-water mark for light heavyweights in boxing history. There was a series of great champions and great contenders. Those who fought in the 175-pound division at that time couldn't get past Saad Muhammad, Dwight

Braxton Qawi, Marvin Johnson, Michael Spinks or Eddie Gregory, who changed his name to Eddie Mustapha Muhammad. Camel, Parlov, Murray Sutherland, Richie Kates, Yaqui Lopez, John Conteh and Jerry Martin—they all came along at the wrong time. In another era, many of those boxers would have won a title.

For Saad Muhammad to lift the crown from Marvin Johnson was an impressive step for his career. Johnson was a first-rate fighter. Four months later in Atlantic City, in one of the earliest big bouts in that resort town when casino-hotels began flexing their muscle as venues, Saad Muhammad had his first title defense. The opponent was Englishman John Conteh, who brought a 33-2-1 record to the match.

Conteh was a tough fighter, another broad-shouldered bomber who was a worthy foe trying hard to fulfill his own dream and capture a title belt one more time before retirement. Conteh was a celebrity in Britain. He had a partying lifestyle that got him featured in tabloids, and he worked as a fashion model part-time. His wilder days might have been behind him at 28, since he was married with two children, and the family accompanied him on a 12-day training mission to the Bahamas on the way to New Jersey, but those times were part of his reputation.

In 1974, John Conteh won the light-heavyweight crown, but he was stripped of the title a few years later because he refused to carry out a mandatory defense. Against Saad Muhammad, Conteh came as close as he ever would to again owning the belt. Saad Muhammad recorded a 15-round unanimous decision, winning on judges' scorecards by three or four points. The key was knocking down the Englishman twice in the 14th round. That, the Philadelphian figured after the scores were read, was the end of Conteh.

Not quite. The World Boxing Council ordered the rematch because of a controversy stemming from action in Saad Muhammad's corner during the first bout with Conteh. His punches opened cuts over Matthew's eyes. His cut man, Adolph Ritacco, was then accused of using an illegal tea leaf solution to stop the bleeding. The WBC suspended Ritacco for life. The New Jersey State Athletic Commission suspended him for two months. Shortly before the rematch with Conteh, the WBC modified its suspension, reducing it to one year.

This maneuvering gave John Conteh another shot at the crown—he realized that it was likely to be his last opportunity. "This is a chance," he said. "I'm going to grab it with both hands."

There was as much infighting before the bout as there was during it. Arguments occurred about Adolph Ritacco's status, the referee and head butt rules (given that Saad Muhammad claimed the cuts Conteh opened in the last fight were from his head, not his fists). At the weigh-in, he and Conteh pretty much just growled at one another. Saad Muhammad, none too happy about the equity decreed in the purse split, predicted a knockout. He had trained like a madman for the return match, fueled by his anger over the controversy. One day, he took a 12-mile training run that included bounding up the steps of the Philadelphia Art Museum just the way Rocky did it in the movie. Matthew was asked if he jumped up and down and thrust his arms skyward like the scene in the movie. "You know I did," he replied, smiling at the recollection. It made sense. Every jogger that passed by did it, so why not a genuine world boxing champion?

George Francis, Conteh's trainer, said that Sam Solomon, one of Philadelphia's bright strategists, was "too fat to be a good trainer." Francis insisted that he was kidding, but Solomon, whose build was definitely on the round side, didn't see much humor in the comment. "Smile now," he added. "After Saturday, they'll be very sad." Conteh said that he was fitter than ever and that fans could expect to see a different fight than the first time.

Conteh was right about that, but not in the way he expected. Saad Muhammad basically beat him to a pulp. There was some feeling-it-out in the first round, but by the second, Saad Muhammad's fists discovered unblocked, clear routes to Conteh's head, and while the fight was scheduled for 15 rounds, just like the previous one, there was no way that was happening. Boom, boom, out go the lights. Saad Muhammad pummeled Conteh quite frequently with every type of punch. In the fourth round alone, Conteh hit the canvas five times. Referee Octavio Meyron waved an end to the proceedings with 33 seconds still remaining in the three-minute session. Right around that time, referees started becoming more conscious of frequent knockdowns, and audiences began to see swifter stoppages of fights.

Sometimes the overhand right scored, coming in like a missile over John Conteh's jab. Sometimes Saad Muhammad got inside and dug left-right combinations to his body. Afterward, Conteh admitted that he had lost count of how many times he tasted the canvas.

"I'm the best light heavyweight in the world," Saad Muhammad declared. At that moment, two defenses into his reign, there didn't seem to be anyone around to dispute him. In fact, Saad Muhammad felt so good after the Conteh fight that he wanted to keep going with another title defense as soon as possible. He ended up facing Louis Pergaud, who hailed from Germany via Cameroon, in Halifax, Nova Scotia. That put the world in the World Boxing Council. Saad Muhammad won on a fifth-round TKO.

In 1980 and in 1981, Matthew Saad Muhammad began expressing broader goals than just being a world-champion boxer. He talked a little bit about his motivations, which seemed two-pronged. He hoped to bring glory to his chosen religion, and he hoped to keep banking six-figure paydays so he could retire at a young age and do whatever he wanted.

"My sole purpose in fighting," Saad Muhammad said at one point, "is to propagate my faith of Islam and to win the other half of the championship."

That other half, at the time, referred to the World Boxing Association. Today there are more alphabet boxing authorities than just the WBC and WBA. The record for light-heavyweight division title defenses was 12, set by Bob Foster, and Saad Muhammad made that his goal as well, declaring "That's my intention." He also wanted to be a retired millionaire by age 30. They were laudable aspirations providing excellent motivation, but while reasonable in theory, they were far distant in reality.

In October 1978, Saad Muhammad faced Alvaro "Yaqui" Lopez in Philadelphia with the North American Boxing Federation crown at stake. He defeated Lopez with an 11th-round stoppage. After dispatching Pergaud rather handily in Canada, Saad Muhammad signed for a second fight against Yaqui.

Lopez was a rugged fighter from Mexico who was living in Stockton, California. He was born under a bullring in the town of Zacatecus, and for years lived beneath the grandstand. His aspiration was to become a matador. However, when Yaqui got his chance at age 14, a bull's horn severely broke his ankle. That's when he turned to boxing. Few top-notch fighters had as much bad luck as Lopez. In 1976, he fought John Conteh for the title in Denmark before the Englishman forfeited it and lost a disputed decision. Twice he fought Victor Galindez in Italy, with both decisions going to the champ. Lopez won most of the time, but he could not halt a champion to take the decision out of the hands of the judges.

By the time Yaqui agreed to face Saad Muhammad for a second time, he was 0-3 in title bouts, but he was viewed as a dangerous and worthy adversary. At only 29, Lopez's face looked like a road map of his travails. He had the tough-guy face of a Charles Bronson. Each little line or crease seemed to represent a close call in his life. Saad Muhammad had tremendous respect for his abilities: "Yaqui's a good boxer. Sometimes a southpaw can make you look bad. He's a thinker. There is meaning in everything he does."

Whether or not he recalled his words from the pre-fight banter, after it was over, trainer Sam Solomon seemed to have the wisdom of Solomon with his analytics. "It'll be pretty tough for a while," he concluded. Of course, Sam went and blew it by saying that Saad Muhammad's second fight with Lopez could resemble his second fight with Conteh. The resemblance between the fights, in what became an epic bout at the Great Gorge Playboy Club in McAfee, New Jersey, turned out to be nil.

The July 13, 1980 bout was scheduled for 15 rounds. It also figured to be a somewhat routine defense for Saad Muhammad, but it was the fight that brought out the best in both men. A remarkable contest that was chosen as *The Ring* magazine's Fight of the Year for 1980, it was likely the most difficult, evenly matched challenge that either man ever faced, and it left the 1,300 spectators in awe of what they witnessed. I was one of those left open-mouthed at various times by the action.

The fight had more twists and turns than a grand prix course, more unbelievable moments than any five other fights, and it demonstrated in a most emphatic way what ring courage is all about. Those who were present still speak of the bout as one of the greatest they have ever seen.

This was Matthew Saad Muhammad's fourth defense of the WBC light-heavyweight crown, and it was almost miraculous that he emerged still in control of the title. The bout probably came within an eyelash of being stopped by referee Waldemar Schmidt—in Yaqui Lopez's favor.

From the beginning, Lopez's hunger to finally capture a world title was on display. He was the aggressor, pressuring Saad Muhammad, and in the first round he opened a cut on Matthew's head. Although Saad Muhammad started somewhat slowly, he did bloody Yaqui's nose and then cut him with blows around the eyes.

It was a brutal war of a fight, but midway through, Lopez seemed in command. In the eighth round, Lopez landed with a huge right and believed Saad Muhammad was about to fall. The wild action had fans roaring and at times thinking the champion's title was going out the window. Saad Muhammad was pinned against the ropes, bobbing and weaving, desperately trying to play defense as the punches rained down on him. Lopez had the upper hand, firing 10 straight punches without a retaliatory response. The barrage continued. There were 20 straight blows from Lopez to Saad Muhammad without interruption over 30 seconds. He was trapped, and looked doomed. It seemed as if Schmidt was going to step in and halt the fight, giving the championship to Lopez. The only thing that saved Saad Muhammad was his ability to duck and avoid some of what Lopez threw at him.

Then things turned so swiftly as to be surreal. Saad Muhammad actually smiled at Lopez and began firing hard left jabs back at him. For a minute or more, Yaqui thought he was king of the world. Now he had no zip left in his punches. His arms were weary and he could barely defend himself. Just that fast, Matthew Saad Muhammad had regained control. From the brink of defeat he roared back. *The Ring* magazine chose this three-minute stretch of stunning action and seesawing control of the fight as its 1980 Round of the Year.

The fight fans who were present will never forget it. This might have been the round of their lives. "I felt truthfully he had me in trouble," Saad Muhammad recalled. "But I felt whatever happened I would be victorious."

At that point, he was probably the only one, despite having a reputation for coming back from difficult circumstances. Yet from there Saad Muhammad captured the next three rounds, making Lopez backpedal and setting the stage for a climactic 14th round. As Lopez weakened, Saad Muhammad grew stronger. Early in the 14th round, he scored a knockdown with an overhand right, a left hook and another right. Lopez climbed to his feet, but appeared shaky.

Sensing the kill, Saad Muhammad bore back in immediately, and more combinations sent Lopez to the ground a second time. Up again, desperately trying to regroup, he could not fend off the champ and went down a third time almost immediately. That made three trips to the canvas. When a fourth journey to the floor followed after a Saad Muhammad straight right, Waldemar Schmidt called it off. Matthew Saad Muhammad retained the title with a technical knockout at two minutes and three seconds into the 14th round.

It had been a very long afternoon for the two combatants, and it got longer when the protagonists stayed in their dressing rooms for lengthy visits with their handlers before emerging to discuss the fight. Yaqui Lopez appeared and seemed somewhat bewildered that he had not won: "I hurt the guy. I hit him good, and he almost went down. I did not pick my shots right. My corner told me what to do, but I'm a hardhead." Lopez held a cold compress against his left eye as he spoke, and he wore a bloody towel over his shoulders.

Matthew Saad Muhammad remained out of sight and contact for 80 minutes after the fight. I didn't think he was going to come out at all to talk to sportswriters. When he submitted to questioning, he spoke so softly that he could almost not be heard. A small group of us surrounded him and leaned in close. He seemed thoroughly exhausted and puffiness surrounded his eyes. He mostly spoke in whispers, and it seemed to be an effort. Matthew said that he was too careless with his own protection in the early rounds, and he admitted that at times "he was hitting me at will."

The victor looked very much as if he needed a rest, but he did recognize that the fight fed his reputation and was not uncharacteristic of his style. "Everyone knows Matthew Saad Muhammad can make wars," he said of himself. "I just fought a very good veteran. Eventually, it can turn into a war."

After this war, Saad Muhammad needed a little bit of peace in his life for a while. He took a four-month break before making a defense in San Diego against Lotte Mwale of Uganda. The boxing world is filled with characters with unusual and colorful back stories—sometimes believable, sometimes seemingly subject to embellishment. Mwale came into his shot at the WBC light-heavyweight title with one of those stories attached to his name.

Lotte Mwale grew up in Uganda and came of age at a time when the mad dictator Idi Amin ruled the land. Among the hellacious crimes Amin was accused of by his people was cannibalism. Supposedly, he saw one of Mwale's fights and visited him in his dressing room after the bout. Amin admired the muscular body of the Ugandan light heavyweight and said it looked good enough to eat. Such a comment coming from a beautiful actress might be considered flirting. In this instance, given Amin's fearsome reputation, Mwale packed a suitcase that night and fled to Zambia. Whether fact or fiction, no one was certain, and although Mwale's record was announced as 17-0, no one seemed positive about that either. When Saad Muhammad's handlers tried to find film on Mwale, who had made appearances in Denmark, they also came up empty. "We are counting on the underground scouting system," Sam Solomon noted.

By the time the fighters reached the ring in the San Diego Sports Arena, Lotte Mwale's record had improved to 21-0. He had had a heck of a training camp. Playing his role to perfection, Mwale entered the ring accompanied by several drummers in tribal dress. It wasn't clear whether they were supposed to psych him up or psych out Saad Muhammad.

Perhaps trying to apply his own mental magic, Saad Muhammad paraded into his foe's corner and placed his forehead against Mwale's. It was an exaggerated stare-down lasting about 30 seconds. Yet for all of that, when the bell rang to start round one, Saad Muhammad started with his typical slow pace. Mwale landed crisp jabs, and Saad Muhammad tossed wild swings and missed. But before the end of the second round, the champ was in charge, pressuring his opponent with big shots.

In the fourth round, Saad Muhammad zipped a hard and swift left uppercut to Mwale's jaw, and the shot flattened him. He fell backward slowly and hit his head hard on the flooring. Mwale was counted out at 2:25 of the round by referee Tony Perez, who would have had time to count to 100. The Ugandan lay still on the canvas as the ring doctor examined him and later reported that he did not even open his eyes for the first 15 seconds. Indeed, even in his dressing room after a decent interval, Mwale sat up groggily, saying, "He just confused me."

During and after, it seemed. A small crowd of sportswriters and Mwale supporters surrounded him as he searched for answers as to why Saad Muhammad had starched him. Mwale's English manager, Mickey Duff, pushed his way through the group to his man, slapped him on the thigh and said rather cavalierly, "Well, Lotte, that's show business."

That was pretty much the last heard from Mwale on the world boxing scene. Later it came out that he was from Zambia, not Uganda, all along. He had been an extraordinary amateur; he posted a 44-9 professional record, and died at age 53 in 2005. Apparently, the Idi Amin–Uganda myth was just show business.

The knockout punch delivered by Saad Muhammad could have been used on an instructional video of how to throw an uppercut. Even he marveled at the picture-perfect nature of it: "That was the best shot I've ever thrown in boxing."

Matthew Saad Muhammad was paid $650,000 for the fight, his biggest purse to that point. He still dreamed of a one-million-dollar payday to fight Eddie Mustapha Muhammad, then the WBA champ, in order to unify the title. At that time, the promoters at Muhammad Ali Professional Sports were throwing around big money to fighters like confetti at a New York City parade, trying to seize control of the marketplace from promoting stars Don King and Bob Arum. Muhammad Ali lent his name to the group for a fee, though he didn't work with MAPS on a daily basis. Nevertheless, he was at ringside to watch Saad Muhammad defend his crown.

Not long afterward, MAPS came unraveled. Founder Howard Smith burst into the news when he was accused of embezzling more than $21 million in funds from Wells Fargo bank. The sugar daddy of boxers disappeared from the scene before he could make as many of them as rich as they hoped, and before he could wrest control of boxing matchmaking from the big guns.

For the moment, Saad Muhammad was quite content with his dominating performance against Lotte Mwale: "If the right don't get him, the left surely will." That was true, although he felt compelled to add the phrase, "I'm not bragging."

Matthew Saad Muhammad, his reputation burgeoning, returned to his home area in Atlantic City for his sixth title defense against Vonzell Johnson of Columbus, Ohio. He had been angling for the big unification bout with Eddie Mustapha, and talk was floated of a $1.5 million payday for that. But no arrangements were made, and he accepted the Johnson challenge on three weeks notice for $300,000. "Come early," Saad Muhammad advised. "He's just another man on my knockout list."

Johnson was trying to avoid such a fate. He was tall at six-feet-four and had a good jab. Vonzell thought flicking it in Saad Muhammad's face was the way to go to preserve his good health and remain upright. He watched enough film on Saad Muhammad (much more readily available than movies of Mwale) to understand that his other most recent foes had the same game plan, but he

Matthew Saad Muhammad's life story was the stuff of Hollywood movies and his fights in the ring were legendary. (Photo courtesy of J. Russell Peltz)

didn't stay with it once he swarmed them. What Johnson did offer was an intelligent analysis of how Saad Muhammad came across in the ring.

"The guy's tough and durable," Johnson conceded. "He's deceiving. It looks like he's ready to go [fall], but he's not ready to go. It takes a little from their heart. He took their best punches. He's got a lot of endurance. You can never get out of your fight plan against a guy like that."

There was no doubt about it that Johnson talked a smart game. However, one of the characteristics of boxing is that it's a lot easier to be reasoned and objective when sitting down studying film than it is after your opponent punches you in the mouth. Somehow, everything you learn gets scrambled upon contact, and all lessons are lost.

Unlike many others who couldn't stick to their strategies for very long, Vonzell Johnson impressed everyone by fighting as wisely as he said he would for the first eight rounds of the scheduled 15-round contest. He did precisely what he intended to—sticking and moving and staying away from Matthew Saad Muhammad's power. Johnson did not get anxious; he did not rush things, and did not fool himself into believing that Saad Muhammad was more vulnerable than he seemed. Eight perfect rounds were in the bank, a classic boxing performance giving him the lead. It was perhaps not so surprising that the 23-1 Johnson followed the strategy he had set out since he was managed by the great Angelo Dundee, who trained Muhammad Ali and Sugar Ray Leonard in their spectacular careers.

Johnson even buckled Saad Muhammad's legs with a shot in the first round. His regular, annoying jab to the face drew blood from the champ's nose. Everything was going Vonzell's way, but it always must be remembered that the championship distance of 15 rounds is a marathon, not a sprint.

In the ninth round, Johnson seemed to develop a sudden onslaught of amnesia. Instead of sticking to the style that brought him that far, he came out of his corner and stood still, ready to mix it up instead of sliding and moving. What happened? Saad Muhammad began to impose his will. The slower his target moved, the more he hit his target. Vonzell slowed and looked weary, and Matthew bore in.

The 11th round had just begun when Saad Muhammad delivered an overhand right that caught Johnson perfectly in the face and knocked him backward into his own corner. Matthew moved in and pummeled Johnson with lefts and rights, and Vonzell flopped to the canvas. He was in big trouble in a hurry, although he was able to climb to his feet ahead of a 10-count. That was an achievement, but he was in no condition to defend himself, and Saad Muhammad pounced on the challenger again and landed several blows before referee Tony Perez halted the bout. "I knew it would be in the later rounds," the winner said of his victory. "As always, Saad Muhammad comes back." Although his goal was to meet Eddie Mustapha Muhammad and round up the other piece of hardware to unify the title, when Matthew was asked after the Johnson bout who he would like to fight, the WBC champ replied, "I'll fight King Kong. I don't care if they come up with the money."

That would be a fine bit of matchmaking for Don King, Bob Arum, J. Russell Peltz or MAPS. Of course, if Saad Muhammad was going to take on a foe as formidable as the skyscraper-climbing King Kong, he wanted to he paid appropriately. Twenty million dollars to be exact.

For whatever reason (Mr. Kong couldn't be reached for comment), that match was never made. Instead, Saad Muhammad defended the title two months later against Murray Sutherland. A Scotsman from Edinburgh, Sutherland favored plaid trunks in the ring and was better suited for the super-middleweight class at 168 pounds, rather than at 175. He did eventually win a world title at the lesser weight, but he gave Saad Muhammad a good scrap before having his hopes for the light-heavyweight crown dashed in the ninth round in Atlantic City.

Murray Sutherland left Saad Muhammad with an unwanted souvenir of their meeting. One Sutherland blow to the face burst the champ's lip open, and he needed seven stitches to seal the cut.

The triumph over Sutherland represented Matthew Saad Muhammad's seventh title defense. In a talent-rich division that was impressive. He was skilled and courageous, although rarely did he ever have an easy fight. His reign was duly appreciated and admired. In July 1981, Saad Muhammad appeared on the cover of *The Ring* magazine. His photo showed a handsome athlete with a muscular torso, black hair closely cropped, and with a pensive look on his face. He came across as a young man with things on his mind, his eyes gazing away from the camera as if looking toward a murky horizon.

Inside, in a package of stories, Saad Muhammad's career was examined along with his life. Editor Nigel Collins was extremely complimentary of the rugged fighter, suggesting that he "has staged more comebacks than Frank Sinatra. Blessed with a deluxe knockout punch, celestial recuperative powers and enough heart to stock a brigade of Marines, he is the prototype of today's sluggers."

The somewhat haunted look on Saad Muhammad's face seemed appropriate given the complicated scenario surrounding his beginnings. At one point, Matthew offered a $10,000 reward for information leading to a reunion with his birth family. Like so many persons from somewhat similar origins, he wanted to know the truth about his past. A woman contacted Saad Muhammad because she thought he bore a resemblance to a neighborhood girl from her own youth. She was right. Eventually, the connection was made between Saad Muhammad and the Loaches—four half-sisters and a half-brother.

There was no DNA testing at the time, but when Saad Muhammad met the group, he was convinced they were for real. The half-brother, now a grown man, was Rodney, the one who had abandoned him on the fateful day he was left alone near the Benjamin Franklin Parkway. The way Rodney told the story, he took the younger boy out, told him they were going to have a foot race, and then he ran away without looking back. That was the last time in more than two decades that he saw his half-brother.

"The story made me cry," the fighter said. "It shocked me." At that time in his life, though, Matthew Saad Muhammad could afford posting $10,000 rewards. He owned a house in the Philadelphia suburbs that had a swimming pool. He was just beginning to obtain some endorsement opportunities. Almost as soon as he became champion, Saad Muhammad stated that he didn't want to continue fighting for too long a time. He wanted to cap his career when he was still a young man and go on to do other things, such as being of help to children growing up without parents. "I don't like to get hit," he admitted. "Nobody likes to get hit."

A couple of years after making that statement, however, Saad Muhammad was still fighting. He was arguably at the peak of his earning power as he turned 30. Boxers never walk away too soon. They always stay too late. Boxers almost never give up a title voluntarily. They lose the title, then retire. Or they lose the title, retire and un-retire, only to fight again. Money, pride and that unflagging belief in their own invulnerability still tend to rule their thoughts.

Saad Muhammad did not wish to relinquish his light-heavyweight crown easily. His next opponent was another Philadelphia-based boxer. Jerry "The Bull" Martin was originally from Antigua, but he left the Caribbean and settled in Philly. The Bull was a strong fighter with staying power who was building a good record, but he did not possess as much pure firepower in his fists as Saad Muhammad, though he believed he did.

After the Sutherland bout, Matthew took five months off from the ring. He needed the time for his lip to heal, and he also got married during that summer of 1981. It seemed that he had honed his sense of humor, for when the boxer was asked about his lip, he replied that his new bride Michelle "says it's kissable."

There was no intimacy between Martin and Saad Muhammad, even if they were both Philly guys. The bout went on into the 11th round before the champ caught up with the challenger. A straight right fist crashed into Martin's face and the impact had him teetering on his pins as if he was about to fall forward. But referee Larry Hazzard rushed in, caught Martin, and signaled that the fight was over before The Bull hit the canvas.

It was a controversial ending, but it gave Saad Muhammad his eighth straight successful defense. Somehow, one after the other, he dispatched worthy challengers. He always took their best stuff, kept on standing, and returned fire sufficiently to put them away in the end.

Was there anyone Matthew Saad Muhammad couldn't defeat? Eddie Mustapha was out of the picture after losing to a rapidly improving Michael Spinks. But a new contender was battling his way to the front of the rankings. Sure enough, he was from the area, too. Dwight Braxton, at the time called "The Camden Buzzsaw," was from the New Jersey city right across the Delaware River from Philadelphia.

Braxton, who later changed his name to Dwight Muhammad Qawi, carried his 175 pounds very differently on his body than did Saad Muhammad. If the latter appeared lanky, Braxton seemed squat. He was large-boned and exuded power. If other fighters gave Saad Muhammad due respect because of his seemingly inexhaustible ability to absorb punishment and still come back, Braxton did no such thing.

"Saad's got the perfect style for me," The Buzzsaw remarked. "He will get his head knocked off. I will beat him unmercifully."

Such talk is commonplace around the fight game. Braxton may have believed every word he uttered, but the bravado could also be seen as a method for drawing out Matthew Saad Muhammad to convince him that the big talker needed shutting up, and the only way to do that was to sign to fight him, putting the title at risk. For those who had watched Saad Muhammad rise through the ranks, take on all comers and polish them off, even when he had to seize victory from the jaws of a looming defeat, Braxton seemed to be simply another contender. He was a legitimate one, for sure, but few saw in him the destructive power that he claimed would be too much for a formidable champion.

At that point, I had correctly predicted the results of 20 or so world title fights in a row. I predicted that Matthew Saad Muhammad would win and retain the title. My winning streak and his ended on the same night.

Saad Muhammad, his handlers, the sportswriters and the legion of fans who loved him in Philadelphia were shocked when all of Dwight Braxton's predictions came true. The title changed hands on August 7, 1982 in Philadelphia. Braxton delivered a fearsome beating to the legendary boxer, stopping him in the sixth round of their scheduled 15-round title match.

It was a painful thing to see, the king being deposed, the champ being brought down by someone who carried so much power in his fists. Saad Muhammad was likeable and popular, and suddenly he lost his status as the light-heavyweight champion of the world. For all intents and purposes, his boxing career ended that day. It should have, but a man who said he derived no joy from fighting and wanted to retire young did not stick to his word.

John DiSanto, a Philadelphia boxing historian who works closely with the Pennsylvania Boxing Hall of Fame, where Matthew Saad Muhammad is

The plaque honoring Matthew Saad Muhammad at the International Boxing Hall of Fame in Canastota, New York.
(Photo by Lew Freedman)

enshrined, said of the onetime light-heavyweight division ruler: "He was my champion. As far as the most exciting fighter of all time, he gets my vote. He's in that conversation. There was a time when it was impossible to beat him. If they didn't pull out a sledgehammer or a gun, they couldn't stop him."

Saad Muhammad was finished as a world-class fighter, but he didn't know it. Almost overnight, he began losing regularly. He did not officially retire until 1992, and most of his last bouts were conducted overseas where his name still had value for a young up-and-comer to face. Near the end, Saad Muhammad fought in Trinidad and Tobago, the Bahamas, Australia, Germany, Serbia and Spain. He lost seven of his last nine fights with one draw, and his final record was 39-16-3. For all of the money he made, which reached into the millions of dollars, nothing was saved. In the end, he kept fighting for the paydays.

Matthew Franklin had begun boxing as a sad story, and Matthew Saad Muhammad ended his time in the ring as a sad story. For all of his skill as a fighter, the former light-heavyweight champion had an even greater capacity to break hearts.

Near the end of his boxing career, Saad Muhammad dabbled in mixed martial arts in Japan. For a little while, he trained young fighters in Atlantic City. The highlight of his retirement came in 1998 when he was inducted into the International Boxing Hall of Fame in Canastota, New York.

Shockingly, in the early 2000s, Saad Muhammad was homeless and living on the Philadelphia streets he once owned. All of his money had evaporated through his own negligence or the chicanery of others, though no specific blame was charged in any legal forum. At one point, Saad Muhammad lived at the RHD Ridge Center, a Philadelphia homeless shelter.

Eventually, the former champion was featured in a front-page story appearing in a street newspaper produced by homeless editorial personnel. When reporters sought out Saad Muhammad and talked to him, they noted that he had been given the key to the city of Philadelphia by four different mayors. It just so happened at the time that he owned not a single building with locks in which he could turn any of those keys.

Saad Muhammad admitted being embarrassed that he was staying at a homeless shelter and acknowledged that he really had nothing to his name. He was looking for a fresh start, and his belief in God was strong. One thing was clear from the interviews he gave—Saad Muhammad believed he still had one more big comeback in him. He thought he could still be a productive citizen and help others. That is, once he could clear his head and get back on his feet. He was determined to do that, and no one ever accused Matthew Saad Muhammad of being short on determination.

Where did all of his money go? Saad Muhammad claimed that he once supported 39 people. The money flew out the window as if it was attached to birds tagged by the Department of Natural Resources. He said that he listened to the advice of too many people, including too many of the wrong kind, and that he lost his way and used bad judgment. He added that he loved boxing, even if he did not use that word when he was in his prime.

From the beginning, the residents—if that is the right word—at the homeless shelter recognized him. Matthew Saad Muhammad was decades removed from the era when he dominated the light-heavyweight division, but it was doubtful that he could walk down Spruce Street, Chestnut Street, or even the Benjamin Franklin Parkway in Philadelphia for very long without being recognized.

It was the street newspaper *One Step Away* that revealed Saad Muhammad's problems, but in addition to other news outlets that followed up, the story led to reconciliation between him and his family members. In 2010, he moved into his own apartment. He then got involved in programs that help draw attention to the plight of homeless people in the city. On May 2, 2012, acting as a representative of the group Knock Out Homelessness, Saad Muhammad threw out the first pitch at a home game of the Philadelphia Phillies.

Yet it still was not precisely clear what was going on in Matthew Saad Muhammad's life. When inquiries were made to seek him out in his new apartment, some of those still in the fight business who had known him believed he was homeless again.

The life of the little boy born in 1954, who was named by nuns but who attained worldwide fame under another name, continued to be a compelling, dramatic tale almost beyond belief. Somehow—on the streets, in the ring, in the company of those who guided him, and by guiding himself—he had persevered and survived. But then he was diagnosed with amyotrophic lateral sclerosis, better known as Lou Gehrig's disease. In the spring of 2014, the world caught up with Matthew Saad Muhammad. On May 25, he passed away in a Philadelphia hospital at the age of 59.

6

JEFF CHANDLER

O ne of the things no one could understand about "Joltin' Jeff" Chandler is how he packed so much power into his fists when he was only a bantamweight, fighting at the division's 118-pound limit. The other thing no one could understand was how he could remain male-model thin without surrendering all of his favorite foods.

Chandler measured five-feet-seven, and he had a washboard midsection. By applicable boxing standards, he was a little guy. For those who must maintain a strict weight limit, Chandler just didn't figure. He seemed to eat whatever he wanted, whenever he wanted, especially when manager "K.O. Becky" O'Neill did the cooking and invited him over for dinner at the South Philadelphia home she shared with husband Willie O'Neill, Chandler's trainer.

Watching Jeff Chandler eat was almost a spectator sport. On one particular night, he downed meatloaf, corn, spinach, bread and three glasses of iced tea. That was not long after he ate two pieces of fruit and announced that he planned to eat again that night before bed. I could testify that the food was good since I was sitting at the same table, but I didn't eat as much as Jeff. K.O. Becky and Willie used to admonish him for eating too much, but when they observed his absence of weight gain and his fanatical training commitment, they stopped worrying that he would eat himself out of contention in one of boxing's lower-weight classes. "He trains hard," Becky commented. "He's always in good shape." "If you give him a day off, he'll run anyway," Willie added.

Chandler grew up as a South Philly guy. The neighborhood was tough and had its share of bullies. Jeff said he had to fight in the streets and also at school, but those were not bouts governed by the Marquis of Queensberry rules. He was 19 years old when, driven by curiosity, he showed up at the Passyunk Gym.

Becky and Willie were the odd couple of Philadelphia boxing. They shared their married life with the young boxers they handled. At four-feet-eight, Becky had a voice like a foghorn, one that could be heard across the street even when she wasn't angry. Willie was more soft-spoken, but he took care of the training details, sometimes with Nick Belfiore, who worked with Chandler. Willie had a chunky build; he could probably sweep Becky off her feet and bench-press her if he wanted to. Although Becky and Willie were white and Jeff was black, they treated him like a son and were like a new set of parents. Not every fighter has been lucky enough to have managers who cared as much about him as the O'Neills did for Chandler.

Watching the couple and Jeff Chandler interact made me think of a family, as if they were all connected by genealogy. Whatever happened behind the scenes, in public forums they were always polite and helpful, and they made you want to root for their clubby little endeavor to succeed. With all of the money being thrown around by big-time promoters, I thought of their association as a mom-and-pop arrangement in which they were struggling to get noticed by the sport's governing authorities and doing things the right way on the way up.

From the first moment the O'Neills saw Jeff in the gym, they recognized that they might have stumbled upon a natural. Chandler said he had no experience with gloves on, but they saw excellent form immediately, and a willingness to learn. Just maybe, they thought, they had somebody special working with them.

It didn't take long for others to see the potential in Chandler as well. He turned pro in February 1976 in Scranton, Pennsylvania. But after that, most of his early fights were on cards promoted by J. Russell Peltz at the Blue Horizon and the Spectrum. The debut bout was a draw, but then Chandler, who sometimes weighed in at between 114 and 116 pounds, well under the threshold regardless of his diet, won every single fight—four-rounders, eight-rounders and 10-rounders.

Heavyweights rule boxing. The bigger they are, the more fans love them. Big guys turn on the crowd. The ticket-buyers want big thumpers. Bantamweights don't carry much sway, maybe because most of the fans are larger than they are. Also, the history of top-notch bantamweights in the United States has been limited. The small fighters thrived in Asia and Latin America. There were not very many highly regarded American bantamweights, so fans did not get terribly excited about the prospects of even a first-class local guy fighting against an opponent who didn't speak English. That meant it was hard for a Jeff Chandler, or any other American bantamweight, to get matches that resulted in big paydays.

Chandler was blessed with good management. He gained experience, made a name for himself in the division, and waited patiently for the opportunity to challenge the titleholder. If he kept winning, he knew it was only a matter of time. In September 1979, Chandler won the United States Boxing Association crown from Baby Kid Chocolate with a ninth-round technical knockout. His improvement was evident. Chandler was a very controlled fighter. He picked his spots accurately, and he carried a great deal of power when he landed. He knocked out enough opponents to have the nickname "Joltin' Jeff" bestowed on him. Chandler seemed almost too skinny to pack so much wallop in his fists, but he never showed up for a fight in anything less than peak condition.

Tall for his weight class, with black, curly hair at the time, Jeff wore a distinctive mustache. He did not brag about his skills, but he had a game plan that he believed would pay off over time, as long as he kept on winning. Chandler felt his time was coming, probably by 1980. If he won a handful of additional fights, he could no longer be ignored. He lived his life with the single-minded purpose of someone sacrificing to fulfill a dream to become the best in the world: "You can't do it unless you sacrifice. My life is built around my training."

The maturation of Jeff Chandler was on display when he annexed the U.S. title from Baby Kid Chocolate. A few months later, he took on Francisco Alvarado of El Paso, Texas. The fight took place in Upper Darby, just outside of Philadelphia. Alvarado was a stubborn foe, but Chandler was an artist in the ring. The Texan may have been hardy, but Chandler was precise. He repeatedly ripped clean shots at the visitor, penetrating his defenses and landing exact punches that gradually weakened his opponent. The fight was stopped in the seventh round as Chandler whaled away at Alvarado, who just wouldn't fall: "He was hard to take out. The guy's tough. I gave him good body shots and good head shots. I was going out to box him, but after the first round, he was easy to hit."

By that time, Chandler was 19-0-1, and he was gaining a Philly following. He might be overshadowed by the big men in the fight game, but when Jeff entered the ring, he provided action, and those who appreciated style recognized the smoothness and slickness of his delivery. As time passed, one did not even have to be an aficionado to realize he was the genuine article. "Jeff was the best fighter I ever had," Russell Peltz maintained, "and he got better all the time. He only wanted to fight good fights."

Peltz marveled at Chandler's dedication, remembering him shoveling snow so he could get into the gym while at the same time it built muscle: "He was a strong fighter for a skinny guy."

Over the decades, the biggest weakness in the sport of boxing has been that it is not governed by a single efficient authority. Politics has played a role in the pairing of fighters since the turn of the 20th century. Often the deserving do not get a shot; at other times, the unprepared are rushed into title fights as cannon fodder. Sometimes it all works out the right way, with the fighter who has earned the chance to be a challenger getting his fair shot. Peltz worked on Chandler's behalf, and Jeff held up his end of the bargain, beating every opponent brought before him.

After Alvarado, Chandler faced Javier Flores. Then in the first half of 1980, Chandler appeared three times at Resorts International in Atlantic City and won three straight bouts. He cracked the world ratings and was ranked ninth by the time he met Andres Hernandez of Puerto Rico at the end of March. Chandler endured a cut over his left eye from Hernandez and could not knock him out. Later complaining that his opponent was a dirty fighter, Chandler was unusually animated in the ring in the 12th and last round. He sealed a unanimous decision by cutting Hernandez and knocking him down twice in the final round.

Chandler's big chance came near the end of the year. At last he signed a deal to meet Julian Solis of Puerto Rico for the World Boxing Association bantam-weight title in Miami. The fight was scheduled for November 14, 1980 at the Miami Jai Alai Fronton.

Five years had passed since Chandler first wandered into the Passyunk Gym. His record was 23-0-1, and on fight night he was rated seventh in the world. Defending champion Julian Solis was 22-0 after lifting the crown from Jorge Lujan of Panama. The 15-rounder was Solis' first defense.

Solis had never seen Jeff Chandler fight. Chandler saw Solis win the title and studied his style. He fully expected to take the title back to Philadelphia along with the $100,000 purse. Married and with a baby, Chandler hoped to use the money to buy a house. He hoped to use the crown to enhance his reputation.

There was no mingling between the combatants in the days leading up to the bout, even though they were staying at the same hotel. Solis spoke Spanish and Chandler English. At their joint pre-fight press conference, Solis waved the championship belt. Chandler playfully tried to grab it, setting off a stream of commentary from the champ—not a word of which Chandler understood.

Jeff Chandler was never excitable outside the ring. He was no Muhammad Ali making rhymes and predictions. He almost always remained unflustered by what was going on around him, inside or outside of the ring. Chandler was not particularly philosophical, but he was thoughtful. And even as he worked his way up through the world rankings, he did not completely forego his job as a construction worker. That type of labor certainly strengthened his upper body, and I once described him as a stork that looked as if it had been lifting weights.

Leading up to the fight with Solis, Chandler admitted that he had spent considerable time imagining what it would be like if he won the title, when he won the title, and how he would react. Pictures floated through his mind of the great moment, but because it hadn't happened yet, he could not really know: "Sometimes I think when I knock the guy out, it will be like any other fight and I won't be overwhelmed. Then, sometimes I think I'll jump out of the ring into

South Philadelphia's "Joltin' Jeff" Chandler won the bantamweight championship of the world from Julian Solis in Miami. In the fight shown here, held in Atlantic City in July 1981, Chandler defeated Solis a second time. (Photo courtesy of J. Russell Peltz)

the third or fourth row. I've envisioned it, but I really don't know how I'm going to act when I win it." It was not clear whether or not Solis got the message when Chandler said he was going to pressure the Puerto Rican champ so hard it was going to feel as if he was being hounded by a swarm of bees.

The scene was colorful. Not too many world title fights have been contested in a jai alai fronton. It was November, but still steamy in Miami. The city, a haven for expatriate Cubans and Latinos from Central and South America, turned out in force to support Solis. The crowd was more than 5,500 strong, vocally backing their favorite. For a while, Solis' girlfriend paraded around the perimeter of the ring, showing off the WBA title belt. Chandler brought his own cheering section, including his mother, Irene, and three dozen or so friends and family members from Philadelphia. Most of them wore "Joltin' Jeff Chandler" T-shirts to make their allegiance visible.

If most of the fans were against Chandler, then so be it. Nothing shook his confidence. He had always been unflappable in the ring, and even though this was a special night, he embraced it calmly, treating it as business as usual. There was nothing to indicate that he was overwhelmed by the moment. It was the moment Jeff had planned for, and he was ready for it.

From the opening bell, it was all Chandler. Near the end of the first three-minute stanza, the challenger dumped the champ onto the canvas with a major league left hook. The stunning blow quieted the crowd, but it came so close to the end of the round that there was no count. It was apparent, however, that Solis was going to be in for a long night of punishment, and that's what occurred. In the third round, Chandler cut the champion over the right eye. Things were going so well for Jeff that in the corner, Willie O'Neill told him to slow down.

The strategy seemed to work. Chandler kept pummeling Solis, and the defending champ rarely had the answer. A swelling appeared under Jeff's left eye, but he blamed a head butt, indicating that he believed that was pretty much Solis' best offense. Chandler's punches became more effective in the 10th round, and Solis' original cut began bleeding as if the challenger had opened a water faucet. The blood began interfering with the champ's vision, and while between rounds his cornermen patched him up, Chandler promptly reopened the cut with fresh blows in the next round.

The 14th round brought the end. Chandler trapped Solis in a corner and just belted away at his head, flinging combinations that scored big. Although Solis did not go down, referee Carlos Berrocal had seen enough and halted the round at one minute, five seconds. Jeff Chandler was the new WBA bantam-weight champion of the world. Julian Solis' girlfriend surrendered possession of the title belt, and Chandler shouted, "I'm taking it back to South Philadelphia!" Chandler became the first American bantamweight champion since 1950.

K.O. Becky started crying from joy, the tears streaming freely down her cheeks at the sight of Chandler as the boss of the division. "It went just the way I thought it would," she declared. For that matter, Jeff really did swarm Solis as he predicted, the pressure from his stalking so intense that the champion could not land his good stuff and was always covering up from the barrage the challenger leveled at him. "I'm going to holler and scream a little bit," Chandler exclaimed, displaying uncharacteristic emotion. "I'm in ecstasy. I'm so happy."

Jeff Chandler came along at a good time in the fight game, when solid money matches were being made frequently in the casinos at Atlantic City, when network television was seeking high-profile Americans to show off on weekend afternoons. An all-sports cable network called ESPN was the new programming vehicle on the block, but it was young and still finding its course. In the coming years, it would revolutionize the way sports are covered by television, but at the time, networks were happy to have title fights on free TV.

Coming from Philadelphia, Chandler had the pedigree of a major American fight town behind him, even if he wasn't a middleweight or a big guy. Prominent bantamweights were nonexistent in the United States, but Jeff was going to change that mindset. He had a world title on his résumé and that was his calling card. The fact that he was an action fighter and an American with English as his first language added to his credentials since most of the key challengers were foreigners who needed translators when interviewed by American TV.

Chandler's first title defense was scheduled for January 31, 1981 at the Franklin Plaza Hotel in downtown Philadelphia. The Art Museum was not much more than a long outfield throw away. Putting up a ring in a first-class hotel not attached to a casino was a peculiar idea, but it did represent a home-field advantage for Chandler when he met Jorge Lujan, Solis' predecessor as titleholder and a boxer who wanted the belt back.

To the little guys of the world, Chandler's victory represented a usurpation of the crown. There had never been any Americans who got title shots, much less won the title. On the world scene, Chandler was something new. This fight in itself represented something new since there hadn't been a world bantamweight title fight in Philadelphia in 40 years.

Jorge Lujan, the oldest of 12 children, had been the champion for three years before Julian Solis bested him, and he made five successful defenses. He was anxious to show that his loss to Solis was a fluke, and many agreed with him. Jeff Chandler recognized Lujan's skills and conceded, "He's gonna pose a problem. He has good stamina. He can go the 15."

Lujan had a 22-3 record and claimed he was fighting for his country. He stated that he badly wanted the title back so that he could bring the belt home to Panama. Now that he had actually corralled the title, though, Chandler was in no mood to give it away. He also started thinking of himself as a representative of the "smaller guys" in boxing. The title and television were providing him with a forum to make a statement: "I want to show people what they've been missing. This is in defense of smaller guys. I want to do good when I'm out there. They [the fans] don't think we can break an egg. It's all constant motion, hit and not be hit."

Chandler could be a bomber when he let loose, but against Lujan he showed off a superior defense. He found it difficult to connect with the challenger's chin as often as he wanted to, but he drove Lujan crazy by eluding all of his best punches. Jeff was like a wisp of smoke—easy to see, but hard to grab. He ducked and slid away in anticipation of Lujan's right hands, he clinched to bottle him up, and connected with a steady tattoo of punches, even if not really big ones.

The fight went the 15-round distance, Chandler's first time going all the way, and he claimed a unanimous decision. Jorge Lujan was a renowned body puncher, but Chandler kept him off-balance. For long stretches of time, Lujan appeared befuddled, trying to figure out how to move in on his opponent, and instead not doing anything. Consistent with his usual "eat-first-and-ask-questions-later" approach, Chandler was quite surprised when he weighed in on fight day at only 113 and a half pounds. Lujan weighed 118, and that's pretty much an unheard-of spread in the bantamweight division. Chandler thought the scale was wrong. Whatever their real weights were, he looked exceptionally slender, and for a small man, Lujan's stomach looked as if he hit a buffet right before fight time.

Chandler also had to put up with a cold, but his stamina never flagged. He didn't pepper Lujan with big shots, but he scored consistently enough to eliminate the number-two-ranked contender. Now Jeff had two victims on his résumé who had recently been world champs. The rest of the universe was beginning to get the word that he was for real and might be around for a while.

Less than three months later, the World Boxing Association ordered Chandler to defend the crown against number-one-ranked challenger Eijiro Murata in Tokyo. The circumstances did not represent particularly friendly treatment of the champ by the WBA, making him fight the chief contender halfway around the world in his own country. The O'Neills definitely worried about whether Chandler could get a fair shake in Japan. Although it was a mandatory defense, Becky drove a very hard bargain on behalf of the champ. Jeff was to be paid $150,000 to make the journey, as opposed to the $70,000 he made against Lujan. The Chandler camp was also very picky about the officials. While K.O. Becky agreed to allow for one Japanese official, it was also agreed that there would be one from Pennsylvania and a third official from a neutral geographic area. "I have enough telegrams to paper my kitchen wall from the negotiating," she remarked.

It took two days to fly to Tokyo, but it took even longer (as in never) to sort out the winner. The Chandler–Murata bout ended in a 15-round draw. That meant that Chandler kept the crown, but it didn't truly settle the matter of who was better.

Just about everyone Jeff Chandler faced on the worldwide scene wanted to face him again. Jorge Lujan said that Chandler never hurt him, and Murata scored a draw. Julian Solis also wanted a second chance. The second Chandler–Solis bout was set for Atlantic City, a rather different environment from the first, though really just another gambling establishment in Resorts International. Chandler still lived in South Philadelphia, so he was among friends, instead of facing a hostile Latin crowd in Miami or an unfriendly Japanese group in Tokyo. Yet he noted that the final preparation week was still tough when he was at home because everyone there knew him: "When you start getting mean for the fight, it's hard to be with people you love."

Julian Solis wanted another piece of Chandler—a piece that he didn't get the first time around. One of five boxing brothers, Solis said he wasn't in top shape for the first encounter because he had tremendous pain from problems with his wisdom teeth. Now his choppers were OK. That may have been, but it didn't matter. Chandler's right hand was lovelier the second time around. He recorded a one-punch knockout of Solis, seven rounds into the rematch. It was such a hard blast that he was checked out at the Atlantic City Medical Center. The count to 10 could have past midnight.

"It was an instant punch" was the way Chandler described his devastating KO shot. It was "the bomb." The explosive overhand right followed a left jab and landed flush on Solis' jaw. He fell forward into Jeff, seeking to grasp him in a clinch, probably on instinct. "I knew he was just about finished. I could see him drop as a dead weight on me," Chandler recalled.

The victory was Jeff Chandler's third defense of the world title, and the next challenger up was also familiar. At least there was a good excuse to face Eijiro Murata again since their first match ended in a draw. This time, for the December 1981 rematch in Atlantic City, it was Murata who took the long flights to reach the bout.

For the first time, Chandler, whose nickname might as well have been "Mr. Buffet," talked openly of the increasing potential for weight problems as he aged. He admitted that he had ballooned all the way up to 120 pounds between fights, and began speculating on a future as a junior featherweight (at 122 pounds). But almost in the same breath, the details of one of his most recent meals were revealed: chicken cordon bleu, baked potato, string beans, ice cream roll with chocolate sauce, and fruit cup.

Atlantic City was more hospitable than Tokyo, and for $125,000 Chandler felt right at home. He may have run into trouble solving Eijiro Murata's defense the first time in Japan, but it was clear that he had learned from one dance with the challenger. Looking crisp and smart, Chandler zipped jabs at Murata's face constantly from the first round on. He slipped away from Murata's best offerings and kept him off-balance. Round after round passed with Chandler completely in charge, piling up points. Only in the seventh and eighth rounds did Murata do well. But those three-minute intermissions were exceptions.

In the 13th round, Chandler, who patiently awaited an opening, smashed Murata with a right uppercut that knocked him to the canvas. The Japanese fighter rose and continued, but his American opponent did it all over again, clobbering him with another right uppercut. This time Murata was finished. To that point, the three judges had Jeff ahead by 12, five and seven points, respectively.

Chandler was on a knockout spree with a variety of finishing blows—from a left hook to an overhand right to two uppercuts. "That was my shot," he noted. "When he bends forward, pick him up." And then, of course, let him down, and not so gently.

Just another notch on the belt, a belt that was beginning to fit better the longer Chandler wore it. "Jeff was a great fighter," Nigel Collins, the former editor of *The Ring* magazine, commented. "He didn't want to fight stiffs. He moved very quickly once he turned pro. He just had it."

After wiping out the most prominent challengers from far away, Jeff Chandler found himself in a most unusual position. One of the other world-ranked bantamweights was also from Philadelphia. In fact, Johnny "Dancing Machine" Carter was from South Philly. The duo went to Edward Bok Technical High School together. Chandler studied welding, but never pursued that as a profession. Carter studied tailoring, and in adulthood he could sew, make pants and taper his shirts.

Jeff Chandler had earned worldwide bragging rights, but all of a sudden, a considerable amount of noise was starting to drown him out in his own neighborhood. The thing that gave Johnny Carter credibility, besides a 23-1 record, was that he defeated Chandler in the amateurs. The famous champ, however, had only had two amateur bouts before turning pro. Carter wanted a crack at the crown, and the match was eventually set for March 27, 1982 at the old Civic Center.

Believing that Philadelphia might not be big enough for two bantamweights, Johnny Carter worked his way into the world ratings mostly by fighting out of Las Vegas. But when it became apparent that his old acquaintance was in the way of his achieving his aspiration as world bantamweight champion, Carter returned to the area.

Johnny aligned himself with gruff-voiced manager Bob Botto. Botto, who at six-feet-four and close to 300 pounds, was large enough to be a defensive tackle for the Eagles, also smoked cigars that were as long as Louisville Sluggers, and sometimes they preceded him into a room. The funny thing was that as deep-voiced as Botto was, he had nothing on K.O. Becky. Chandler's manager described herself as "four-foot-eight, 82 pounds, and I have a voice that sounds like 10 tons of gravel [but] I don't come up to his waist."

Botto was an energetic salesman for his fighter, although his gestures could be a bit grand. When I informed him that was I taking a particular weekend off to get married, he wanted to give me a wedding present of a side of beef. I politely declined, saying that I had nowhere to put it. My bride and I joked that for our tiny wedding at home in our condo, we should utilize Big Bob's services at the front door, asking "Friend of the bride or friend of the groom" in his intimidating voice.

Botto owned a meatpacking plant in Mount Royal, New Jersey, and Johnny Carter worked part-time loading sausage on a wrapping machine. When he wasn't packing either meat or punches, Carter took voice lessons, and Botto swore he could be the next Nat "King" Cole when he concluded a life of throwing jabs. In June 1981, Botto announced that he was close to a deal for a World Boxing Council title fight between his man Carter and the champion, Lupe Pintor, but it never came off.

When the deal was struck to bring the two Philadelphia fighters together once more, Chandler offered nothing but respectful commentary about his rival. "John Carter is a much tougher opponent than all of them," Jeff said of those he handled in his recent string of title fight victories.

Carter leaned a little bit more toward trash talk: "His style hasn't changed a bit. He never fought a guy like Johnny Carter." As was consistent with his nickname, Carter was light on his feet and moved agilely in the ring. It was going to be Jeff Chandler's task to slow him down with jabs and body punches and then let fly with those big right hands.

At that point in the 25 years of Chandler's life, Carter was the only man who had defeated him in the ring as either an amateur or a pro. Carter was hungry to win the title. Chandler was hungry to avenge the loss. "That is the only thing I do have to motivate me," he remarked. "It's the only loss I have."

Chandler couldn't erase the defeat, but he could make up for it. It didn't take him all that long to do so. As expected, Carter came out dancing over the first two rounds of their scheduled 15-round fight. His talent was in his elusiveness, and he stayed away from the thunder in Chandler's fists. A patient man when he had to be, Jeff studied Carter's movements over those six minutes. By the third round, he was getting busy with some hard shots. In the fourth round, Carter forgot all about his intelligent game plan and tried to slug with his opponent. That was a major error. Chandler not only staggered Carter with big blows, he fired so many rapid punches that Johnny could do nothing but cover up.

Chandler proved that he was boss of the old neighborhood, and not incidentally, of the whole wide world. After winging left hooks at Carter's head, the challenger was shaky enough to provoke referee Frank Cappucino into halting the bout at two minutes and 28 seconds into the sixth round. That was the last time that anyone from South Philadelphia, no matter how tight they were with Carter, suggested that anyone but Chandler was the best around.

Afterwards, Willie O'Neill began to say, "I expect Jeff to be the champ…" But before he could finish his sentence, Chandler cut him off and laughingly added, "forever." K.O. Becky chimed in with "and ever."

Of course, there is no such thing as forever, except perhaps in fairy tales. Certainly not in boxing as fighters age and lose their edge, as new hotshots come along, and as flukes occur. After two more defenses, as he had previously suggested, Jeff Chandler began experimenting with the next higher weight class, the 122-pound division. He twice fought at that weight, winning once and losing once, and then he dropped back down and successfully defended the crown two more times.

On April 7, 1984 in Atlantic City, Chandler faced up-and-coming Richie Sandoval. The bout went to 15 rounds, but he lost on a technical knockout and surrendered the title. Sometime before that contest, eye doctors said that Jeff was developing cataracts and that if he continued to fight, he might risk blindness. After the loss, Chandler retired with a record of 33-2-2 and underwent surgery for the problem. He never boxed again.

Johnny Carter remained an active fighter until 1989, but he never got another shot at a world title. He retired with a record of 33-8. In 2012, he was inducted into the Pennsylvania Boxing Hall of Fame and was one of several inductees feted at a banquet in Philadelphia.

Carter hasn't been a bantamweight for a while. He still was in touch with the sport, though, working as a trainer at the Marian Anderson Recreational Center in Philly. On his induction day, Johnny sported some fuzzy chin hair and wore a skullcap. He lamented the absence of Bob Botto for this special occasion. Botto had died at his home in Swedesboro, New Jersey in February 2007 at age 73. "I kept in touch with Bob from time to time," Carter recalled. "Me and Bob had some of the best times."

Johnny, who was surrounded by family members at his table at the banquet, intended to deliver prepared remarks, but he couldn't do it because he got so emotional when it was his turn to talk. "I had a speech, but I choked up," he admitted. "I couldn't even read the paper. I wanted to thank my mother and father. I was very emotional."

Thinking back 30 years to the bout with Jeff Chandler, Carter said he felt as if he was at the peak of his game at that time. He proved himself a winner in Las Vegas and believed that since he beat Jeff as an amateur, he could do it again.

"I came back home and I became a top contender," Carter reminisced. "I was proud of myself. I was almost on top. I wanted to do that, fight Jeff. I thought I won the first five rounds. But you can't keep that pace up that I had. It was like a rocket. It was going to come down. It had to come down. It's very ironic that it happened that Jeff and I were from the same school. We were the same everything. But it is what it is."

Carter was a John Travolta–style dancer in his prime, and he loved his nickname "Dancing Machine." It was different for sure. He loved being in the boxing world, too, and that's why he still trains more than a dozen young people: "It keeps me in the game. I can really show them." Proud of what he accomplished in the ring and proud to be a Philadelphia fighter, Carter said the label is a great one. "It carries that legacy with it," he added.

Jeff Chandler was just 28 when he retired after holding the bantamweight title for three and a half years. He was planning for a rematch with Richie Sandoval, who knocked him down in the 11th round of their title fight for the only knockdown of his pro career. During his eye surgery, Chandler had a plastic lens implanted in his left eye, and when that was publicized, the heads of the boxing commissions of Pennsylvania and New Jersey said they would not grant him a license to resume fighting.

The chorus for Chandler's retirement grew louder. Promoter Russell Peltz and K.O. Becky O'Neill also said that he should stay out of the ring. "I kissed Jeff's eyes and told him he'll always be my champ," Becky said at the time. Chandler said he didn't want to retire, but that it became an issue that was out of his hands.

There are so many instances of boxers who make ill-advised comebacks and endure devastating defeats that it was reassuring to those close to him that Jeff Chandler did not. In 2000, Chandler was inducted into the International Boxing Hall of Fame in Canastota, New York. It was a hallowed and satisfying moment for the onetime bantamweight king.

In 2012, Chandler was living with his girlfriend in Delaware, an easy ride from Philadelphia, but far enough away from Center City that he kept a low profile. He was the father of three sons aged 23 to 30. His two sisters, one a Philadelphia lawyer, and a brother were still close to him. Chandler's hair was very close-cropped, shorter than military regulation, and he had some gray in a

The plaque honoring Jeff Chandler at the International Boxing Hall of Fame in Canastota, New York. (Photo by Lew Freedman)

tightly cropped beard. He wore glasses, but was easily recognizable as his old self. Jeff said he was shocked one day when he stepped on the scale and it read 144 pounds, but he did something about it to lose some of the weight.

Still, Chandler overlooked his diet during a visit to a favorite Italian restaurant a few blocks from his home. He said that growing up in South Philadelphia made it easy to get into trouble on the streets, but that his father, who worked at the Frankford Arsenal, was enough of a disciplinarian to keep him scared. He kept telling his children that he didn't want them to end up dead or in jail. Such a tragic ending would have been entirely possible in the neighborhood, and some of Chandler's childhood friends ended up that way.

When Jeff was a teenager, although he hadn't really played other sports, he thought he would like to be a basketball player. Then he looked in the mirror, assessed his height and weight and realized that wasn't going to happen. Jeff walked into the Passyunk Gym, he claimed, entirely "on a whim."

Johnny Carter, who had something like 80 amateur fights, beat Chandler in his second amateur bout. But he was too impatient to stick with the amateurs in order to gain experience. If he was going to get punched, Chandler wanted to make money.

The first manager for his first few fights was Arnold Giovanetti. "He was killed," Chandler recalled, "but he told Willie O'Neill that if anything ever happened to him, 'Could you do something with my boy?'" Jeff noted that Willie had seen him fight, and he ended up with the O'Neills as his guardians in the sport: "It don't get no better than Becky and Willie."

Chandler was right. They weren't big-time managers, but they cared about him and knew enough of the right boxing people to guide him to the top. Russell Peltz thought of the team of Willie and Becky O'Neill the way I did, as the ultimate mom-and-pop boxing operation. Willie died of a stroke at age 78 in 1994. K.O. Becky, who was born Rebecca Ruth Birenbaum, died in 2005 at age 81. When she was a younger woman, before meeting the husband who turned her on to boxing, Becky worked in vaudeville. Chandler misses both of them terribly:

"It's tough. It's been a pretty hard time. Boom, they were both gone. They were two people who did so much for me. I became a Hall of Famer because of them. That's my mom and pop. They treated me like that. They took care of me all of the way. I loved those people. It was a big loss. They loved me to death. They were good people. I do want their memory kept alive. I really miss them."

Willie O'Neill showed Chandler the way to the championship. Almost from the moment he first began working with him, Willie offered encouragement. "Let's get it" is how he spoke. Chandler was inexperienced and had to work his way through the ranks and learn his trade, but he had the will to do so and O'Neill saw that in him.

"I had thoughts about whether I could become world champion," Chandler admitted. "'I'm going to keep working hard to do this' is how I thought. I won the U.S. Boxing Association title and then the North American title. I had an undefeated streak going. Then it was, 'Wait a minute, I think I can do this. Am I there yet? How much does it take to get there? I can do this.' It took some time."

In Chandler's mind, the turning point came when he bested Baby Kid Chocolate to win that USBA title. It was a step up in class compared to the fighters he had been battling: "When I put a whipping on him, I thought, 'Maybe I can do this. Maybe there's a place for me.'"

Living in South Philadelphia wasn't always the easiest thing, even after Chandler became a contender. At one point, he was charged with cocaine possession and was placed on probation. Another time, he was involved in a street altercation and was stabbed in the back. It was not as serious an injury as it could have been, but he was scarred. "I knew I was going to fight for the title," he recalled. "All I knew was that I did my running. I trained every day. I kept myself clean."

One day the dream came true. One night in Miami, Chandler grabbed the bantamweight championship from Julian Solis. His first thought was, "It's unbelievable."

Probably the most mature thought Jeff Chandler ever had in his life came upon him soon after. He had been on a long journey and fulfilled the goal of winning a world championship. But he wanted to keep that world championship, so instead of letting down, instead of celebrating too long, instead of letting his training slide, he worked harder because he knew that arriving at the destination wasn't a dead end: "I was trying to be the best in the world. Beating Solis took me a little bit higher. But here I come into 1981 and we're still climbing up that ladder. I was telling myself, "'You are the best in the world, but you've got to get better.'"

Chandler did that. He beat Solis a second time. He handled Jorge Lujan, the former champ, and he twice took on Eijiro Murata. He fought like he wanted to keep the title forever, just as he said that time when Willie provided the lead-in sentence. The Johnny Carter thing was there—old business that he had to dispose of in order to quiet the Carter factions in Philadelphia. Under World Boxing Association rules, he probably never would have had to face Carter, but Chandler thought it was best to do so:

"He wasn't even on my level. It was to settle an old score. He was a good fighter, but I was a 15-round fighter and I beat him in six. I was ready. I put something on him in the third or fourth round. I could see the distress in his face. He realized he got himself into something he couldn't handle. He deserved the shot and I deserved the win."

For most of his career, the put-it-in-front-of-me-and-I'll-eat-it Chandler had little difficulty making weight. For one fight he came in a pound over. He wondered about moving up permanently to 122. "Before I was making weight so easy. I was in tip-top shape almost every time I fought. I was trying to be the greatest in the world and it paid off."

Chandler was 56 when he was reminiscing and he looked sharp. He liked to wear nice clothes after he won the title, and he looked quite impressive in a suit. His children were on the verge of having children, and although Jeff did not keep much memorabilia around in his Delaware house, he said he had a lot of films of his fighting. One day, when they got old enough, grandpa planned to show the grandkids what he was like in his prime, when he was the best in the world at what he did.

Just for a moment, Chandler rose off the couch in the living room and began shadowboxing. He could still work his hands like a pro, digging into those imaginary foes. Hard training was so long ago, but he swore that when he took his long runs on Broad Street, in Fairmount Park, and all over the city, he ran up the Art Museum steps before Rocky ever thought of doing it.

Jeff Chandler won the WBA bantamweight championship, and he defended the title nine times. It is a record that he is proud of, a record that won him acclaim not only from the Hall of Fame in upstate New York, but another Hall of Fame in Los Angeles, and the Pennsylvania Boxing Hall of Fame as well. "I haven't seen anybody since Jeff Chandler who could have beat him," Russell Peltz declared. That's nearly 30 years of bantamweights.

The absolutely most pleasurable moment of Chandler's career was the night at the Miami Jai Alai Fronton. When he won the title and made the belt his, he jumped in the air and then his rooters from Philadelphia rushed into the ring and hoisted him on their shoulders: "That was the best night I ever had in boxing." And going into the Hall of Fame in Canastota was the best night of retirement: "My God is great to give me something like that. That was wonderful, man. I hadn't thought about being in a Hall of Fame."

Many former fighters look back with bitterness to bouts they believe they should have won. They didn't always save their money. They retire and fall out of the public eye. Not Chandler. He achieved his goals and became world champion; he says he is OK for money and has fond memories of all that he accomplished: "I had a good career. Great times. Every time I open up that Ring boxing book, I look up my name."

It says there in black and white, just the facts without embellishment, that Jeff Chandler of Philadelphia was for a time the best in the world.

7

THE FLETCHER BROTHERS

When it comes to nicknames, few boxers can compete with the monikers applied to Frank and Anthony Fletcher, and even fewer can offer up a mother who was so theatrical outside the ring that she deflected attention from what her boys did inside the ring.

Frank "The Animal" Fletcher came out of prison to become a shooting star on the world middleweight scene. Anthony "Two Gun" Fletcher, his younger brother, is in prison on death row, though certainly not for what he did in the ring. Mother Lucille, probably the most animated fan of boxers in American history, not only shouted out her belief in the kids, she even banged her high-heeled shoe against the canvas in a fevered demonstration of rowdy support. The TV cameras could not resist the Fletcher clan.

As somewhat of a wild kid, Frank Fletcher gravitated toward trouble. Lucille taught him how to box and survive. On good days it took, but on other days, Frank could still get into trouble. In 1976, when he was 22, he made his professional boxing debut. Displaying a merciless and relentless but crowd-pleasing style, Frank pummeled foes into submission. He was the type of guy that, had he been serving in the infantry, would have waded into machine-gun fire to take out an enemy nest with a grenade. It was all or nothing with Frank, and few could stand up to his sledgehammer punches.

Once discussing what he thought about in jail, Fletcher mused, "Always the ladies." The comment was accompanied by a deep sigh. He was arrested frequently as a youth because he got a kick out of stealing, but he spent two years at Holmesburg State Prison for assault.

Frank had a one-inch scar on his nose, and anyone might guess that it was put there by a nasty, knife-wielding thug. He said that the cut was made by a razor blade in a gang fight in 1975. There was a gap between his teeth when he smiled, but with lips pursed and impassive eyes staring out, he could be downright handsome in photographs. Not that he was likely to remain that way if he wasn't careful; Frank took his share of blows to the face in trade for the twice-as-many punches he threw. His vicious pursuit of foes, pinning them in corners and wiping them out, earned him his colorful nickname, "The Animal." In some professions, that would be a liability; in boxing, it was an image enhancer. I found Frank to be entertaining in and out of the ring.

Like most boxers, Fletcher was anonymous during his first several professional fights. Being from Philadelphia, he appeared on cards at the Blue Horizon and ventured into Rahway State Prison to fight Tony Braxton of Camden, New Jersey, in two six-rounders. Braxton, the brother of Dwight Braxton, who became light-heavyweight champion as Dwight Muhammad Qawi, won one and the other was a draw.

While Braxton served his time, Fletcher rose from unknown to prominent middleweight, his reputation growing by the minute in televised fights that packed more action into them than a James Bond movie. Frank punched out Ben Serrano, Jerome Jackson, Caveman Lee and Randy McCready, and he kept right on rolling. Sammy Nesmith and Norberto Sabater also tasted knuckle sandwiches delivered by The Animal. He was a phenomenon. There wasn't a more exciting fighter around.

None of that "basic art of self-defense" stuff for Frank Fletcher. He was built for free-for-alls, able to take anything that any opponent landed, but with concrete in his fists that could take out a man once he cleared his own head of any cobwebs. He bludgeoned people, often at times when it was least expected. Before the end of 1980, Fletcher owned an ESPN Tournament title and in 1981, he went after fellow Philadelphian Ernie Singletary in a defense of his United States Boxing Association middleweight title.

Singletary's résumé contrasted with the stereotyped image of a boxer. Yes, he had won Golden Gloves trophies so he had boxing credentials, but he was also studying to be a lawyer. Over the decades, many more boxers needed the services of a lawyer than thought of becoming one. To help support his family, Singletary, who brought a 24-2 record into the August 31, 1981 fight at the Sands Hotel Casino in Atlantic City, also worked part-time as a carpenter. He was looking for more fame from his boxing career than he had already received. Well known in Philadelphia, Singletary was on the radar screen of *The Ring* magazine with a number 15 middleweight ranking, but just barely.

In his mind, Frank Fletcher had stolen his thunder. At the moment, Fletcher was only 27 years old and was already ranked number six, though he hadn't put in nearly the amount of time that Singletary had. His record was 12-2-1. Ernie was a textbook boxer, not a flashy puncher. Frank was the darling of the middle weights of the sport because he was the opposite—a devil-may-care leather thrower. That kind of irritated Ernie, who was already 29. Actually, it really irritated him: "It bugs the hell out of me to see someone [like Fletcher] take the shortcut when Ernie Singletary takes the long way around. I think he's sloppy. There's no class to his fighting. He's never been up against a fighter like Ernie Singletary."

Well, Ernie Singletary hadn't ever been up against a fighter like Frank Fletcher either, and for good reason since there really was no one else around like The Animal.

Fletcher didn't give his opponents much time to think about things once the bell rang. He was on them and punching and trying to ring their bell. Ernie sought to fight his way, but he had to fight Frank's way. But he acquitted himself quite well with that style. Blasting away and exchanging blows to each other's face for three minutes a round, the two boxers engaged in a true slugfest. In the end, Singletary had his right eye virtually shut and was unable to see Fletcher's punches coming. The ringside physician stopped the fight because Ernie was taking too much punishment. But it wasn't as if Fletcher got away unscathed; blood was pouring down his face. "The Philadelphia Story" ended in the eighth round of the scheduled 12-round bout.

"His punching wasn't nothin'," Fletcher declared in a statement of bravado afterward, though he had to step back from those words. Frank had been cut pretty badly and that was hard to ignore. What did not come out until later was that Singletary and Fletcher both spent time in different hospitals recuperating from their intense exertion.

On the same card, Fletcher's brother, Anthony, chalked up a solid eight-round decision over Livingstone Bramble. He had served in the Army and launched a lengthy amateur career that tabbed him as someone to watch. Anthony's record was 159-12 and he won the National Amateur Athletic Union lightweight championship before turning pro in 1980, ahead of his 23rd birthday. At five-feet-nine and a half, he was a little bit taller than his brother, though he was thinner and competed in lower weight classes.

In early 1982, Frank Fletcher met Tony Braxton for a third time, with the USBA title at stake. This time Braxton no longer lived behind walls topped with barbed wire. He was released from Rahway State Prison in August 1980 and was trying to build upon the boxing career he began behind bars. By then brother Dwight had captured the light-heavyweight championship. It was during this

Philadelphia middleweight Frank Fletcher (*right*), before he shaved his head, became a swift sensation in the early 1980s because of his ferocious style. Here he is besting Tony Braxton in a 1982 bout in Atlantic City. (Photo courtesy of J. Russell Peltz)

period that Tony Braxton admitted that he was really older than Dwight by a couple of years, not his younger brother.

Tony admitted that he had been in trouble with authorities from the time he was a truant at age 13 and did his time for armed robbery. "I grew up in reformatories and I never was able to cope with society," he stated with remarkable candor. "I went through all of the reformatories in New Jersey and all of the prisons. Drugs were one of the problems. Soft stuff to hard. That was one of the problems. It was the same people, the same crowd you run into. I wasn't assertive enough to tell them no."

When meeting guys like Fletcher and Braxton, and hearing them out, they seemed like different people than the ones who committed the crimes that earned incarceration. I found it difficult to imagine their split personalities, one minute friendly to sportswriters, the next minute courting trouble. It happened with many boxers.

Braxton sought help from manager Dan Duva and got clean of drugs at the Damon House, a rehab facility in Paterson, New Jersey. Tony liked it so much—the program made him feel so much better—that he kept living there. He had already begun work as a counselor to 14- to 18-year-olds who experienced the same kind of growing-up difficulties that he had faced.

Tony may have been a prison fighter at first, but when he got out, he notched a big win over Clint Jackson. Braxton was a more natural 154-pounder, a junior middleweight, and was ranked number eight in the world by The Ring. But the Jackson victory set up an attention-getting, televised opportunity against Frank Fletcher, and given his record against The Animal in their first two meetings, he wasn't going to be scared.

Not that Frank Fletcher feared anything. But leading up to the fight, he did show a new side of his personality. Much like Muhammad Ali, who made the practice famous, not only because he could rhyme, but because he was accurate, Fletcher doodled out a poem predicting how the fight with Braxton would end. It read: "I am not the greatest, but the latest. Braxton is a bum, I don't know where he comes from. Neither will I care, because I will be right there. The fight is for certain and I am for sure...Tony Braxton will fall in four." Not exactly Robert Frost, but clever enough for a boxer, even if he wasn't right in his round prediction.

Fletcher was indeed right there—he proved that by leading with his face. Braxton was as tough as ever, and he and Fletcher traded bombs, connecting fists to heads, drawing blood, gritting teeth and plowing on. The fight went the 12-round distance and once the blood was mopped off the scorecards, Fletcher had a unanimous decision and his 10th straight triumph. That left Frank undefeated for the last two and a half years, or since his Rahway loss to Tony Braxton.

Braxton, who seemed to be preparing for a longer run near the top, followed his brutal bout with Fletcher with consecutive losses to two more Philadelphia middleweights: Ernie Singletary, on the rebound from his loss to Fletcher, and Curtis Parker. And then Braxton left the sport with a 10-4-1 record.

Meanwhile, as Frank Fletcher invaded living rooms all over the country, enrapturing and energizing fight fans with his always-on-the-edge style, his mother became a personality in the fight game just from her over-the-top, fight-day shenanigans. Lucille dressed colorfully and she could raise her voice like a soprano. She couldn't stay in her seat any longer than a kindergarten student, and she never failed to mesmerize spectators.

For those who believed she was the ultimate Little League know-it-all (a.k.a. know-nothing) parent, it was surprising to learn that Lucille Fletcher was actually a licensed amateur boxing judge. In one of the great off-the-wall, deadpan descriptions that could contend for a spot in *Bartlett's Familiar Quotations*, Frank Fletcher's manager, Marty Feldman, assessed her this way: "She's a mouth, but a knowledgeable mouth." That may well have been a compliment.

One of 11 brothers and sisters, Lucille never grew larger than five-feet-two with a weight of about 140. But she was tougher than many of the boys in the family. That included brother Dick Turner, who became a world-ranked welterweight in the 1960s. In becoming the most visible and best-known fight fan in the land as Frank ascended the middleweight ladder, Lucille Fletcher was dismissed as crazy by some. But everyone knew who she was. Almost always attired in a pants suit that permitted freedom of movement, carrying a Teddy bear that symbolized "The Animal," and occasionally employing a megaphone, though she didn't really need one to be heard, Frank's mom was hard to miss at his bouts. In fact, at the height of Fletcher's career, *Sports Illustrated* wrote a feature story on Lucille. She may have been an objective amateur judge, but there was not the slightest hint of objectivity when her son was fighting.

Fletcher was on a great run. Every time he strapped on those bright red gloves, he banked a six-figure payday, usually between $100,000 and $150,000, and that was without holding anything grander than the USBA title. Although just about every bout seemed to be an ordeal as Frank took on prominent names while waiting for a shot at the title against Marvin Hagler, no matter how they cut him up, he emerged victorious. A 12-round decision over Clint Jackson and a six-round KO of James "Hard Rock" Green completed Fletcher's 1982. He thought there was no way he could be kept out of a title fight, but instead he was matched against Wilford Scypion in February 1983. The winner of this bout was in line for the title bout against Hagler.

Unfortunately for Frank Fletcher, this is where his winning streak ended. It was a hard-fought, go-the-distance, 12-round bout, though not as wild as some of Fletcher's recent fights. It was Wilford Scypion, 27-3 at the time, who scored better and won a unanimous decision. The loudest detractor of the result was Lucille Fletcher, who first at ringside and later at Scypion's press conference, kept shouting, "He was robbed!"

Trying to celebrate what may have been his greatest triumph, Scypion did not take kindly to the constant interruptions or the vilification of the decision. "Everybody thought Frank Fletcher was going to beat my brains out," he recalled. "All the people were downing me by talking about who was gonna beat Hagler. It was 'Fletcher, Fletcher, Fletcher.' Now it's Scypion. It was destiny."

This was one time that Frank admitted to being embarrassed by his mother's outlandish behavior, and he asked her to cool it.

Wilford Scypion did get his long-awaited chance for the title, taking on Hagler a few months later. But Marvelous Marvin knocked him out in four rounds. For Fletcher, it turned out that his devastating knockout of James Green had pretty much been a last hurrah. Although he won a subsequent bout over the lesser-known Curtis Ramsey in his comeback fight after Scypion, Frank never regained his mojo, his indestructible image, or his status as a darling of the networks.

Fletcher was knocked out in six rounds by Argentine contender Juan Roldan. He squeezed out a 10-round win over Jimmie Sykes, but then was blasted out in a fourth-round knockout by John Mugabi. His career was ended in two rounds by Philadelphia middleweight Curtis Parker on February 4, 1985 in Atlantic City. "He's the kind of street fighter who can be controlled by a good boxer," Parker predicted.

Frank Fletcher might well have kept on fighting if he could have. However, he was on probation and while visiting his probation officer later in 1985, he thought he was going to be arrested on an unresolved assault charge. Fletcher ran from the office and became a fugitive. His legal problems resulted in the end of his boxing career.

Alas for Frank, once he stepped away from the world of organized mayhem, he went right back to living a life of real risk. By 1987, he was behind bars again, incarcerated in Graterford Prison outside Philadelphia. Even worse, as an inmate, he was stabbed by another prisoner. The incident apparently had its roots in an argument that Frank attempted to win with a punch. Only there was no referee in the immediate vicinity to step in and stop the fight.

Fletcher, who was serving a five- to 10-year sentence for aggravated assault, told a sportswriter that he thought he might end up in a prison fight in which he killed someone and then got sentenced to life. This time around, Fletcher was not only too famous for his own good, he was famous for fighting, and the other tough guys wanted to challenge him. For a man with a temper and a propensity to solve problems with his fists, this was not a good situation.

When the website Philly Boxing History plucked a quote out of Fletcher's repertoire to illustrate his career, the sentence chosen was not about a particular fight, but his general lot: "I've had so many problems in my life that I've often thought the only place you can get peace of mind is a graveyard somewhere."

By 2012, it was not clear just where Frank Fletcher was. He had become a somewhat legendary figure around Philadelphia, and not solely for his successes in the ring. Depending on which Philadelphia boxing figure was asked, the answer to what Fletcher was doing usually involved incarceration in one prison or another, thousands of miles from Pennsylvania. He had been sentenced to a fresh 22 years and was sent to a prison in Colorado after being caught following the probation violation.

"I was told, 'You've got to keep Frankie busy,'" promoter J. Russell Peltz remarked. "He made a lot of money in a short period of time. We made a mistake putting him in with Wilford Scypion. Roldan was another chance to get to fight Hagler. We definitely had Hagler. Frankie was all blood and guts and his mother was part of the act."

For all of the fanfare surrounding his fight years, Frank "The Animal" Fletcher's record ended up at 18-6-1, numbers that do not do justice to the hold he had on the boxing public and the prominence of his career at its apex.

Anthony Fletcher was actually in bigger trouble than Frank. For years he had lived on death row at the State Correctional Institution in Greene County, Pennsylvania (SCI Greene). When the younger Fletcher turned pro, his nickname was "Two Gun." Somewhere over time it morphed into "Two Guns," which was at least two guns more than he needed in the eyes of the Pennsylvania justice system.

Anthony Fletcher was a slick boxer. He was a southpaw and that confused many of his opponents. Taller and thinner than Frank, he also did not pack the same kind of wallop and usually boxed his foes into submission. Between 1980 and 1990, Anthony compiled a record of 24-4-1. In 1987, the younger Fletcher was arrested and charged with cocaine possession. While he was still active, he also suffered an attack of Bell's palsy that left him with a speech impediment, and at one point his boxing career was derailed by a detached retina.

In 1989, Anthony still harbored hopes of winning a world championship. However, on a Philadelphia playground that year, he was shot five times and left for dead. He and a friend were watching a basketball game in his car when someone attacked them. Fletcher's friend died in the shooting. It was first reported that the assailant accused Anthony of being part of a drive-by shooting, though he wasn't present at the scene. Later, he said that it was a case of mistaken identity involving the belief that he and his friend were members of a rival drug-selling gang.

After 11 months off, Anthony Fletcher returned to the ring. He won once and lost twice, but felt that his skills were diminished. In February 1993, Fletcher was convicted of shooting Vaughn Christopher, a 26-year-old Philadelphia man. On the fateful day at issue, he spotted Christopher on the street, got out of his car and confronted the other man, demanding the return of $40 that he said Christopher stole from him at gunpoint in a craps game a week earlier.

Christopher pulled a gun, according to Fletcher. Claiming that the man was trying to kill him, Anthony supposedly grabbed Christopher's gun in self-defense and it went off in the struggle. However, the jury did not see it that way, and Fletcher was sentenced to die by lethal injection. At one point, in March

2001, Anthony was officially informed that he was to be executed in May of that year.

Originally, Fletcher was offered a plea bargain with a sentence of 10 to 20 years in prison. He refused the deal because he wanted his innocence proved in court. He lost his case. Fletcher was stunned by his sentence and has fought it ever since. In 2004, three Philadelphia lawyers, working pro bono, got the conviction overturned. Two medical examiners changed their testimony in the new trial and provided information more favorable to Fletcher.

There was conflicting evidence at trial of how the confrontation between Anthony Fletcher and Vaughn Christopher played out, and new evidence was introduced that Fletcher's defense counsel was ineffective. The prominent law firm of Wolf, Block, Schorr & Solis-Cohen took on the case pro bono and attorneys Jarrett Decker, Lindsey Pockers and Joe Crawford spent three years trying to help Fletcher. Crawford was the son-in-law of the late Philadelphia cut man Eddie Alliano, who had worked in Fletcher's corner during his career.

In 2005, despite the efforts of Fletcher's attorneys, his conviction was upheld for a second time by the Pennsylvania Supreme Court. The Court ruled that the changed testimony of the medical witnesses would not have changed the outcome of the case and that the argument of ineffective counsel did not hold water.

By 2006, Fletcher was residing at the Curran-Fromhold Correctional Facility on the outskirts of Philadelphia. Longtime members of the Philadelphia boxing community wrote letters of support, held fundraisers and played a role in trying to help clear Anthony's name. His lawyers challenged the original sentence and got a judge to listen and act.

Time passed and Fletcher remained in prison. His conviction was upheld, but it took more time for his sentence to be examined. After the Supreme Court rejected all of the arguments of his attorneys, he was sent back to death row. A new execution date of August 18, 2010 was set, but that too was set aside.

Recognizing that he is in a fight for his life, Anthony continued to insist that he did no more than defend himself against Christopher. He continued to amass paperwork that he hoped would one day clear him. Fletcher spoke to members of the media. He attracted the assistance of a Canadian group, the Crime and Justice Project, and new attorneys expressed a willingness to fight alongside him and try to shift his case into federal court.

A note written by Anthony surfaced on the Internet and was reproduced by the Canadian organization. In part, it read, "The fight continues and it will be long and hard-fought. I pray that you all will continue to believe in me." The Canadians also circulated an online petition for readers to sign which was to be sent to the governor of Pennsylvania, asking for the commutation of Fletcher's sentence.

In 2012, Ivan Goldman, a former columnist for *The Ring* magazine, wrote a lengthy series about Fletcher and his case. He viewed the entire matter as a miscarriage of justice and pointed out several flaws in the prosecution's case. Like others before him, he noted that the testimony of a key witness that Fletcher shot Christopher in an execution-style slaying from several feet away should have been considered tainted by the fact that the witness was a drug addict. Goldman joined many others in the boxing community in the hope that one day Anthony Fletcher would walk free again.

By 2012, some 30 years had passed since the heyday of the Fletcher brothers in the ring, comparatively carefree days when both Frank and Anthony could aspire to boxing success, bigger paydays and the prospect of world renown. Those were the days when it seemed the worst that could happen to either of them was that their mother might embarrass them with her enthusiasm.

8

RANDY "TEX" COBB

I t was obvious that anyone whose nickname was Tex did not grow up in Philadelphia, not even South Philadelphia. But wherever Tex Cobb came from, it was also apparent that he was one of the funniest men in boxing history. Hanging out with Cobb could be good for the soul. Most of the time it was good for a few laughs.

Even when he was serious, which he hardly ever was, Cobb could produce a chuckle here and there. Randall Cobb was born in Bridge City, Texas, so the roots of his nickname were real. He played some college football at Abilene Christian, a school that also sent a running back named Wilbert Montgomery to Philadelphia, where he starred for the Eagles. Cobb also worked as a bouncer at a bar and said he was very scrupulous about checking the identification of the girls who wanted to come in: "Not a single 18-year-old girl got in without her giving me her phone number."

After his football days, Tex, who stood six-feet-three and was a real heavy-weight at about 230 pounds, tried kick boxing for a while, recording nine bouts. He also had a black belt in karate. Cobb made his debut in the ring in El Paso, Texas in 1977 against an opponent named Pedro Vega whom he stopped in one round.

The majority of Cobb's earliest fights were in the West, but he eventually relocated to Philadelphia, a bigger fight location, to hone his skills and improve his opportunities. Cobb could punch and his scowl was ranked number one in the world, even if his fists barely lodged him in the top 10.

Randy was big and he had power. He could look scary when he stared at an opponent. His biggest shortcoming was that he was slow and going up against swifter foes was a risk. But his stamina was immense, his ability to withstand a punch was legendary, and because he could make chatter with a talk-show host, fans loved him.

Almost as tangible proof that he was a genuine Texan, Cobb frequently wore a cowboy hat in public. However, unlike the old movie stereotypes, he wore a black hat even though he was not a bad guy: "I just can't keep a white hat clean." That was something you never heard from the Lone Ranger.

Cobb, who had dropped out of Abilene Christian, was still only in his late 20s when he began living in Philadelphia, but he applied the bemused attitude of an older man when coming to terms with the big-city view of him. He said he got called "Cowboy" a lot. He added that people wanted to touch his hat, which was pretty much a hanging offense in Texas: "They're not mature enough to realize their danger. It gets difficult to bring manners to these people." If these guys went to Texas and did the same thing there, "No, they wouldn't live." I loved talking with Cobb because you never knew what he would say, but you could bet it wouldn't be a cliché.

There was no doubt that Randy Cobb knew what he was doing and saying when he talked about his earlier life, but his deadpan delivery usually caught northerners off-guard. Of Abilene he said it was "a long way from what you people describe as a metropolis. But it's a good size for that part of the country. I think they had two elevators."

Cobb said he was never called Tex in his home state, where anyone could be known as Tex, but that trainer George Benton started calling him that in Philadelphia because he "just can't remember white boys' names." Randy rarely cared much about what he said or who he insulted. He figured that anyone who knew him understood he was really just kidding.

After his football career was stillborn, Cobb drifted to kick boxing. He joked that while he was called a professional, he used the term loosely because the most he ever made—only once—was $100. When he was rounded up to make his boxing debut, Cobb was supposed to be a "nobody opponent," but he not only broke the other guy's nose and cut his chin, he got $50 out of it, too.

Tex was in a try-anything mood early in his career. Some people thought he'd be OK in the movies. With curly hair, an expressive face and bright blue eyes, Hollywood found some use for him. In the remake of the movie *The Champ*, Cobb played a boxer who fought Jon Voight. He returned to the movies with more vigor later on.

Living in Runnemede, New Jersey, a Philadelphia suburb, Cobb commuted to a Philly gym and subjected himself to the management of George Benton and Joe Gramby. Moving to Philadelphia was a no-brainer after people told Cobb he could make it as a boxer: "It was the place to go if you wanted to rumble."

Tex recalled that left to his own devices between fights, all he did was drink and hold court at Dr. Watson's Pub. At times when he went into serious training for a big fight, Cobb retreated to the Montgomery County Boys Club in the Philadelphia suburbs. It was military-style living with bunk beds in a barracks where the residents of the moment focused on their running, their sparring and their swatting of the speed bag. When asked what he did the rest of the time in the isolation ward there, Cobb replied, "Oh, I go into town and drink and fuck and take drugs." I spent the night in the barracks once as part of a story, but I never witnessed any activity that would have required me to be placed in the witness protection program for my safety.

George Benton was once an accomplished fighter who could not get a shot at the title even though he compiled a 61-3-1 record as a middleweight in the 1950s and '60s. He was renowned for his defense and his assignment with Cobb was to improve the big guy's "D," to help make him a more complete fighter. "He learns fast and he's got a champ's heart and a champ's jaw," Benton remarked.

He was also a talking machine, and if Cobb had a few more of Muhammad Ali's attributes, he might have been a heavyweight champion. Tex, who admittedly liked to party, developed as a regular at selected saloons, although boxers were never supposed to say things that implied they weren't in training year-round. Cobb was an import from the Lone Star State, and while he liked Philadelphia and appreciated its boxing scene, he did not adopt all aspects of the local culture. He was not into soft pretzels, but decided he could put up with Schmidt's beer: "Schmidt's ain't bad beer. I can get along with Schmidt's, especially after a six-pack."

Cobb's motto was that there are always good, friendly people everywhere, and certainly that applied to Philadelphia. Tex was a magnet for crowds because while he was on the huge side and could look menacing, his banter coupled with a wide grin that turned his eyes to slits when he laughed made him approachable. Coming to Philadelphia did not seem to make for much of a reunion for Cobb and Wilbert Montgomery, not because they didn't like one another, but because they didn't have that much in common. Montgomery was soft-spoken and kept to himself, while Cobb was the life of the party. "He just likes to smile and run for touchdowns," Randy said of his old teammate.

Cobb's athletic prowess instead led to his separating other big, tall men from their senses and teeth. He flew back and forth between Philadelphia and Texas for many of his early fights, which kept him busy, but also undefeated. The zero in the L column led to a fight with former top contender Earnie Shavers. Shavers was probably the most dangerous puncher in the history of the heavyweight division. He had so much power that he could probably break a brick with a jab or crack a truck windshield with an overhand right. For many boxers, signing to fight Shavers was like writing a suicide note.

Shavers, nicknamed "The Black Destroyer," won 74 fights in his career, and 68 of them were by knockout. He was getting older when he faced Tex Cobb at Joe Louis Arena in Detroit on August 2, 1980, but he was only three bouts removed from a title fight against Larry Holmes. Tex stopped Shavers in the eighth round of a scheduled 10-rounder. "All I was doing was throwing punches and then I'd look to see if he was dead yet," Cobb recalled.

It was the pivotal fight of his career. Cobb was only 17-0, but he was now on the boxing world's radar screen, a better-known quantity, and a fairly rare one in that he was a white contender in a field dominated by African-Americans. He knew that the pigmentation of his skin could be an asset. "It's a wonderful selling point that I seem a racist pig," Cobb remarked, although in person he gave off the vibe that like Will Rogers, he never met a man he didn't like. "I had the good taste to be born white. That seems to be the most saleable factor. I have the ability to absorb punishment. I have the ability to hit hard. I have good reflex action. I'm not uncoordinated. I don't have trouble moving."

About that punishment thing... One reason George Benton was trying to hurry along Cobb's ring education was because the fighter had no amateur career, the traditional learning curve, and he was gaining in popularity. That meant that soon he would be matched against better fighters. "I have the least amount of experience of any heavyweight I know," Tex noted. "The rest of it is a learning process."

Cobb recognized that beating Earnie Shavers was a big notch on his record: "Any time you beat a boy like that, you get to the top 10. I can actually pay the bills now."

Bigger paydays loomed. Cobb was viewed differently by the boxing establishment after beating Shavers. He was only a step or two away from a title shot against Larry Holmes, provided he could beat the one or two right people in the way. A big opportunity came through. Cobb was matched against Ken Norton, who had one of the few victories over Ali. "He's a big name," Tex admitted. "He's important. He's a good fight for me."

Anyone who fought Norton in a television fight not only stood the chance of moving up in the rankings closer to the top and a bout with Holmes, but was also going to get a decent paycheck out of it, even if not the millions that the really big guys received. "I'll certainly get enough money to get drunk for a month," Cobb remarked in his own unique way.

Ken Norton briefly held the World Boxing Council heavyweight championship belt, but he was even more famous for his three-fight series with Muhammad Ali. Norton broke Ali's jaw in one of those bouts and was one of the few men ever to defeat the man that some call the greatest fighter of all time. Norton, whose son was also named Ken and became a pro football linebacker, dabbled in television commentary, and it so happened that he was the color analyst for the Cobb–Shavers fight.

The two boxers signed to fight in San Antonio—Cobb country—on July 11, 1980. For Norton, it was a comeback fight. He had retired and been out of the ring for 13 months, but he decided to give it another go. He had to lose 26 pounds to get into fighting trim. But Ken Norton long before proved that he was a warrior, and a victory over Randy Cobb could return him to top contender status and make him an attractive opponent for Larry Holmes. Norton owned the crown that Holmes had held for eight months. It was awarded to Norton following a win over Jimmy Young of Philadelphia when the title was vacant. In Norton's first defense, he lost it to Holmes.

Cobb was on the rise, but he needed a few more wins over big names, it was felt, before the public would see him as a contender. With their back stories colliding, there was a lot at stake in the scheduled 10-rounder for both Ken and Tex.

When the bell rang, the combatants commenced a war for survival that featured seesaw stretches, huge exchanges of bombs by both sides and a roaring crowd of 9,000 fans that was pro-Cobb. Tex was hot from the get-go, wading into Norton and connecting with big shots to the head. In the third round, it seemed as if Norton was ready to drop to the canvas. Cobb delivered brutal punishment, but the former champ somehow stood in. In-between the big rights, Cobb kept Norton off-balance with his left jab and one time even staggered him with that. Ken looked very rusty from his layoff.

Norton snapped to, however, in the middle rounds, and the exchanges of swift, hard punches made the fans gasp. His best round was probably the seventh. He stood in, battering Cobb with lefts and rights over and over again. Astonishingly, Tex took the heat and never once seemed close to a knockdown. It was known that he had a concrete chin, but now he was showing that he had a concrete head, too, impervious to another world-class heavyweight's hardest shots.

In the ninth round, it seemed as if referee Tony Perez might stop the fight. Cobb unloaded, delivering an incredible onslaught that pinned Norton on the ropes and left him unable to retaliate in the face of perhaps 40 unanswered punches. It was an amazing display by Cobb, and it was equally amazing that Norton did not go down. In the 10th and last round, Norton inhaled some fresh air, straightened his shoulders and came out for the last three minutes with the determination to finish off Tex. Time after time, Norton belted Cobb cleanly, but nothing fazed him. He did not wobble or stagger; in fact he barely reacted.

The fight was one of the most action-packed bouts between big men in years. It was a stunning battle that exhausted even the watchers, never mind the contestants. Clearly unmoved by absorbing Norton's best stuff and smashing him back with a clear plurality of clean blows, Cobb looked as if he might be moving into position for a title shot.

But there was one problem. When the result was announced, the Philadelphia-via-Texas heavyweight was declared the loser by split decision. It seemed to be an impossible ruling given the amount of punishment Cobb dished out: "I thought I won about eight rounds," he asserted. "I guess I would have had to knock him out to win."

Cobb was discouraged by the judges' decision, especially since the first thing Norton said to him when the final bell sounded was, "Man, you really kicked my ass."

I was more shocked by the scoring than Tex was, figuring that he had defeated Norton easily. It's still one of the biggest miscarriages of boxing justice I've ever seen.

Instead of going right back to Philadelphia, Cobb took some time off in Texas. He visited with his mother, Norma, and his brothers. When Randy did go back East, he joked about what he was doing, pretty much making it sound as if he was drinking up all of the beer in the land: "Somebody gives me a pocketful of money and I don't come back until I've spent it."

After his vacation, Cobb reviewed the Ken Norton fight. He still believed he won, although he admitted making mistakes by not trying to hit Norton more to the body and not doing his best on defense. At that time, Tex had no idea what was next for him and who his next opponent might be: "It doesn't make any difference to me. Some wash woman. Some SOB in shorts and gloves."

That was very Cobb-like commentary from the heavyweight contender, who ended up fighting the wrong guy next. He deserved the decision over Norton, but in black and white on paper a loss is a loss. He was not going to move on from a Norton fight to a title fight after a defeat. It might have been best for Cobb to fight a few additional lesser fighters to pad his record, but instead he met Michael Dokes in Las Vegas. Originally from Akron, Ohio, Dokes was powerful and had fast hands. He was also the WBC's third-ranked contender. His nickname was "Dynamite," and he seemed not only to be on the road to a heavyweight title fight, but also appeared to have the goods to win the crown.

Michael Dokes won his first 17 fights, including a triumph over Philly's Jimmy Young, before drawing with Ossie Ocasio. In a rematch, he knocked out Ocasio in the first round. He eventually would win the World Boxing Association heavyweight crown in 1982; he won another bout and then agreed to meet Cobb. Another thing Dokes was known for was tossing long-stemmed roses to the women seated closest to the ring. Cobb was 17-1 and fresh off his loss to Norton, though he was still ranked 10th by the WBC. Tex saw the Dokes bout as an opportunity to get back on the right road after being detoured.

It was a difficult fight and Dokes beat Cobb by majority decision, which set back the big man's ambitions. Tex definitely had to rebuild and put a few more W's on his résumé. He topped Harry Terrell and then went up against Bernardo Mercardo of Colombia in Pittsburgh on the undercard of the Larry Holmes–Renaldo Snipes heavyweight title fight in November 1981.

This was yet another case where Cobb needed an iron jaw when he faced an opponent who stood his ground and went all out for all 10 rounds. Like the Norton fight and the Dokes fight, Tex was embroiled in a doozy of a bout where it seemed possible that neither man would have permitted himself to go down even if smacked with a baseball bat. The decision went Cobb's way, but he just could not believe that Mercardo stood up to the heaviest punches in his arsenal: "Tonight that sucker was willing to die, and it damn near killed me."

Bernardo Mercardo was clearly in danger of hitting the deck in the sixth and seventh rounds as Cobb unleashed a massive barrage of punches that staggered but couldn't topple him. When a sportswriter asked Tex to attribute a reason why Mercardo wasn't knocked down despite the onslaught, he seemed to consider the question seriously for a moment, but then said, "I thought it was amphetamines. I asked him what they gave him and if they had any left."

It was a good show and it elevated Cobb's profile. Talk began that he might be in line to fight WBA titleholder Mike Weaver. Weaver certainly seemed less formidable and more beatable than Holmes, although he did have a torso so chiseled that his nickname was "Hercules." Cobb admitted that it seemed such a deal was very close to being signed, and he was truly hoping for it. For one thing, Tex believed he could handle Weaver because his style was made for him: "I'll get dead in the middle of his chest and see how long he can last. He's a guy who believes in the big bomb. He doesn't run." Pretty soon, however, all talk of Cobb's next opponent in the ring vanished because of the opponents he met in the street.

Tex was a great pal of *Philadelphia Daily News* columnist Pete Dexter, a scribe known for his intelligent prose and fearless commentary. But Dexter's opinions were not always popular. There were many murky details about what occurred leading up to the infamous street fight that resulted in Cobb's taking a break from the Marquis of Queensberry style of fighting for a while.

As a rough summary, Dexter was apparently discussing something he wrote with a man who was unhappy Pete wrote it. Discussion escalated to yelling, which escalated to fisticuffs and violence. Dexter, Cobb and a few other friends were obliged to take on a contingent of about 15 antagonists. Supposedly, Dexter was knocked unconscious, suffered a broken hip, and had to be rushed to a hospital by Tex. He suffered a broken arm in the brawl from being hit with a tire iron.

The unfortunate battle royal resulted in Cobb's being shelved and losing out on his chance to fight Mike Weaver and earn perhaps a million dollars. Instead of hitting the heavy bag, he was ordered to rest his right arm, which was encased in a cast from the tips of his fingers to his elbow. Intricate details of the brawl were kept quiet, and only the general story was told, though the results, from injuries to the interruption of Cobb's career, were pretty specific.

"You can't get mad," Tex maintained. "It don't help nothin'. I don't think there was a smart move made all night. It was just a mistake, just like any other mistake made by poor judgment and lack of concentration."

Pete Dexter eventually left Philadelphia to become a newspaper columnist on the West Coast and then a full-time novelist. In one of his novels, a character is involved in an incident very much like the real-life confrontation that involved him and Cobb in the street fight.

The title opportunity evaporated while Cobb was recuperating and then Weaver lost his crown to Dokes. While this was going on, the gigantic Gerry Cooney, at six-feet-six and 235 pounds, was rising like a rocket through the ratings. Cooney, who was from Long Island, had much of his popularity ascribed to the fact that he was white and it was said that he had not really paid his dues and beaten top fighters.

Cobb's name was floated as an opponent for Cooney. Word leaked out that Tex was being offered $200,000 for the bout, more than twice as much as he made for fighting Ken Norton, his highest payday. Manager Joe Gramby, though, kept arguing that his client was worth even more, somewhere between $400,000 and $500,000.

Cobb was tracked down and asked to weigh in on the matter, most particularly the expanding belief that he was holding up the works by demanding more money. Not so, he replied. "I'd fight Gerry Cooney for 25 cents and a blow job." This was offered as a casual but vivid remark that could not be printed word-for-word in any family newspaper. "And it'll probably have to be in his living room with his brother, his uncle, and an in-law for the judges." I had difficulty in not laughing for so long that I needed a pitcher of water to wash down Cobb's words.

One can pardon Cobb's cynicism, but he was probably right that Gerry Cooney's handlers would work extra hard to protect their asset. In fact, they protected him so well that the fight never came off. Instead, Cooney polished off a trio of heavyweight old-timers—Jimmy Young, Ron Lyle and Ken Norton—with consecutive knockouts in four rounds or less.

That was good enough to get Gerry Cooney ranked high enough for Larry Holmes to bother with. The scheduled 15-round fight was stopped in the 13th—and with Cooney having three points deducted for low blows—and was a pretty easy win for Holmes. The loss was Cooney's first, but his career ended a handful of bouts later with consecutive knockout losses to Michael Spinks and George Foreman. He was knocked down twice in each contest.

There was a tremendous buildup for the Holmes–Cooney fight in June 1982, a lot of the blather focusing on Cooney as "A Great White Hope," or being ridiculed for being "A Great White Hype." Once Holmes disposed of Cooney's challenge, though, there was no logical next opponent. There was a weak crop of heavyweights scrapping to climb into the top 10 at that time, but hanging around, whatever reputation he had built still intact, was Cobb.

So Holmes' next defense, in November of that year, came against Tex. For a while it seemed his loyalty to a friend may have cost Cobb his only shot at the heavyweight championship, but now, although Holmes was a tougher opponent than Weaver, Cobb was actually getting his chance. The fight was scheduled for 15 rounds on November 26th in Houston. It was another Texas fight for Tex.

It wouldn't have mattered where this fight took place—in Abilene in Cobb's old backyard, in North Philadelphia in Joe Frazier's gym where he trained, or on a football field—no place would have given him enough home-field advantage to defeat Larry Holmes.

Holmes, "The Easton Assassin" as he was known for his hometown some 60 miles from Philadelphia, was probably the most underrated heavyweight champion of all time. He was fast on his feet and possessed a wicked jab. Once he wore a man down, he could chop him into submission. Cobb had the size to stand in with Holmes, and he had a cast-iron chin that afforded him a layer of protection when foes got close.

Larry Holmes was distinctly favored, as he should have been, and Tex was game, as always. But no one foresaw the way the fight would play out. Holmes' superior skills were evident early, and his hand speed kept Cobb off-balance. Despite everything George Benton sought to teach him, Tex could not play a big-league-caliber defense. Whatever he tried was futile.

For 15 rounds, Holmes stalked Cobb. He picked him apart with his jab. He mixed in combinations that bludgeoned his foe. Cobb's face turned into a bloody mess. Yet the one thing Holmes could not do was knock Tex off his feet. The encounter made for tortuous theater. Holmes kept hitting him, and Cobb kept climbing off his stool following his one-minute rest breaks between rounds to take more punishment.

Howard Cosell, announcing at ringside, railed against what he saw, begging for an official stoppage. But it never came. The fight went the distance and in a rare circumstance for a 15-round fight, it was nearly a shutout on the scoreboards. Two officials had it at 150-135 on the 10-point must system, and the other gave Cobb one round, scoring the bout 149-136.

Cosell, the most famous sports announcer in the country at the time and one of the creators of *Monday Night Football*, expressed his disgust over the event and said he would never work another boxing match. He stuck to that pledge. Cosell seemed to take Cobb's defeat more to heart than the boxer did because Tex was his usual self in the moments, hours and days after the bout. As intelligent and sharp as he was, Howard Cosell probably wouldn't have wanted to match wits against Cobb—even after Tex had had his brains beaten in for 15 rounds. There was a year when Cosell was voted both the most popular and the most disliked sportscaster in the nation, so not every sports fan was pleased with his denunciation of Cobb, who was viewed as a warrior who gave boxing his all. "Hey, if it gets him to stop broadcasting NFL games, I'll go play football for a week, too," Cobb quipped, calling his sending Cosell into exile "a gift to the sport of boxing."

Tex Cobb may have suffered the most lopsided decision in heavyweight title history, but like Rocky, he went the distance and he was never knocked down. In fact, some people saw the match-up as a real-life replay of Sylvester Stallone's Rocky Balboa versus Apollo Creed.

One remarkable question that Cobb was asked was whether he would be interested in a rematch with Larry Holmes. He replied that the champ's "hands could not take it." That was the one and only time that Tex Cobb got a shot at a title. He fought with regularity until 1993, winning most of his bouts but scoring just one more victory over a name fighter when he bested former titleholder Leon Spinks.

A match against Sonny Barch in September 1992 in Fort Lauderdale that was declared "no-contest" produced longstanding repercussions. *Sports Illustrated* wrote a story that accused Cobb and Barch of conspiring to fix the fight and of taking cocaine together. Cobb sued the magazine for libel over the story, which was headlined "The Fix Was In," and a federal jury in Nashville awarded him $10.7 million in 1999, five years after the lawsuit was filed. However, *Sports Illustrated* took appellate action and the 6th U.S. Court of Appeals threw out the verdict in 2002 on the grounds that the magazine showed "no actual malice" against Cobb when it wrote the story. His final bout was in 1993 in Winston-Salem, North Carolina, and he retired with a record of 43-7-1, in addition to the no-contest with Barch.

Long before this, Randall Tex Cobb had established a presence in the movies and he kept active in Hollywood, at times during his fight career and when he had finished. Among the films Cobb appeared in are *Raising Arizona, Ace Ventura, Police Academy 4, Naked Gun 33$^{1}/_{3}$, Diggstown* and *Uncommon Valor*. He also appeared in a number of popular television shows, including *Miami Vice, Married...with Children, Walker, Texas Ranger* and *The X Files*.

The onetime college dropout from Abilene Christian went back to school in his fifties and earned a degree from Temple University in Philadelphia in 2008. The local media took note at the time, and Cobb was up to the challenge of the occasion by issuing a memorable observation. He said it felt strange to be cheered by a crowd when he wasn't in a boxing ring and even stranger to have a fresh opportunity to wear a robe in public, "to step up there and not to have to worry about bleeding."

Although Cobb's degree was in sports and recreation management, given his background and personal history, he might have been better off choosing a career as a standup comedian. He was an improvisational type of guy, so that may have worked out.

It was more than 30 years ago, when he was still a fighter on the way up with the dream of getting a title shot and becoming a heavyweight champion that Cobb remarked, "I'm not going to fight the rest of my life, but I sure am going to laugh the rest of my life. I guarantee you, I will have a good time the rest of my life." If the past is a predictor of the future, then Randy Cobb got it entirely right.

9

MICHAEL SPINKS

A lthough he won an Olympic gold medal, the light-heavyweight championship of the world, and the heavyweight championship of the world, boxing was only at best Michael Spinks' second-favorite sport. Pushed to choose, Spinks would probably lean toward bowling.

That's right, bowling. It's what happens when you grow up in St. Louis. Spinks was not a Philly guy, but he pretty much became one once he captured the World Boxing Association light-heavyweight title. Living in Philadelphia, Spinks fought so often in Atlantic City that he probably ate saltwater taffy for dessert after every meal. And when he retired, he settled in Delaware, only an hour or so from Philadelphia. Spinks made himself into a Philadelphia boxer by proxy.

It was not terribly surprising that Michael Spinks moved to a new city as an adult. His childhood memories of St. Louis were not comforting. Raised in the Pruitt Igoe housing projects, all his youth did was remind him of hard times. Fatherless and raised by his mother, Kay, Spinks and his siblings were threatened by bigger kids stealing their lunch money and picking on them at Vashon High School. They were so poor that at times there were meals of only donuts and water.

"In its way," Spinks recalled, "it was like a prison. Except the ghetto doesn't release a person like the prison systems do after a person serves time. The ghetto holds onto you forever. The only way to get out is to escape." Movies show prison escapes all of the time, whether it is tunneling beneath the walls or going over them. Escaping poverty-stricken neighborhoods requires a different kind of resolve and will, taking advantage of circumstances and working to make oneself into a success.

Spinks became nationally known during the 1976 Olympics when the United States sent its greatest amateur boxing team to Montreal for the Summer Games. He and his older and slightly larger brother, Leon, each won gold medals. It was a great story. Two brothers from the same household who had grown up in poverty were living the American dream. They were so poor that their mother couldn't travel to the Games to watch them until an anonymous benefactor paid her expenses. At the time, Leon was the king of the light-heavyweight division and Michael was the boss of the middleweight class. But the Spinkses were still growing.

The story grew in magnitude when in only his eighth professional fight, Leon scored the greatest upset in heavyweight history by winning a 15-round split decision from Muhammad Ali to capture the heavyweight crown in 1978. Leon held the title for just six months, losing it back to Ali in a rematch.

During that period, Michael was overshadowed by his big brother, who also had a propensity to get into trouble in minor incidents with automobiles. Although he was three years younger, Michael seemed the more mature and stable of the brothers. He was also quieter. But soon enough he began making noise in the light-heavyweight division. At first, the Spinkses appeared on the same card as pros and enjoyed that arrangement. "I like it when Leon's there," Michael remarked. "It motivates the hell out of me when I know he's watching me. Leon roots for me and we inspire each other."

Michael Spinks rose to prominence in the 175-pound class at a time when it was arguably at its strongest ever. The World Boxing Council champ was Matthew Saad Muhammad. The World Boxing Association champ was Eddie Mustafa Muhammad. Former champs Marvin Johnson and Mike Rossman still lurked in the rankings, prepared to waylay any hopefuls, and Dwight Muhammad Qawi was on the rise. There was no easy path to a light-heavyweight crown.

Michael Spinks was soft-spoken and had a slight gap in the middle of his front teeth. He was lankier than Leon, but he had a powerful right-hand knockout punch that when delivered came with the description, "The Spinks Jinx." Spinks turned pro in 1977, and rather than align his future with Don King or Bob Arum, the two most influential promoters in the sport at the time, he signed with Butch Lewis, who was more of an underdog in the promotional ranks. Lewis hustled and was trying to build a name as he guided a small client base highlighted by Spinks and heavyweight Greg Page.

By 1980, when Michael first fought in Atlantic City against Yaqui Lopez, he was positioning himself for the light-heavyweight title. He had to travel to Las Vegas to tackle Eddie Mustafa, but he lifted the WBC crown at the Imperial Palace hotel and then defended the title six straight times in Atlantic City.

Spinks owned wins over Ramon Ranquello and Murray Sutherland, but by beating Lopez, a reliable trial horse, his stature in the division was elevated. By then he was living in West Philadelphia, training at Joe Frazier's Gym in North Philadelphia, and he had worked his way up to a number-one contender rating in both the WBC and WBA. At the start of 1981, Spinks was biding his time for a title shot against either Saad Muhammad or Mustapha Muhammad, who were planning a title unification fight.

To keep busy, Spinks, then 15-0, took on Willie Taylor on January 24th. The match was held in Philadelphia at Martin Luther King Arena, and it was a surprisingly good one for a stopgap bout. Spinks prevailed with an eighth-round TKO in a scheduled 10. Four years since the Olympic glory that produced such pro champions and top contenders as Sugar Ray Leonard, Leon and Michael Spinks, Leo Randolph, Howard Davis and John Tate, Michael was the only one who hadn't yet had a title fight. He was slowed by a knee injury incurred in training, but he was getting impatient.

The knee injury lingered and frustrated Spinks, and he confronted the risk of falling out of shape as he recovered. As a youngster, Michael had been nearly as avid a roller skater as he had been a bowler, and after years away from the activity, he resumed skating all around the Philadelphia area. He learned that roller skating was a terrific way to maintain his condition without putting stress on his knee. For 11 months, roller skating was a cornerstone of his exercise plan. "I hadn't been on skates for so long," he admitted.

It was an unexpected aid in his recuperation, but all the time Spinks was idle, he saw his U.S. Olympic teammates collecting big money and in the case of Leonard, Leon, Randolph and Tate, championship belts. "I'm the only one who hasn't lost among the 1976 Olympians," Spinks noted. "Everyone had a title shot except for me. I want the shot and I'll do all I can to keep anyone from keeping me from it."

Such a statement made in the world of boxing is brash because things often occur to make matches fall through. Sometimes a fighter gets injured. Sometimes the area of dispute is money. Spinks was banking on becoming the mandatory opponent for either Muhammad following the reunification bout they planned for February 1980. Only the fight never happened, the men never met, and the titles remained split.

Instead of fighting for either version of the crown, Spinks accepted a date with number-two-ranked Marvin Johnson, the Indianapolis boxer who twice held the crown and wanted it back. On paper it was a marvelous match, and it was difficult to see how the winner could be ducked by a champion. Michael already had the number-one ranking and could advance his case only a little. But since Marvin was the best man out there not wearing a big, flashy belt to hold up his pants, Spinks thought he should fight him.

Johnson said he had plenty of respect for Spinks and he talked that way, not using inflammatory words at all. There was a lot at stake, but Marvin remained calm in the pre-fight going. Spinks was almost always calm. It was promoter Butch Lewis who sometimes took the offensive and got worked up in meet-the-press sessions. He probably felt he had to because Spinks was ice, not fire.

From the 1970s on, it seemed, promoters derived satisfaction from coming up with catchy slogans to name the title fights they organized, and this one at Resorts International was billed as "The Rumble at Resorts." Johnson said he intended to fight Spinks the same way he fought his other opponents, which was to say he was adaptable. Marvin could box or slug, and did damage on the inside.

For the first three rounds, Johnson's superior experience seemed to be a telling factor. He did swarm Spinks; he stepped inside and mauled him. Marvin defended well, blocking Michael's jab, and he seemingly went for an early knockout. Matters changed abruptly in the fourth round. Johnson was doing well, executing a well-thought-out game plan. However, Spinks interrupted with a lightning quick, out-of-nowhere left uppercut/left hook that caught Johnson flush on the chin and knocked him flat on his back.

Referee Joe Cortez waved the fight over at one minute and 22 seconds into the fourth, and while Johnson got to his feet, he again slumped in his corner and required a long visit from the ringside doctor before being taken to Atlantic City Medical Center for treatment of a concussion. "I saw it right there," Spinks said of the opening in Johnson's defense. "It was like I took a picture of it and I threw a punch."

Down went Johnson. And out the window went his chance at a title shot. Although the consensus was that Spinks was behind when he fired the knockout blow, he didn't view it that way. He said that although he couldn't get into a good rhythm, he didn't think he was losing, either. Still, he shifted his approach: "I went to what Michael Spinks knows." What Spinks knew was that his fists had stopping power.

Four months later, in the baking desert heat of Las Vegas in July, Spinks got his chance at the WBA crown. The opponent was Eddie Mustafa Muhammad, who had been born Eddie Gregory and debuted as a middleweight after winning two New York Golden Gloves titles. A few months before the Spinks bout, Eddie made an ill-advised foray into the heavyweight ranks and lost a split decision to Renaldo Snipes. Mustafa Muhammad, used to fighting at the 175-pound limit, weighed in at more than 201 for the Snipes fight. When the fight was announced weeks earlier, he said he knew he was going to have to add some weight to fight as a heavyweight, but that he would not be able to break 200 if he ate nothing but candy bars between then and fight night. Wrong. He must have really enjoyed all those Tootsie Rolls.

Then Mustafa Muhammad had to turn around and lose all of the weight to qualify to defend his title at 175. The fighters' camps agreed to a midnight weigh-in, at 12:01 a.m. on fight day, instead of getting their charges up early. I was far ahead at the roulette table when the weigh-in time crept up on me. Duty called and I left my wife in my seat, instructing her to put two dollars on black with every spin until I came back.

Once in a while, a champion comes in too heavy for the weight limit, and when that happens, he is given extra time to lose weight or else forfeit his crown. Mustafa Muhammad missed the cutoff by a pound or so. All women were asked to leave the weigh-in room, and Mustafa Muhammad stripped to lose a couple of extra ounces along with his cast-aside underwear. But it wasn't enough.

So after Michael Spinks weighed in at 173 and three-quarter pounds and went off to bed, Mustafa Muhammad was forced to stay on site and fight the scale before he could fight Spinks. For half an hour, Mustafa Muhammad worked up a sweat jumping rope and thinking of other ways to burn calories. Finally, he made weight and the fight was on. The weigh-in dragged on so long that by the time I returned to my seat at the roulette wheel, my wife was nowhere to be seen. It turned out that she lost all of the money and vacated the table. As much as I liked Eddie Mustafa, I was not pleased with him at that moment.

This extra tension seemed to leave Mustafa Muhammad more vulnerable, but he didn't show it in the ring, carrying the bout the full 15 rounds. Still, it was Spinks' day. He grabbed the WBA light-heavyweight title after closing his foe's right eye with a punch in the eighth round and knocking him down in the 12th. "Oh, I feel so good," Spinks declared after his win and after sharing a good cry with brother Leon in his dressing room when the scores were read.

In another area of the hotel, a party revved up for Spinks, who was several days shy of his 25th birthday. But he gave himself the best present in the world, something not even the Neiman Marcus catalogue could have delivered at Christmas. There was a cake waiting for him with the words, "Congratulations, Michael Spinks, World Boxing Association Light-Heavyweight Champion," written on the icing. He attended the post-fight party still wearing his shorts and fight robe.

By then, Spinks had been a Philadelphia resident for more than four years and the idea of defending his title in Atlantic City, a short car ride away, instead of hopping on a jet to fly thousands of miles, had a strong pull. And he was right on time. The competition for matches with big-name champs was intense among the casinos. Instead of choosing between cities, Spinks and Butch Lewis could just hold out for the best deal offered by a casino. The boardwalk seemed just fine to Michael.

Spinks was proud that he and Leon had won Olympic gold medals at the same time, and had followed up with world boxing titles. Michael stood six-feet-two and had long limbs. He did not seem to have difficulty maintaining weight, and he was joyful at the notion that he had fulfilled a dream. He wanted to spend a little bit of time savoring the triumph. Always friendly, Spinks seemed more at ease as well. Once he captured the crown, he visited his mother in St. Louis and took a trip to Disney World. The Disney visit was more about fun. Showing his face again in St. Louis was more about pride. Over a five-year period, Spinks had won Olympic gold, moved to Philadelphia, and become the world light-heavyweight champion. His pledge to himself was not to go back to St. Louis until he had accomplished his mission of demonstrating that he could be somebody. By returning to the old neighborhood as the possessor of a prize medal and a prize belt, Michael felt he got his message across.

After winning the title, Spinks also competed in the *Superstars* competition that pitted champions from different sports against one another for a made-for-TV show in sports that were not their specialty. At that time, the show was all the rage. It was kind of an early version of the modern-day reality show. Former heavyweight champion Joe Frazier made a notorious appearance on the show, infamous because he couldn't really swim and nearly drowned in the pool. When asked how he fared, after the show was taped but before it was aired, Spinks remarked, "I swim much better than Joe Frazier." He would probably have been wise to keep quiet about that, because Frazier might not have let him back into his gym.

Of all things, Spinks had taken to wearing cowboy hats and with some of the loot from the Mustafa Muhammad fight, he bought himself a new one made of gray felt. "I did my best to spoil myself," Michael said of the purchase and travel experiences following victory in the title match. But then he returned to Philadelphia and resumed business as usual.

Spinks' first defense was against Vonzell Johnson, one of the solid light-heavies in the division who were born at the wrong time to win a title. Johnson was tough and could beat most of the other contenders, but he came up short in title fights against the very best. This was the first of Michael's series of title fights in Atlantic City that left him far too familiar with the Atlantic City Expressway connecting the shore community to Philadelphia.

It went into the books as a seventh-round knockout at the Playboy Hotel & Casino, but it ended controversially. Vonzell Johnson and Michael Spinks were in a clinch and were ordered apart by referee Larry Hazzard. The men followed orders, but Johnson had a lapse in his mental concentration. As he backed away, Vonzell dropped his hands. Spinks immediately seized upon the opening and delivered a hard left hook, followed by a strong right and a second left hook. That was all she wrote.

Anyone who has ever walked near a boxing ring, read anything about the sport, or listened to a trainer speak knows that the absolute number-one rule of the game is to protect yourself at all times. "I made a cardinal sin," Johnson admitted after his head cleared. "I was taught ever since I was knee-high to a puppy to come out of the clinches low." Although Johnson's handler, Angelo Dundee, was not happy that Spinks landed a sneak punch, he also had to admit, "You keep your hands up at all times." There were some rumblings about how Spinks gained the upper hand, but he swore, "I didn't cheat."

That wrapped up a very satisfying 1981 for Michael Spinks, and what was apparent to close watchers of his development was that he was getting better all the time. Spinks also recorded a very good 1982. He wasn't going to let go of that WBA title easily. In succession, he topped Mustafa Wassaja of Uganda, Scotsman Murray Sutherland, Jerry Celestine of New Orleans, and Johnny Davis of Hempstead, New York. Four up, four down, and there wasn't a slouch among them.

Besides polishing off everyone put in front of him that year, Spinks faced another interesting challenge. Author John Hersey penned a novel called *The Child Buyer*; its premise was that everyone has his price, whether it is money or something else he cherishes, and for that something he would be willing to sell his soul.

In the months after Spinks won the WBA crown, he claimed to have been approached several times by promoters with deeper pockets than Butch Lewis, the man who had been at his side and directed him to the title. Those promoters wanted to throw riches at him and sign him to their stables. Spinks spurned their offers. "I have a few guys trying to buy my soul," he stated. "But I don't sell my soul. I don't like being owned by anybody. Nobody owns Michael Spinks and no one ever will."

It was a telling illustration of character, but so, too, was Spinks' low-key demeanor even after becoming champion. Many boxers acquire rather large entourages of hangers-on once they become famous. He was not interested in such bandwagon pals: "You can call me champ, but I prefer Mike. I like being just regular old Mike."

The level of Spinks' gentlemanly behavior far exceeded the norm in a tough sport, but if anyone felt that his outward appearance indicated weakness, they were in for a shock. Michael was made of steel inside, and his confidence was unshakeable. He just didn't need to broadcast it.

Spinks and Butch Lewis angled for a chance to unify the light-heavyweight title with a bout against Matthew Saad Muhammad, but their efforts were in vain, and Michael's fellow Philadelphian later lost his World Boxing Council 175-pound title to another great light-heavyweight from the area. From Camden, New Jersey, Dwight Braxton, who was soon to change his name to Dwight Muhammad Qawi, was fighting his way to the top of the rankings. Eventually, Braxton got there; he got his fight with Saad Muhammad and won the title. Negotiations opened with the Braxton camp for a unification fight, one that would be classified as the biggest light-heavyweight bout of all time, paying more than a million dollars in purses to each of the champs as they risked their belts. The match was set for March 18, 1983.

This fight would test Spinks like no other, and he needed to be in top shape physically and mentally for the showdown. However, that was not possible because his fiancée, Sandra Massey, with whom he had a daughter, was killed in an automobile accident. Michael continued to train and renewed his commitment to follow through with the bout, but he was definitely not himself. He met with a small group of sportswriters in Atlantic City while training, but before he engaged them, Butch Lewis told the writers that the painful subject of the deceased fiancée was off-limits. After several minutes of fight conversation, though, one reporter injected a question about Massey. Spinks began to break down and cry and Lewis hustled him away.

It was that backdrop that pressed in on Spinks as he tried to focus solely on Braxton. Although each man could weigh no more than 175 pounds, Michael was six-feet-two and Dwight was about five-feet-seven, the shortest man ever to win the light-heavyweight crown. While well-muscled, Spinks still appeared slender. Braxton was big-boned, with wide shoulders, and squat. In some ways, they did not seem to fit into the same weight class. Braxton reached his level of prominence by dominating foes with his power. Spinks boxed, moved well, and then unleashed surprising power to finish off his opponents. At the time, Dwight Braxton's record was 19-1-1, while Michael stood at 22-0. This was one case where the light-heavyweights stole the spotlight from the heavyweights, a rare occasion in the fisticuffs world.

As predicted, the Braxton–Spinks battle was a rugged one. It went the 15-round distance and "The Spinks Jinx" prevailed over "The Camden Buzz-saw," giving "regular old Mike" both belts and gaining him recognition as the undisputed light-heavyweight champion of the world. Spinks was paid $2.1 million for the fight and jokingly made reference to the old TV show, *The Untouchables*, with Robert Stack as Eliot Ness. "That's how I wanted to be tonight," he remarked after the decision was announced. "I became untouchable."

Spinks had the benefit of watching Dwight Braxton stop Matthew Saad Muhammad twice, so he learned what not to do against the WBC champ: "I couldn't let him get close. If he wanted to get me, he had to run and jump like a cat." For Braxton, the strategy of his opponent drove him nuts. He was trying to hit someone who stayed just out of reach much of the time. "He didn't beat me," Dwight noted. "If anything, I beat myself."

The oddest part of the fight was the eighth round. Braxton was trying to work his way in close for some body punching, and all of a sudden, Spinks fell down. Referee Larry Hazzard ruled it a slip. Then almost the identical thing happened again. This time Hazzard called it a knockdown for Braxton. Spinks fell still a third time while swinging and missing at Dwight. It was weird theater and fans in the crowd laughed. Spinks said later that Braxton was stepping on his feet. Dwight admitted that was true: "I kept stepping on his feet accidentally because they're so big." Braxton seemed a bit baffled by all that had occurred, but afterwards Spinks seemed to have a Cheshire cat, all-knowing grin. "I think I fought a superb fight," he declared.

Of Michael's 10 most recent bouts, nine had been in either Atlantic City or Philadelphia. The only away game he played was the Vegas fight with Eddie Mustafa that earned him the title. Between November 1983 and June 1985, Spinks defended the light-heavyweight title four more times, three of them by knockout and two of them in Atlantic City. He almost could have qualified for residency in A.C.

Counting the bouts with Eddie Mustapha Muhammad and Dwight Braxton, Michael Spinks had won 11 light-heavyweight title fights. It seemed if anyone was going to pry the belt away from him, it would have to be done by blowtorch while it was around his midsection because no one had thought of a way to best him in the ring. By then, Spinks had also solidified his standing in Philadelphia. He was an adopted Philadelphian, but a longtime resident.

After all of those defenses, Spinks and his co-conspirator Butch Lewis hatched a scheme that when revealed had people shaking their heads, wondering if they were crazy, wondering if they were reaching too far. Michael, they decided, was going to build his body into the heavyweight division and challenge Larry Holmes of nearby Easton, Pennsylvania for the heavyweight crown. Other light-heavyweight champions—from Billy Conn to Archie Moore to Bob Foster—had tried to do the same, but no light-heavy had ever won the heavyweight title. The move up in weight had been attempted 13 times by nine different men, and they had all failed to conquer the heavyweight king.

Michael spent months carefully adjusting and monitoring his diet. He lifted weights and put on muscle weight. His frame was always big enough to handle the heavyweight size, but he had been brilliant as a light-heavyweight, so why mess with success? Spinks had pretty much run through the prime contenders in the light-heavyweight class, and the prestige, money and uniqueness of the challenge in going after Holmes seemed worth the risk.

By September 1985, Holmes had been in possession of some version of the crown for seven full years. He had defended it 20 times and had one of the most distinguished runs in the history of the division. Holmes fought comfortably at about 218 pounds, around 40 more than Spinks. He was six-feet-three with good reach, one of the best jabs in heavyweight history and enough power to complement that flicking left. The only visible advantage for Michael was that Larry was pushing 36.

With Spinks living in Philadelphia and Holmes in Easton, it could be argued that the Spectrum would have been the best place for the fight, but it was arranged for Las Vegas, the gambling Mecca that still managed to pick off the biggest fights of all. Holmes weighed in at 221-plus pounds. Spinks weighed 199-plus and was visibly more muscular than he had been at 175. Boxing experts wondered if the added weight would slow him down. Boxing experts wondered if the 48-0 Holmes could still wield his size to overpower Spinks. Larry was a 5-1 favorite in the famous betting town.

Michael was very savvy about his diet. His camp hired an expert nutritionist who somehow figured out a way for him to eat 4,500 calories daily, but have it be good for him. "I'm eating nuts, bolts, screws, razor blades and sledgehammers," he joked. As long as they qualified as members of the vegetable family, it was OK.

What fans got was not what they expected. The fight went all 15 rounds and the unanimous decision went to Spinks, terminating Holmes' reign. It was a shocking result, especially since many at ringside did not think that Michael did enough damage to out-point the champion. He moved well and stayed away from most danger, but Holmes stung him often. He could not land flush, however, and could not put Spinks away. Michael threw punches from different angles, catching Larry by surprise. When it was over, it didn't really appear as if Spinks had done enough to swipe the title, but in the eyes of the judges he had.

Spinks was jubilant as he held up the championship belt in the ring, but he did not lay on boastful talk; he was too honest: "You know, I never saw myself winning this. Well, once. Once, I saw myself knocking him out. Hey, he couldn't hit me. I gave him a totally confused person. He must have thought I was having a fit. He was totally frustrated."

Holmes was very much frustrated and in the immediate aftermath, he said he would fight no more. That didn't take, however, and after a decent interval with the heavyweight championship belt residing in Philadelphia rather than in another Pennsylvania town, a return match was agreed upon for April 1986.

Also held in Las Vegas, the second Spinks–Holmes fight also went the distance. Even though he was fighting with a broken right thumb suffered in the third round, Holmes landed harder shots and more of them. He almost had Spinks out in the 14th round, and yet fell for the second straight time, in this case on a split decision. By now, Michael was staying at heavyweight. He tipped the scale at 205.

Spinks defended the title once in 1986 against Steffen Tangstad, and once in 1987 against Gerry Cooney. He stopped both of the challengers. It was not hard to see that Michael was working his way toward retirement, taking a full year off after that. He had moved to a more spacious home in Wilmington, Delaware, but prepared for his next defense in June 1988.

There was a new face on the scene, a man with a growing reputation as a big puncher and someone destined, it seemed, to become heavyweight champ. Not even Spinks, though, could foresee what lay in store when he agreed to fight Mike Tyson. Butch Lewis negotiated the sweetest contract of Michael's career, and he was paid the astonishing sum of $13.5 million.

It was not a good match of styles. The hungry Tyson, young and strong, overpowered Spinks in the first round. He knocked him down swiftly and then knocked him out just 91 seconds into the fight. The belt was handed over and with a 31-1 record, Spinks, then 32, promptly retired.

Although he remained in the Wilmington area, very occasionally making appearances at Philadelphia boxing events (surprising one crowd when he was introduced at a Blue Horizon fight card), for the most part, Spinks avoided the limelight completely. At his New York retirement press conference only a month after he lost the title to Tyson, Michael said he would never be tempted to come back—and there was never the slightest indication that he was.

Spinks walked off into the sunset the winner of an Olympic gold medal, two light-heavyweight championship belts, and with the knowledge that he was the first light-heavyweight ever to ascend to the heavyweight championship. In 1994, after Michael Spinks had stayed retired for six years, he was elected to the International Boxing Hall of Fame in Canastota, New York.

10

DWIGHT MUHAMMAD QAWI

A ll anyone had to do was look at the big arms and the immense fist and decide that the best thing to do when encountering Dwight Muhammad Qawi was to run the other way. Sometimes when a fighter gets a nickname, the person who bestows it gets it just right, and this was one of those cases. "The Camden Buzzsaw." That was Dwight, whether he called himself Braxton (the name he was born with) or Muhammad Qawi (the name he switched to), because Camden, New Jersey, just across the Delaware River from Philadelphia, was his home.

Actually, it is little-remembered that Dwight was born in Baltimore, even if he grew up in South Jersey. Much of Camden was a poverty-stricken, troubled community at the time, and he and his brother Tony, who also became a fighter, drifted into crime at an early age. Sent to juvenile detention at age 13, Qawi was convicted of armed robbery and sent to Rahway State Prison in Avenel, New Jersey when was 19. He was an inmate in the maximum security facility when he turned to boxing. "I didn't have my head on straight," Dwight said of his youthful days. "I'm not too proud of it. I don't speak of it too often."

In the late 1970s and early 1980s, Rahway offered boxing as a main element of its recreational program, and one inmate, James Scott, became a star whose abilities attracted attention beyond the walls. In an unusual arrangement, Scott was able to fight other prominent light-heavyweight fighters inside the prison and have the bouts televised nationally.

As a byproduct of the attention showered on Scott and the program, and as a way to find new direction, Qawi took up the sport. When he was released from prison in 1978, Dwight had earned his high school equivalency diploma, completed a couple of semesters of college credit, and decided he would stick with boxing. He began training at Joe Frazier's Gym in North Philadelphia. As he sought to gain experience and carve out a career, Qawi began at 1-1-1 as a pro.

He learned the ins and outs of the sport and although he was short for his weight, the naturally big-boned Qawi demonstrated enormous power. There was some debate over Qawi's height, variously reported at as little as five-feet-six and three-quarters and as much as five-feet-seven and a half, but in any case it tabbed him as the shortest man ever to win the light-heavyweight title. Qawi also had large, expressive eyes, a closely cropped beard and what seemed like the ability to stare a hole through an opponent's forehead. That is, if he wasn't punching a hole in an opponent's forehead. I never took punches from any of the top light-heavyweights of the era, but Qawi's power always impressed me. He seemed as if he had the strength to put his fist through a wall at will.

The one early loss was to Johnny Davis, but then Qawi went on an experience-gaining spree under co-trainer and co-manager Quenzel McCall and won 10 fights in a row before scheduling a rematch with Davis. As McCall noted, Qawi really didn't need the fight because he had won an ESPN tournament that guaranteed him a bout with a top-10-ranked opponent. For a while, the choice to take the 10-round bout looked like a mistake. Qawi got off to a slow start and

Dwight Muhammad Qawi of Camden was one of the hardest punchers in the light-heavyweight division, and he later became cruiserweight champion as well. (Photo courtesy of J. Russell Peltz)

dropped the first three rounds. However, once he gained his rhythm, his Brooklyn foe was in trouble. Twice in the ninth round, Dwight almost scored a knockout, and he had Davis staggering around the ring. "I know I had to come from behind," he acknowledged. One way he did so was to concentrate on body punches that hit Davis so hard they made fans in the third row grimace. After winning the decision, Qawi was on the division's fast track, and he stepped up his level of competition. From then on, his résumé was dotted with big names.

Dwight next handled Al Bolden over 10 rounds in Philadelphia, and then in a crucial career step, he was matched with Mike Rossman at Resorts International in Atlantic City. The former light-heavyweight champ, originally from the South Jersey town of Turnersville, won his crown from Victor Galindez on the undercard of the Leon Spinks–Muhammad Ali second title fight, but he lost it back to Galindez. Rossman was nearing the end of his 44-7-3 career when he agreed to dance one-on-one with Qawi in May 1981.

When Qawi stopped Rossman in the seventh round, he solidified his reputation. The next foe involved some irony. He was matched with James Scott inside Rahway prison. A pre-fight press conference that sent Qawi to Newark in person to converse with Scott, speaking from prison via a telephone box, was punctuated with Dwight screaming at the absent Scott directly, but not to his face.

There did not seem to be any indication of friendship between Qawi and Scott, based on their shared time at Rahway. Dwight Qawi spent more than five years in jails, and half of them in Rahway. Why he would want to go back to the site of his incarceration for even one three-minute round was not clear. He made certain to say it was not for a reunion, not for a vacation, and not to see old friends; it was a business trip.

If fighting a highly rated foe inside a maximum security prison gave other fighters the creeps, Qawi at least had going for him that he had been there and done that, even if he didn't want to hang out very long: "In a way, it will not be strange. And in a way, I will have a funny feeling. I'll go in saying it's only a matter of an hour. I'll do it and get out. I don't really want to stay an hour at Rahway."

"I'm not going around shaking people's hands, Dwight continued. "I'm not politicking for nothing. I've had time to prepare for it. I don't have fond memories of it, but I don't have fond memories of the ghetto either, and I go back there after every fight. The atmosphere won't bother me."

Something about James Scott did bother him, though. Qawi began shouting at the squawk box that delivered Scott's voice. "Just be there Saturday!" he yelled. "Don't escape. You say any more and I'll smash this box." Qawi claimed that Scott had stiffed him for two days of sparring partner wages some years earlier, but he also said he lost respect for Scott because he was out of prison and fighting at the start of his career, but then got sent back behind bars. Qawi said it was very difficult for him when he first emerged from prison and had no income, but he resisted any temptation to break a law that would have sent him back.

The September 5, 1981 unanimous 10-round decision over James Scott did not require even an hour to complete, but it sent Dwight Qawi to a higher level in the rankings. The loss to Qawi was also the last time Scott fought in his career. The World Boxing Association, which had listed him as one of its top-10 light-heavyweights, decided that a man with a felony conviction living in prison should not be welcome in its ratings.

There were times during the bout when Scott seemed to have the upper hand, but he fought more defensively than offensively and he didn't score enough points with that style. Qawi couldn't land more precisely to put Scott away, but he kept trying: "It's a good feeling coming back here as a success—a true success. I rolled up my sleeves and worked hard. He's slow as molasses; it's just that he's tough." Qawi made one thing clear—this was definitely a farewell tour of Rahway for him: "This is the last time I'm coming back here."

With the ESPN title in his pocket, a victory over ex-champion Mike Ross-man accounted for, and a win over the hard-to-beat Scott, Dwight Qawi's value zoomed. All of a sudden, he was a blue chip stock. His record was only 15-1-1, but he had credibility and a World Boxing Council number-five ranking. Champ Matthew Saad Muhammad was willing to give him a shot at the title on December 19, 1981 at the Playboy Hotel & Casino in Atlantic City.

Saad Muhammad was 27 years old and had a record of 31-3-2. This was his ninth title defense. Although Matthew had nearly been beaten a few times, he always managed to come back and grab victory. His resilience, coupled with his big-fight experience, made him a favorite over Qawi. Those tough fights had only solidified Saad Muhammad's belief in his own invulnerability. He was like one of those watches that could take a licking and keep on ticking: "I don't care what it takes, I'm going to be victorious." It was a comment that perfectly illustrated his actions in the ring.

Saad Muhammad had had too many close calls to believe that he would keep the title forever, but I didn't think Qawi was going to take it at this meeting. Like many others, I was wrong.

Dwight was no ballerina in the ring. He didn't slide and move, stick and run like a Muhammad Ali. He was a straight-ahead charger whose heavy punches took a toll on those at the receiving end. Saad Muhammad was renowned for his stamina, but Qawi seemed inexhaustible, too. What he did was to bore in on a guy and ignore the punches that were supposed to flatten him or slow him. He just kept on coming; he was a wrecking ball with feet. "I've had harder street fights," Qawi recalled. "I've been hit with a stick harder than he can imagine. If he punches harder than a mule kicks, I'll be there for an hour taking it." That was not necessary. The situation was reversed on a bad day for Saad Muhammad, one that went wrong hours before he climbed into the ring.

During his preparation for the bout at the 175-pound limit, Matthew Saad Muhammad and his handlers relied on their own scale in training camp to make sure he had trimmed down enough to meet weight requirements. However, at 6 a.m., when Saad Muhammad awoke and stepped on a scale in Atlantic City, it registered a shocking 181 pounds. Matthew was six pounds over the limit two hours before the official 8 a.m. weigh-in. He began sweating off pounds, but there was only so much he could do that fast. Saad Muhammad weighed in at 177 pounds.

Under New Jersey State Athletic Commission rules, Matthew had two hours to be re-weighed and come in under the limit or he would have to forfeit his title. Again Saad Muhammad went to work and with five minutes to spare, he officially weighed in at 174 and a half pounds. It could not be determined how much this energy loss impacted Saad Muhammad in the fight, but it was a Qawi day all the way.

In a result that rocked the boxing world like a 7.0 earthquake, underdog Dwight Qawi dominated the fight. He bulled into Saad Muhammad and pushed him around as his sledgehammer blows wreaked havoc on the champion's face. Qawi sliced up Saad Muhammad, drawing blood from both nostrils and his lip, and swelling shut his left eye. By the 10th round, Qawi's onslaught of left jabs, overhand rights and left hooks had Saad Muhammad teetering. Rapid-fire delivery of two rights and two left hooks put Matthew Saad Muhammad on the canvas for the first time in his career. Referee Arthur Mercante waved the fight over in that round.

"A lot of people thought I didn't have it in me," Qawi recalled. "I *am* the Camden Buzzsaw. I do saw, and when I cut, all you can say is 'Tim-ber!'" Matthew was so severely battered that he immediately left the premises for the hospital where he sent back a statement that in part read: "He went to the bank and borrowed my title. It's just temporary, I'll get it back." Then and now, Qawi believes, "Saad Muhammad left himself wide open" for the big punches that finished him off.

At the time, Saad Muhammad had been looking ahead to a soon-to-be scheduled unification bout with Michael Spinks that would have paid him about two million dollars. That match was down the tubes. It was Qawi, making $50,000 to Saad Muhammad's $300,000, who was going to be in line for bigger paydays.

The ascent to the title had come quickly for Qawi, only about three and a half years after he turned pro, and while he had been vocal in his confidence beforehand, not long after the bout ended, he was spotted walking through the casino and shopping area of the building, wearing a sweatsuit with his new belt tied around his waist. Many passersby did double takes, then smiled and offered congratulations. One man yelled, "There's the champion of the world!" While Qawi did not spin around and look behind him, he was still processing his next exalted status. "Thank you, thank you," he repeated to the well-wishers before going up to his room to take a rest and contemplate a promising future.

Dwight Muhammad Qawi's title defense came against another Philadelphian, demonstrating the remarkable depth of talent in the area's light-heavyweight division. Jerry "The Bull" Martin was the foe in a bout that probably made the most sense for the Spectrum, and certainly would have been a hit in Atlantic City, yet took place in Las Vegas.

Even stranger, before Qawi left for Nevada, he moved out of Camden into an anonymous South Jersey motel because his home was broken into and his car was vandalized. It seemed like the kind of mischief he indulged in as a teenager, but was disrespectful to the new light-heavyweight champ who wanted to share some of his success with his hometown: "I wanted to give Camden credit. They didn't appreciate it. That's a shame. It's their loss." It was a prime example of the old adage, You can't go home again. So Qawi went elsewhere.

Headlining at the Showboat Hotel & Casino, Dwight finished off "The Bull" inside of six rounds in March 1982, and then offered a rematch to Matthew Saad Muhammad, this time at the Spectrum, in August, and defeated him more handily in six rounds. After three title defenses, Qawi was offered the unification bout with Michael Spinks that Saad Muhammad had been nearing.

Leading up to the bout, *The Ring* magazine solicited first-person commentary from both Qawi and Spinks about how each would beat the other man. Dwight was pictured on the cover of the January 1983 issue, bare torso in a fighting pose, taped hands shaped into fists, his championship belt around his waist. In part, Qawi's story read this way: "Michael Spinks is in serious trouble. I'm not kidding when I say this. He made the mistake of a lifetime by agreeing to fight me, and he'll pay a painful price for that decision. Constant pressure, that's always been my style of fighting, and I don't intend to change strategies against Spinks." He didn't really, but it didn't work. It was a good, close fight, but the performance did not produce the result Qawi counted on.

On March 18, 1983 in Atlantic City, Michael Spinks won a unanimous 15-round decision to take possession of the World Boxing Council crown and add it to his World Boxing Association title. By then, Qawi was examining his life again. He adopted his Muslim name, changed trainers, changed managers and chose to forego the 175-pound weight class for the cruiserweight division.

This was a very difficult time for Dwight, and it didn't all have to do with boxing. His father was killed, he was going through a divorce and to calm himself, he drank a lot and became addicted to drugs. He knew he was at risk of

The aptly named "Liberty Brawl" in 1982 at the Spectrum pitted Matthew Saad Muhammad against "The Camden Buzzsaw," Dwight Muhammad Qawi in one of the most important light-heavyweight bouts in the division's history.
(Photo courtesy of J. Russell Peltz)

losing what he had built and needed to get himself clean. That was a task, but Qawi also embraced a new path within his sport.

The cruiserweight class was new at the time, an added division spanning between 176 and 190 pounds (although it was later defined with a 200-pound weight limit). The first world cruiserweight title fight was sanctioned by the WBC in 1979. Although he fought several of the top light-heavies in a division heavy with talented boxers, it was becoming more challenging for Qawi to make weight. Also, the depth of talent at cruiserweight was thinner, making it seem easier to pick off a title.

Qawi worked his way through a short list of cruiserweights and then got a deal to challenge for the title. His name and his achievements as a light heavy-weight helped him obtain the bout against champ Piet Crous, but the catch was that he had to travel to the titlist's home country of South Africa for the match. Dwight remembers taking an 18-hour flight to a country that was the symbol of racism against blacks, agreeing to fight a white champion for the prospect of bucking the odds to capture the crown. The music they played when he climbed into the ring was Bruce Springsteen's "Born in the USA." It probably never sounded so good to him in the hostile environment. All of the effort, the adjust-ment, the shift of focus to the new weight class all paid off when Qawi won another world crown by stopping Crous in the 11th round of a scheduled 15-rounder. "I had my second title," Dwight declared.

Qawi knocked off Rick Enis in Atlantic City and then in Reno, he defended against Leon Spinks, Michael's older brother and the former heavyweight champ. Dwight won in under six rounds. Next up was Evander Holyfield, and the holder of two different organizations' cruiserweight belts wasn't going to give them up. It was a close, hard-fought match, but Holyfield prevailed with a 15-round split decision. That bout was a full-fledged trench war. The only time off either contestant took was the one minute between rounds. There was no resting in clinches, just a steady bombardment in both directions.

A second shot at Holyfield didn't go much better, and Qawi lost in four rounds. Unhappy over the result, Dwight tried an ill-advised experiment. He let himself gain more and more weight and at 232 pounds, he met heavyweight George Foreman in March 1988. Foreman still looked like a giant next to Dwight, and he scored a technical knockout in the seventh round of a 10-round bout. Qawi continued fighting sporadically through 1998 when he was 45, and he retired with a career record of 41-11-1.

Qawi admitted he took some fights just for the cash and wasn't truly pre-pared. He had bouts of depression, sometimes as often as bouts with other box-ers, and although he boxed with men, he still wrestled with alcohol and drug abuse (more with alcohol than drugs, starting when he downed celebratory drinks at his own post-fight victory parties).

"I lost myself," Dwight said of what he was like at this point in his life when he was in his mid to late 30s. "I drank when I won and I drank when I lost. I couldn't just take a shot. I'd get wasted."

In 1990, angry at himself for not being able to control his impulses, Qawi put his future in the hands of an organization called The Lighthouse in Mays Landing at the South Jersey shore and accepted treatment for his problems. It was a life-altering move. Not only did Qawi get clean, he moved to nearby Somers Point and later became a full-time drug and alcohol counselor for the organization, which has 60 patient beds. When he finally did hang up his gloves, a decision that was somewhat overdue, a few years passed before Qawi attained the ultimate recognition in his sport. In 2004, he was voted into the International Boxing Hall of Fame.

Dwight said he got the call informing him of his election from director Ed Brophy at about midnight. It woke him up. "I was numb, excited," he recalled. "Oh, it was a special moment. You don't know how special. It's a big deal." At the induction ceremony, someone introduced a fan of his who had traveled from Europe to be there in the little town of Canastota. "That meant a lot to me. It's an honor."

Qawi was pleased by the recognition that brought him to upstate New York for his induction, but he was both philosophical and reflective about his career in the ring—which he launched without benefit of amateur experience—and how he almost lost everything because of his addictions. Dwight was grateful for the validation of his career represented by the ceremony, and although he later split with them, Qawi praised the help that Philadelphia trainers and managers Quenzel McCall and Wesley Mouzon had given him. "The Hall of Fame means a lot to me in terms of what I did as a boxer," Dwight acknowledged. "It's saying you did your best and you did good. There's closure." There is never true closure for a real addict, who does not describe his status as cured, but only as recovering. Helping others recover became Dwight's calling once he fully retired from boxing after his can't-let-it-go dabbling of the 1990s.

Dwight Muhammad Qawi works the night shift at The Lighthouse, and one day in March 2012, he stopped at his favorite International House of Pancakes not far from the office to talk about his days as a boxer. He was on crutches, recovering from foot and ankle surgery, and at 59, he was a heavyweight again. The Dwight of the present still had his neatly trimmed, short beard, but like his hair, its darkness was being invaded by flecks of gray.

Qawi thought back and said it felt as if he just fell into boxing after he got out of prison. He considered being deposited at Joe Frazier's Gym a lucky break. The Philadelphia fighters who hung out and worked out there were skilled and prominent, from Bobby "Boogaloo" Watts and Willie "The Worm"

Monroe to Bennie Briscoe and heavyweight Duane Bobick. "I walked in and there was a lot of action," Qawi remembered.

When he lost for the first time against Johnny Davis, Dwight thought, "Boy, this is a hard way to make a living." No one who has boxed for long would doubt the veracity of that statement. No one who has tried it would deny it. Anyone who thought otherwise, because he watched too much TV and took too few jabs to the face to realize it, was a fool. But Qawi stuck with boxing anyway, adding "I went to school." That meant training hard with Mouzon and McCall. Quenzel knew what he needed—more maneuverability: "He had me sliding around looking for more angles."

Trying to settle the height issue once and for all, Qawi proclaimed himself five feet seven and a half. He said that he never felt being shorter than the other light heavies was a disadvantage and that he had knocked out some six-footers in his time: "What I had was a vision of what I could do, and I would do it."

Any objective viewing of the light-heavyweight picture of 30 years ago provides a dazzling list of the men who split the title, shared the title, unified the title and dominated the division over a period of approximately six years, including Marvin Johnson, Mike Rossman, Matthew Saad Muhammad, Eddie Mustafa Muhammad, Michael Spinks and Dwight Muhammad Qawi. But usually unsaid is the fact that not only did they have to wade through one another, but there were other light heavyweights lower down in the ranks like Yaqui Lopez, Jesse Burnett, James Scott, Jerry Martin and Eddie Davis, who in another era might well have been world champions. That's one reason why Qawi is so proud that he fought when he did and rose to the top. "I tell people a guy like Jesse Burnett would have been a champion at another time," he noted. "There were a whole bunch of guys like that. Eddie Davis, I put him down like a tree, but it took me 10 more rounds to win."

When Dwight fought Michael Spinks in the unification bout, he said after the fight that he had had trouble breathing because he had a cold. It turns out that was not the real problem. Qawi admitted much later that he had a deviated septum. He couldn't afford to have the fight postponed, which would threaten the loss of the opportunity and a big payoff, so he didn't say so at the time. "If he touched my nose, it hurt so much," Qawi recalled. "After the fight, we went right to the doctor. They fixed my nose and it healed in two weeks. I thought, 'Why didn't we do it before the fight?'"

When Dwight decided to become a professional fighter, he knew he was old at 25, and he knew he would have to make up for his time in prison and lack of an amateur career, so he tried to soak up every bit of experience and information at Joe Frazier's Gym. He felt that he could succeed, but also that he had a narrow window of opportunity: "I looked at it as a science. I always had a good right hand, but I became a student of my game. I moved up fast. The ESPN tournament, that's what made me. I wasn't that easy to hit. People said I was a Joe Frazier type. I was pretty fast. I had good defense. I learned my trade."

One of the basic precepts of boxing is that no matter what a fighter learns in the gym, he is susceptible to amnesia once he gets hit in the ring. If he forgets what he is taught, chances are he will get clocked and afterward be asking himself the same questions the reporters and public are asking, such as: Why did you do that if you knew better? But there is a lot of pressure on a man in the ring; there are bright lights, important things at stake, crowd noise, cornermen yelling and punches coming at his head. It's not always easy to make sound, split-second judgments. Sometimes a boxer will get into a rut, make mistakes and not realize he has gotten away from the good habits that he developed when he was winning.

After he lost to Michael Spinks and moved up to cruiserweight, Dwight Muhammad Qawi did OK for a while. But he did not fight that wisely against George Foreman, and just couldn't get past Evander Holyfield. Near the end, when Qawi should probably have been retired, he lost to others.

"You know, the jab, I should have done more of it," Dwight admitted. "As I got older, I abandoned it. I regret that." The left jab has always served as the appetizer, the setup for the overhand right finisher, and Qawi began rushing, getting ahead of things by throwing some rights before the stage was set. "My right hand was my pay-dirt. It was just natural. That made up for me not having an amateur career."

Camden was a very rough place to be when Dwight was growing up. There were pockets or danger zones where simply walking down the street wasn't very good for one's health. A kid learned to navigate through certain areas, but if he was looking for trouble, he could find it easily enough. Qawi was born into a family of 13 kids and their playground was on the streets where bigger kids fought for odd reasons, or no reasons at all, and it was mandatory to defend oneself. "Camden always had gunslingers who could fight," he noted. "There were rivalries on the corner. There were no gangs at the time. You had to hold your own. I was 19 when I made up my mind to give up that attitude."

Unfortunately for him at 19, Qawi was going to prison and that development was what was scaring him straight. He had five years to think things over and come out from behind concrete walls, determined never to be locked up again. He stayed true to his commitment and made a good life out of boxing: "I have patience now I wish I had as a teenager."

While Dwight was tentative about walking into a gym full-time because he didn't know what professional boxing was all about, he had watched some fights on television. When Qawi saw a Mike Rossman–Victor Galindez bout on the tube, he felt, "I can beat both of them at the same time." Then later he did beat

Rossman: "I felt like it validated me." Once Qawi polished the skills he had with gym time, he gained even more confidence. And he attached a winning streak to it, ripping off 18 straight victories: "If you can see it, you believe it, and you can achieve it."

For anyone who watched Matthew Saad Muhammad rise through the ranks and defend his light-heavyweight title time after time while living on the edge, a feeling grew that one day some hotshot fighter was going to catch up to him and lift that crown. But there was not a widespread belief that the fighter was going to be Qawi. He didn't seem to have enough experience. But he had faith and it was never shaken once the match was made.

"I've never been so mentally ready for a fight," Dwight stated. "I used to run around the Cooper River and it was cold out. You could always change your mind and go in, but I did it. I always tried to do extra. Against Saad Muhammad, even my barber counted me out. He said, 'We like you, Champ, but we don't know about this one.'"

Defeating Matthew Saad Muhammad was a career-defining triumph. Qawi was the underdog. He beat a renowned champion. The win gave him the title. Not a bad day's work. Of course, then he did it again. But it was the first win,

Former light-heavyweight and cruiserweight champion Dwight Muhammad Qawi in 2012. In addition, Qawi is a member of the Boxing Hall of Fame. (Photo by Lew Freedman)

actually claiming the belt, that was the most important bout of his life. The fact that a young man rose from poverty and hardship, and overcame adversity and mistakes made early in life, to gain world recognition was something that spun Qawi's head.

"I was numb," he recalled. "It was unbelievable. I suddenly became champion. Everybody around me was calling me 'Champ.' I still had relatives in Baltimore, and the next day a friend loaned me his Cadillac to go see family and I backed it up into a pole. That brought me back to earth."

At that point, Qawi started to make real money. He was going to be able to afford to pay his friend's repair bill and buy his own Cadillac if he chose to in order to replace his older, shabbier car. Dwight proudly turned his life around, but life also threw him a few curves after he became champ. He wonders about the timing of that old nose injury and his father getting killed. "Fate turned on me," he added.

Qawi got bursitis in one shoulder. He had his troubles with booze and somewhat with drugs: "Things started getting to me." This was at odds with his new self-image. He had become invulnerable, and then things got shaky: "I was thinking, 'I'm a rock.' Then those other things wear on you."

Born Dwight Braxton, Qawi adopted his new name several years after he first became interested in being a Muslim. In his worst moments (and his best), religion has sustained him. "Qawi" means "strong," he noted, and that refers to spiritually as well as physically strong. It is a comfort, he added, to believe that there is something "bigger than anyone, something higher" out there in the world than merely what men do. He picked a new last name at the urging of a religious friend, and he picked Qawi because "I always identified with that name. Religion is the biggest part of my life. It's dear to me."

His has been an adventurous life with both highs and lows, but the one thing Qawi returns to that gives him stability is his faith in God: "It gave me peace and serenity. It's solid. All the rest of this is fleeting."

Some of the people who had known him for a long time weren't keen on the name change. "We know you as Braxton," he was told. "That doesn't matter," Qawi responded. "When everything else is gone, it's between me and God. I wanted to be strong. I've been tested, like everybody."

Strong. It takes being strong to fight back against addiction, to conquer such a life-strangling problem. "I had a chemical problem," Qawi admitted. "I'm 22 years sober. That was a ghost from my past. It can haunt you."

Now he is strong for others. His counseling work began in 1992. At first, Qawi spoke to kids. Now he counsels adults. He said he worked with former heavyweight champion Mike Tyson for a month after Tyson got out of prison.

Dwight considers his counseling work his calling. Boxing was his first career, when he reveled in the glory, made a name for himself, built his self-esteem and recovered from the mistakes he made that sent him to prison. Now he does something every day that he considers meaningful for others: "It feels good that I am helping. It's letting me give back. I've seen so many people's lives destroyed. I'm invested. I really believe the more I stay around, the more I believe in the work I do. People ask me all the time, 'Is there any hope?' Yes, there is."

Once a world-famous boxer, now a full-time healer, Dwight Muhammad Qawi has managed to encapsulate those two immensely important parts of his life into a single summary sentence: "I used to break people up, now I put them back together." One last word would unify the remaining all-important aspect of religion in Qawi's life with those two things: Amen.

11

LARRY HOLMES

History has been kinder to Larry Holmes than the press was during his prime. He suffered from the inconvenience of following Muhammad Ali in the public eye. He was always better than many people gave him credit for, and he probably rates third among the top heavyweight champions of all time, just behind Ali and Joe Louis.

Those who missed Holmes in his best years, when he was heavyweight champion, probably still don't realize what they missed. At six-feet-three and about 215 pounds, he was a perfect size for his era. Holmes utilized an orthodox stance and cocked his head to the side as he studied his foe's defenses. The laser-like left jab opened opportunities, and the big-fisted right hand capitalized on them.

Although Holmes ill-advisedly said aloud that Rocky Marciano, the only champ to retire undefeated with 49 straight victories, couldn't carry his jock, in a certain sense Larry was right. Marciano was a great champion in his era of the 1950s, but compared to Holmes, he was slow and small. If both men met in their prime, Holmes would have jabbed Marciano to a state of distraction and then likely stopped him in the late rounds with a technical knockout. The only sure-thing heavyweights who were better than Holmes in his prime, and better in their own, were Joe Louis and Muhammad Ali. Anybody else would have been no better than a "pick-em" with Larry.

Although he was born in Georgia, Holmes grew up in Easton, Pennsylvania, about an hour north of Philadelphia. Larry never left and today he probably owns half the city. One thing Holmes did with the millions he won in prize money was to invest in local real estate. Larry was considered a local by the

Philadelphia media since he was based just 60 miles away. It was close enough when talking about world prominence. That was one thing Holmes had. He won the heavyweight title in 1978, and he held it for seven years—one of the greatest runs of all time.

Holmes was usually friendly, often expansive, and sometimes too blunt for his own good. But the main times he got cranky were when someone questioned his ability compared to past heavyweight champs or dismissed the value of his achievements by suggesting that he had not beaten quality fighters. It was wearying to put up with such nonsense.

A broad-shouldered frame and a big trunk created the illusion that Larry Holmes was larger than he really was, and it served as an advantage from the start of his career. Holmes dropped out of school in seventh grade and worked in a car wash, and he was working in a steel mill when he turned to boxing. Larry made his pro debut in Scranton, Pennsylvania, and had several of his early bouts there. He was impressive from the start and ripped off victories in his first 26 fights to position himself for a World Boxing Council heavyweight bout eliminator against Earnie Shavers, the great puncher. Holmes, whose left jab was the cornerstone of his success in the ring, used that valuable weapon to prevent Shavers from landing his huge right-hand shots, and he won a unanimous, 12-round decision.

The win set up Larry for a title shot and he took advantage, scoring a 15-round split decision over Ken Norton. To some extent, until that glorious moment, some downplayed Holmes as a serious contender. They dismissed him as merely a onetime sparring partner for Ali. That was a gross underestimation of his talents, and he set out to prove it during one of the finest reigns in heavyweight history. Holmes defended the title 20 times. Caesars Palace in Las Vegas became his home away from home. Few could have predicted that Holmes would hold the heavyweight crown for so long. Reigns of such length are very rare in boxing at any weight class. Only Joe Louis exceeded Holmes' staying power. Louis held the heavyweight crown for the better part of 12 years, with time off in the middle for World War II, and he made a record 25 successful defenses after winning the title from James J. Braddock in 1937.

Holmes won the title in June 1978, and defended it for the first time against Alfredo Evangelista in November. Then he got busy, knocking off Ossie Ocasio and Mike Weaver in 1979 before culminating his year with a September rematch against Earnie Shavers in Vegas. Much was at stake in terms of opportunity the first time Holmes and Shavers met. Now Larry was ascendant, the owner of the most prized belt in boxing, and Shavers' career was on a precipice. That was not a secret. At the weigh-in, Holmes flaunted the WBC belt and told Shavers, "This is your last chance."

Running into a Shavers right hand was like a furry little animal on the highway encountering a Mack truck. For many of Shavers' opponents, when facing the bald-headed wonder, their main objective was not to be turned into road kill. Shavers, who hailed from Warren, Ohio, was then 35, and already had 56 knockouts to his credit. Although he could look fearsome with his shining head, walrus-style mustache and powerful body, Earnie was usually nice to talk with. Even Holmes admitted that Shavers was a good guy, though he did suspend his naturally genial personality in the ring. That didn't mean that the Easton Assassin was going to take it easy on him. When Holmes was asked how this rematch was going to differ from the first bout between the two men, he said, "It ain't." Holmes was a realist. He knew how to beat Shavers—by steering clear of the thunder in his right hand.

Holmes did walk into a Shavers right and it put him on the seat of his pants in the seventh round, but for the rest of the night, he pretty much had Shavers where he wanted him—standing in front of a flicking, irritating and sharp jab. It was almost as if Holmes was stinging him with shards of glass. The jab was lethal, carving Shavers up and drawing blood from several spots on his face. Some of the blood, coming from above Shavers' eyes, distorted his vision. The fight ended in the 11th round, short of the 15-round distance, but pretty much what Holmes had predicted for length.

"Earnie's a strong man," Holmes admitted. He stood up to strong punishment. As the rounds passed, it was apparent that Shavers' defense was flawed, and Holmes could keep on pounding the challenger. But because he liked Earnie, he kept telling him that he should quit before he got hurt. Shavers didn't take the advice. Blood flew from his skull into the first two rows at ringside, and Holmes said to referee Davey Pearl, "What have I got to do, kill him?" Pearl stopped the bout, and Holmes was 32-0.

One thing about Larry Holmes: he was democratic. He felt he had been shunted aside in the title picture for a couple of years after he was ready for a shot, but pledged he would not be that way when he won the title: "I always said I would fight all comers." At 29, Holmes, once shy in public, was clearly maturing. He was at ease chatting about his career and his sport. When he wore his wire-rim glasses, he looked positively professorial, although he saw it a different way: "They make me look handsome. I'm trying to improve my image."

When Holmes said he would fight anybody, he was serious. The next anybody who appeared on his dance card was Lorenzo Zanon, the European heavyweight champion from Italy who reached the peak of his fame when his name became associated with Holmes' as a title challenger. On that trip to Las Vegas, Holmes looked particularly crisp. He beat up his sparring partners so effectively that they were practically being carried out on their shields one after another as if part of a parade. Then in the real bout, Zanon followed them. After a few rounds of feeling out the somewhat anonymous stranger, Holmes unloaded with right hands in the fourth round and drove Zanon to the canvas twice. He showed some surprising resilience in the fifth round, but it didn't last. In the sixth, Holmes got him counted out after a left and right connected, and he dropped Zanon. That was the end of the Italian Stallion.

Less than two months later, also at Caesars in Las Vegas, Holmes took out Leroy Jones to raise his record to 34-0. Then, for a change of scenery, Holmes signed to fight Scott LeDoux in Bloomington, Minnesota. In 1980, the Met Center, which held about 17,000 fans, was primarily the home of the Minnesota North Stars of the National Hockey League. It has since been demolished, and now that area is a part of the site of the Mall of America. Fighting in the Met Center represented a home game for LeDoux, who trained in his garage in a Minneapolis suburb.

A onetime bartender and truck driver, Scott LeDoux always acted like just a regular guy, not someone ranked fifth in the world by the WBC. He was trying to hold things together with two small children and a wife who had cancer. He wanted to be businesslike about getting his big chance at the title. LeDoux regularly made appearances for charity in his community and was very recognizable. But his favorite watering hole, a place he had been visiting for 10 years called The King of Clubs, was admittedly a rough bar. Fights were known to break out there sometimes, and even friends from the bar teased LeDoux about his own toughness: "What's it like to be ranked fifth in the world and 15th at The King of Clubs?"

Some world champions globe-trot and really see the world. Some like to stay close to home, or regularly fight in one location. For Larry Holmes, a trip to Minnesota was about business, not sightseeing. He made a million dollars to LeDoux's $250,000, but the hope was that LeDoux, as a local, would increase the gate. At one point leading up to the fight, Holmes met with a group of kids. One teenaged girl squeezed one of his biceps and said, "Wow!" He did the same to her. There were homespun appearances in various locations in the Midwest.

Among those providing entertainment, although he was not on the boxing card, was an intrigued and intriguing observer—Muhammad Ali. Ali had been in retirement, but was making noise about a comeback in 1980. A lot of noise, really. Up until then, Holmes dismissed Ali's antics, but he no longer thought he could. When he said that Ali was old, out of shape and not a serious contender, those without wax in their ears heard him clearly. But those who let nostalgia cloud their judgment believed that Ali had one more miracle lurking in his body. During the weigh-in versus Scott LeDoux at the Registry Hotel, Ali appeared and when his face was seen, a few hundred witnesses began chanting his name.

The LeDoux fight was Holmes' seventh title defense, but the drums began beating for a Holmes–Ali bout. The rumors of where such an event might be staged were wide-ranging and sometimes fanciful. Among the places mentioned were Madison Square Garden, Las Vegas and Rio de Janeiro. The most eye-opening suggestion was that Holmes and Ali travel to Cairo, Egypt for a so-called Peace Fight. A peace fight—was it possible that no one saw the irony in such a designation?

There was usually a flicker of annoyance in Larry Holmes' eyes whenever Muhammad Ali's name came up. In his mind, Ali represented the past, and this was his time. He just couldn't shake the ghost, and Ali was making it impossible to do so. Larry repeatedly warned Muhammad to stay retired for his own good, but Ali wasn't listening. Accompanied by a heavy sigh, Holmes was convinced that he was going to have to fight Ali to show him—and the world—that the legend's day had passed and that Larry Holmes was the best heavyweight of all in 1980. "A lot of people in the world think Ali's still Superman, still God," Holmes noted. "But he's not here forever. People come and go."

I heard Holmes' logic and understood it. Especially in boxing, the skills erode and the history of those who made comebacks was dismal. Yet with Ali people imbued him with almost magical powers, so the more he talked, the more people believed an Ali–Holmes fight was credible.

Holmes stopped Scott LeDoux on cuts in the seventh round, his seventh straight heavyweight title fight stoppage. LeDoux didn't win a round on any of the judges' cards, and the end was in sight by the sixth when Larry scored a one-punch, right uppercut knockdown and had LeDoux bleeding. Once again, as he had in the Shavers fight, Holmes asked the referee—the same referee, Davey Pearl—to rescue the warrior who was being beaten to a pulp with no retaliation. Holmes said afterwards that Pearl told him to "Shut up and fight." It was not long after that admonition that Pearl did step in.

After he was back in Pennsylvania to rest, Holmes and promoter Don King announced that what Larry never wanted to happen was indeed going onto his schedule in early October, just a few months away. There was going to be a Larry Holmes–Muhammad Ali heavyweight title fight after all. They were not going to see the pyramids, however. The closest that they would get to the ancients was Caesars Palace, which had a bar named Cleopatra's Barge. It would have to suffice, though there was no more mention of a Peace Fight. Promoters probably should have put the fight in Philadelphia. Although it had been some time before, Ali had once lived in Cherry Hill, New Jersey, just a short drive away. But while Atlantic City was stealing much of Vegas' thunder in the boxing game, Vegas still owned mega-fights like this one.

In some ways, the idea of Holmes fighting Ali was just a consolation prize. Long before he agreed to fight LeDoux or even had Ali on his radar screen,

Larry wanted to fight John Tate, the World Boxing Association champ, in a unification bout. In October 1979, Tate, who was a U.S. Olympic bronze medal-winner in Montreal three years before, journeyed to South Africa to fight Gerrie Coetzee for the title.

Holmes was disconcerted by the entire situation. He did not think Tate worthy of being called a heavyweight champion and he was appalled that Tate, a black man, had traveled to South Africa to fight during the apartheid era. "I want to make it clear to you people that Larry Holmes is the heavyweight champion of the world," he declared. "John Tate is not the quality fighter I am. Let there be one champion. Let him go down the street in New York and see who the people recognize as champion."

Holmes was correct on every count. Figuring that he deserved his first defense in his own hometown after his trek to South Africa, Tate took on Mike Weaver on March 31, 1980 in Knoxville, Tennessee. For almost the entire 15 rounds, Tate out-boxed Weaver, but then in the last minute of the fight, Weaver landed a picture-perfect shot and Tate fell like an axed tree flush on his face and was counted out while lying on the canvas in front of a shocked crowd.

Essentially, Mike Weaver did Larry Holmes a favor. Since Holmes had already topped Weaver, there was no outcry for a unification fight. That's when attention heated up for an Ali-Holmes fight. In Minnesota in July, Muhammad Ali, a noted hobbyist magician, performed magic tricks for children in hotel lobbies. It is probably my fondest moment of Ali, when he played games to tease and entertain the wide-eyed kids.

Some believed Ali's ability to cast himself as a legitimate contender all over again, after a two-year layoff without a tune-up bout, was the masterpiece in his bag of magic tricks. Also, in Minnesota, Muhammad had became a thorn in Larry's side, part of a hardcore publicity campaign to get the world to take him seriously again. Ali said that he taught Holmes everything he knew about boxing and that if they ever met in the ring, he would destroy Larry. Gradually, the chatter got on his nerves. Holmes said that Ali was "an old man" and exclaimed "to hell with Ali." He didn't need him to make money or to validate his hold on the heavyweight championship.

Eventually, despite Holmes' initial resistance, Ali swayed the public and got the deal signed. Despite being 38, Ali worked out hard and transformed his body from an out-of-shape blimp to a flat-bellied athlete at 217 and a half pounds. He looked great, but no one could account for ring rust or aging reflexes. This was one time that Holmes was not the center of attention for one of his defenses. Larry also knew how important it was for him to win, so no one could ever say again that he was merely a belt-holder for Ali in between the famous man's willingness to claim it.

Holmes trained like a madman and leading up to the fight, he broke with his usual habits of conducting public workouts and holding court with the press at the gym or in his hotel suite, going into a type of seclusion. A rumor went around that he had been thumbed in the eye while sparring and might pull out of the fight. Finally, one afternoon, he was tracked down in the Caesars casino playing craps. Cornered by sportswriters, Holmes was his usual genial self. "Are you guys looking for me?" he teased. "I bet you this is the first time you had a press conference at a dice table." He probably had us there.

Lighting in casinos is often compared to an eclipse, so the room wasn't the brightest in the Western Hemisphere, yet Holmes wore dark glasses. He came clean and said that he had been thumbed while sparring, but that it was a very minor incident and wouldn't affect the fight. Holmes said he ceased training because he was in prime form and didn't want to overdo it. Then he led everyone up to his hotel suite. There was a prop in his room that couldn't be missed. It was a plastic toy stand-up figure bearing Ali's facial likeness. Someone not only blackened the eyes, presumably because Holmes' supporters felt that was how Ali would look come fight night, but also wrote on the toy, "Little Porky was 255, now 225." It really was quite hilarious, if not at all complimentary, though Ali had said much worse about his opponents in the past.

"I never thought I'd have to fight Ali," Holmes admitted. "I don't dislike him. I don't care too much for him. I find Ali very amusing, a comic, a clown."

When Larry laughs, his eyes become slits and his whole face joins in the joy. When pensive, he can be soft-spoken. During this friendly exchange with sportswriters, Holmes bounced his six-month-old daughter Kandy on his knee. "I'm a nice guy," he reflected. "I'm a very nice guy. I get up in the morning and say, 'Hello, how are you?' I'm two different people. Don't mistake my kindness for my weakness."

Still, twice in the ring in recent months, Holmes, whose job it was to knock opponents out, had asked officials to stop fights when he was tearing up another man. That demonstrated a streak of compassion, if nothing else, one not required by a man in a profession that demands that he protect himself at all times.

Before he carved his own swath through the heavyweight division, before he acquired any kind of national reputation, Larry Holmes worked for Muhammad Ali, getting paid $500 a week to spar with him. Holmes was young and rough around the edges. Ali was in a class of his own. But Ali got older and stepped away from boxing, and Holmes came into his prime and got better. Ali decided he wanted to make it back to the top of the fight game and the top of the world, so he agitated for the bout with Holmes. Many times, whether they are local turf fights, TV fights or world title fights, combatants will box the first rounds with their mouths, saying nasty things about the opponent and how they really don't like him.

Like most of the world, Holmes understood where Ali was coming from. He wouldn't be Ali if he didn't talk up his chances, and talk down Holmes'. Larry tried not to get caught up in verbal warfare with Ali. For one thing, few people outside of a Billy Crystal would have a chance of winning such an exchange.

Seven defenses into his own title reign, the most prominent sports figure in Easton, Pennsylvania seemed more at ease in his own skin, more secure with his role in his sport's hierarchy. Larry Holmes had not wanted to fight Ali, but was pursued and cornered into making the match. Holmes did not want to box Ali, nor did he wish to insult a man that many consider the greatest fighter of all time, and one who became a hero to African Americans across the nation and the world.

"He's a great man," Holmes admitted. "He's done a lot for his country and black people. You can't knock him." No, you couldn't knock Ali, but you could knock him out, and Holmes was going to try and do that for sure. But he was smart enough to know how that would be received. "When I whip Ali, they're going to say I whipped an old man. And they'll be right."

Ali was trying to win the heavyweight title for the fourth time, and he was paid eight million dollars for the shot. Inappropriately, as champion, Holmes, was paid four million dollars. Larry said he would knock out the legend by the eighth round. Ali, his voice carrying almost as if magnified by a loudspeaker, declared, "When they made the odds against me, they forgot my name was Muhammad Ali."

There was a time when Holmes, at age 30, considered Ali to be his idol, but the days of hero worship were long gone and Larry was the favorite. There were stars in the eyes of the average fan, but not the bettors. Tickets were bought by 25,000 fans and the fight was shown in 100 countries, but it didn't take much more than one three-minute round to demonstrate that Larry Holmes was the superior fighter.

These were two heavyweights who lived by the left jab, but it became evident almost immediately that Holmes could stick and sting, and Ali could not reach him. Ali looked trim, but closer inspection revealed stretch marks on his belly. This was the clash of two eras, and Holmes had the advantage. Round after round, he peppered Ali with jabs and hard right shots. The challenger mustered little in response. Gradually, as the rounds played out, the crowd became quieter and quieter. They had come to witness a resurrection, an Ali miracle, but they saw Holmes turn into the avenging angel for all of Ali's ring victims of the past.

The fight was scheduled for 15 rounds, but Ali could not answer the bell for the 11th. By then, Holmes was showing mercy to his onetime mentor, hitting him often enough and hard enough to capture just about every round, but not viciously smashing away to put him out. Larry later admitted taking it easy at times, but he added that it was not a case where he could have KO'd Ali at will. "I couldn't have knocked him out at any time. If I could have, I would have knocked him out in the first round." Leading up to the fight, Holmes recognized that Ali was a shell of his former self. Even if the ex-champ put on a good show in the run-up, "He fooled all you people."

Afterwards, Ali was a beaten man. He wore dark glasses to his post-fight press conference. His face was puffy, and there were suggestions of broken ribs. When he was much younger and taking the world by storm with his ring speed and fast talking, Ali would come into such sessions, point to his face to demonstrate how remarkably unmarked it was, and insist he was still pretty. He was not so pretty after the Holmes bout. Nearly always glib in every circumstance over the 20 years of his career since the Rome Olympics in 1960, Ali spoke slowly and softly at this moment of defeat. "After the first round, I knew I couldn't win."

As thorough as the defeat was, Ali made no retirement announcements, and as soon as he was healthy again, he stunningly spoke of a rematch with Holmes, or of beating a contender. Ali did fight again. He found that contender, and that contender found his chin. The fight was called "Drama in the Bahamas," and Ali was 39 years old and still hoping. Trevor Berbick won a 10-round decision, and this time Ali retired for good.

Holmes went right on repelling challengers. He beat Berbick next, then Leon Spinks in Detroit. The match with Spinks was held at Joe Louis Arena in December 1981, and the fight was dedicated to the memory of that former heavyweight champion, who had died about eight months earlier. Holmes overwhelmed Spinks in three rounds. He was the fourth former heavyweight champion that Larry Holmes defeated. "I have to convince you day in and day out that no one in the world can beat me," Holmes noted, perhaps forgetting that was the purpose of the sport of boxing.

Renaldo Snipes was the next foe up in Pittsburgh, the next man who thought he could lift the crown from Larry Holmes. He could not, but Snipes did his best, looping a huge right at Larry's head in the seventh round to knock him down and jeopardize his hold on the title. Otherwise, the champion pretty much controlled the action. He was far ahead on scorecards when referee Rudy Ortega stopped the fight in the 11th round. Although Snipes and his seconds protested the stoppage vigorously, Holmes was winding up and banging the challenger with unanswered blows that looked devastating. Cornermen were screaming, fans at the Pittsburgh Civic Arena were howling, and Snipes was jostled when an attempt was made to cut his gloves off. Instead, the scissors pierced his arm and he had to leave the scene for medical attention. Holmes shrugged off the momentary embarrassment of the knockdown: "I wasn't hurt. I was more surprised. I was aware of where I was." He quickly cleared his head and finished off Snipes.

What followed was an ugly buildup to a showdown with Gerry Cooney. Cooney, a Long Islander who was blessed with good management, was the latest flavor-of-the-month contender. He was a big, hulking heavyweight with power in his punches, particularly his left hook, but short on experience against top fighters. It was suggested that he was rushed to the top of the rankings because he was white.

In the early part of the 20th century, Jack Johnson became the first black man to win the heavyweight championship. Appalled at Johnson's achievement, the white men who controlled the sport conspired to find a new white boxer to win it back. Thus began the search for "The Great White Hope." Ultimately, Johnson was besieged by legal authorities, less for his prominence as a fighter, but rather because of his attitude of superiority and his habit of dating, bedding and marrying white women. He was eventually convicted of violating the Mann Act, transporting a woman across state lines for sexual reasons, and was thrown into a no-win title defense against Jess Willard. Much of the repugnant story was documented in a variety of books and then told in a Tony Award–winning Broadway play and a highly acclaimed movie.

Over the decades that followed, when Joe Louis was champion, and in the 1960s and '70s when black fighters owned the heavyweight division and America's racial relations were still tense, some boxing people remained on the lookout for a potential white heavyweight champion. The phrase "Great White Hope" was not used as frequently, but came out of the closet when Gerry Cooney moved into the scene. The feel of that description was much in evidence as Cooney got his chance against Larry Holmes on June 6, 1982, again in Las Vegas. Holmes stopped Cooney in the 13th round to retain the title, and that was pretty much the last time that the idea of a "Great White Hope" was conjured up in connection with a heavyweight title fight.

While they may not have been his most difficult fights, beating Muhammad Ali and beating Gerry Cooney were two defining bouts of Larry Holmes' career, ones that he had to win for himself. From Cooney, Holmes went on to score additional title defenses against Randy Cobb (of Philadelphia), Lucien Rodriguez, Tim Witherspoon (of Philadelphia), Scott Frank, Marvis Frazier (of Philadelphia), James "Bonecrusher" Smith, David Bey and Carl "The Truth" Williams.

Those wins built Holmes' record to 48-0, and he needed one more to equal Rocky Marciano's 49-0 heavyweight best record. But Holmes lost a controversial decision and his title to Michael Spinks in 1985 and then lost another controversial decision to Spinks in a 1986 rematch. After laying off for more than a year and a half while Mike Tyson knocked out Spinks to unify the title, Holmes challenged the younger man. But Tyson stopped him in the fourth round for his third straight loss.

Larry Holmes continued fighting and had other chances to regain a piece of the heavyweight title, but he could not do so. Since Holmes actually took a fight and won it over Eric "Butterbean" Esch in 2002 when he was 52 years old, one might say he stuck around boxing a little bit too long. Even then, Holmes did not know it would be his final fight. He retired with a record of 69-6 and was elected to the International Boxing Hall of Fame in 2008.

When he chose to venture into the limelight, Larry Holmes was a full-fledged celebrity who could command fees to open businesses, to sign autographs at sports memorabilia events, or to give talks. When he wished to stay out of the spotlight, Larry stayed in Easton, or he went fishing. He loved that fishing time. At one point, Holmes had a two-million-dollar boat.

Now in his 60s, Larry does not plan another in-the-ring showing. He remains content to live in Easton, where he has an office and owns a bar and many other properties. The office, on a side street on the outskirts of downtown Easton, is decorated with photographs and posters that are memorabilia from his outstanding career. Holmes was 62 years old on a May afternoon, and after

Former heavyweight champion Larry Holmes at home in Easton, Pennsylvania.
(Photo by Lew Freedman)

spending much of his retirement life acquiring property with the winnings from his boxing victories, he pondered the national recession and the housing slump and wondered if just maybe he shouldn't consider downsizing his portfolio.

"I don't want to go on chasing houses and another three acres of land," Holmes reflected. He wasn't talking about investment property, but the house he shared with his wife, Diane, now that their kids were grown. "Do we really need it?" He was just another empty-nester trying to figure out what to do with all of that space. If Holmes pulled out of Easton, the city would have a lot of empty buildings. Larry had heard for a long time, "It's great that you give back to Easton." But he seemed a little bit weary of playing that role.

With the passage of time since Holmes' 20-defense reign as first World Boxing Council and then International Boxing Association heavyweight champion, it's more obvious than ever that he is one of the greatest fighters of all time. So it was a bit sad to hear him say, "I didn't get to enjoy being heavyweight champion of the world as much as I should have."

For some years, boxing people whispered that Larry Holmes was not as good as Ali, that he was not as good as he thought he was. Holmes used that as a motivator. He beat Ali when he had to fight him. He beat Cooney when he was put in front of him. Holmes employed a left jab that was as good as any. He showed heart when he was knocked down by getting off the canvas to win.

There is no doubt that Holmes is the most famous person in Easton, but he is also one of the most respected heavyweights of all time when people paused to compare what he did with the 30 years that followed. "I did enjoy being heavyweight champion of the world and I enjoyed making money," Holmes admitted, stepping back from his previous statement of blanket non-enjoyment. "They can't take that away. I was champion for seven and a half years. That's longer than anyone else except Joe Louis."

It was all about timing. It would have been tough for anyone to follow Ali because not only was Ali great, but he was also a one-man publicity machine. It was like Gene Bartow following John Wooden as UCLA basketball coach. No matter what the next man did in the job, he was going to struggle living up to the accomplishments of a legend.

"I didn't have the PR that Ali had," Holmes noted. So who was the best heavyweight ever? "Don't ask me that question. I'm going to say me. The others were great in their day. I was great in my day."

One of the biggest days of Larry Holmes' life was winning the title in the 15-round showdown against Ken Norton at Caesars Palace in 1978. The fight was oh-so-close and a split decision gave Holmes the crown. What a feeling that was. The transplant from Cuthbert, Georgia couldn't stop thinking about how his friends and family in Easton, Pennsylvania would react. "I was going, 'What are the people going to say when I get back home?' I'm the heavyweight champion of the world." A great moment of accomplishment, fulfilling a dream, can make a man reflect on where he has come from, and Holmes first thought of being poor in Georgia. "We had nothing," he recalled. "We were on welfare. We were sharecroppers. We got our water in the well."

In Easton, the whole town celebrated with him. "They came out," Holmes remembered. And he stayed, investing millions of dollars in the town, accepting civic and community awards along the way, a family man married 32 years, raising his kids in the town. Fans from around the world know where to find him, and they would write for autographs and send letters in many different languages. When they come in Spanish, they are translated and read to him, and the words from boxing fans with long memories are gratifying. "They want to tell me how great I am," Holmes noted. Wouldn't that make any man feel great?

Even when his job was to knock other men out, Larry Holmes was a generally affable fellow outside the ring. He could be fun to listen to when he spoke about his sport, and he knew how to make a joke. Larry used to say that he was a nice guy when he didn't have the gloves on, and he generally was to all appearances. He still says so. "I like people. I drink with them at the bar [his bar, next door to the office]."

Holmes still seems surprised by the amount of flak he took over that Marciano remark. "They made such a big deal out of it. I don't know how good he was. I felt I was the damned best. You know, Marciano was short." So was Mike Tyson compared to Holmes, and he beat Larry. But Holmes was aging and didn't train as he should have. "Tyson gave me the utmost respect. He called me 'Mr. Holmes.' I said, 'Don't call me Mr. Holmes.' I fought for pride. I wanted to win."

The entire premise surrounding the ascent of a boxer becoming heavyweight champion is that he is the toughest man in the world. He is supposed to be unbeatable. Until a boxer grasps the title, he can think he's the best, but not know it for sure. Once he owns the title, he can claim it. Of course, then he has to defend the title, and the label, so to speak. "I never had any doubt that I would become heavyweight champion," Holmes maintained. "But I had doubts a lot of times when I was champion. You train harder. You always have doubts. Someone can hit you with a right hand or a left hook." There's no doubt that the proper combination will put doubt in any man's head if that combination hits him in the head.

"I'm happy with what I did in the game of boxing," Holmes contended. "There was too much racism and bullshit, and people out there that didn't want you to accomplish things. I did it because I was allowed to do it. If I didn't have the skills, I wouldn't have been there in the first place. I had talent. The jab was natural and I developed it. As it went on, I got good at it. I perfected it. That's what made me."

That jab was a thing of beauty and menace. "I threw 70 or 80 punches a round," Holmes recalled, "and maybe 40 of them were jabs. It kept a lot of people off me. Not only was it quick, it was hard."

The theme of the event when Holmes met Michael Spinks the first time, beside being his 21st title defense, was that with another victory, Holmes would tie Rocky Marciano's 49-0 record. From the hindsight of many years, Larry said, "it didn't bother me" that he didn't equal Marciano's mark. "I was 200 percent relieved when I didn't break his record. I was between wanting it and not wanting it. When I lost, the pressure was off."

From the hindsight of many years, it can be said that it didn't really matter because the singular aspect of Marciano's mark was that he retired undefeated. If Holmes got to 49-0, he wasn't going to retire. Sooner or later, whatever the number turned out to be, if he fought long enough, someone was going to beat Holmes.

In the big picture, nothing in his inability to match Marciano really diminished the overall impact of Larry Holmes' career. He still defended the heavyweight title more times than anyone but Joe Louis. He still held the heavyweight title longer than anyone but Joe Louis. He made enough money to take care of himself and his family for life. And he was still elected to the International Boxing Hall of Fame.

And there is still a street named after him in Easton: Larry Holmes Drive. It was a gesture of respect and appreciation—two traits that the great boxer rates highly.

12

THE FAMOUS COME TO ATLANTIC CITY

Marvelous Marvin Hagler knew he had to take detours through Philadelphia and vicinity on the path to becoming acclaimed as the best middleweight boxer in the whole damned universe. No shortcuts for Marvin. He was born in Newark, New Jersey, grew up in Boston, but as the song goes, he wanted the whole world in his hands.

His hands were good enough to give him the world, too, as long as he could negotiate a route through the minefield of matchmakers, promoters and men of equal weight who were hungry enough to be genuine obstacles in his quest. But Hagler was a little bit better than even the best of them, and he was a little bit hungrier than even the most starved of them. To prove it, Marvin not only beat up everyone in the division who would fight him, he legally changed his name to Marvelous. It was superfluous and yes, a bit showy for a meat-and-potatoes guy who was blue collar at heart, but Hagler didn't want to leave any doubt.

You couldn't blame him, really, because Hagler was so good that a significant segment of the 160-pound class was scared of him. Not only did those fighters not want to get into the ring with him, they were ready to cross the street if they saw him coming. Hagler was in his 51st professional fight before he got a shot at the title.

In the late 1970s and early '80s, several of the best middleweights in the world owned Philadelphia addresses. Hagler wasn't yet a big enough name to make them come to him, so he went to them. It's not clear if the Brockton, Massachusetts fighter ever bothered to eat a soft pretzel or a cheesesteak while he was visiting the area, but he did cut an angry swath through the best of the local middleweights.

Marvin Hagler (*left*), the Brockton, Massachusetts middleweight who became one of the best ever in that weight class, had to battle his way through a swarm of top Philadelphia fighters like Willie "The Worm" Monroe to get a title shot. Monroe won this battle in Philadelphia in 1976. (Photo courtesy of J. Russell Peltz)

The first time Hagler ventured to Philadelphia in 1976, he fought Bobby "Boogaloo" Watts and got a lesson out of it, losing a 10-round majority decision, one of only three bouts he lost in his entire career. Hagler came back for more just two months later, taking on Willie "The Worm" Monroe. And he lost that one, too, in a unanimous decision. If ever there was an illustration of how demanding it was to be a middleweight at the time, the results of those two bouts in Philadelphia proved it. Whether or not they recall the details of the bouts, Philadelphia fight fans still remember that their best beat Hagler. Ultimately regarded as one of the best boxers ever in the division, he came in to the Spectrum, fought twice and lost twice—well, that was something.

To Hagler's credit, he didn't shy away. He was back in Philadelphia later the same year to meet Eugene "Cyclone" Hart. That time Hagler was a winner, and when there was a rematch against Monroe in Boston in early 1977, Marvin won that too. They fought a rubber match later that year at the Spectrum, and Hagler beat Monroe for the second time.

One might think that Hagler had seen enough of the 160-pound residents of Philadelphia to last a lifetime, but no one could ever accuse him of taking the easy way. In August 1978, Marvin was back at the Spectrum once again. He seemed to appear there as often as the 76ers or Flyers. This match-up was against Bennie Briscoe, the fight went 10 rounds, and Hagler notched a unanimous decision. That was the last time he fought in Philly.

Of course, as the new decade dawned, that was one of the last times anyone of note fought in Philadelphia for quite a while. The economics of the sport were changing and Atlantic City, just 60 miles away and fronting the Atlantic Ocean, became the new boxing hot spot of the area. Atlantic City was really just an extension of Philadelphia's backyard, but the new casinos going up one after another on the boardwalk took the risk out of promotion.

The casinos had the rooms for entertainment. They had high rollers who would come in on a Saturday or Sunday to play, even as they took a couple of hours off to watch the fights as honored guests. The networks were after programming to fill their time slots. The closer drivers got to Atlantic City on the A.C. Expressway from Philadelphia or the Garden State Parkway from New York, the more billboards they saw advertising the entertainment playing in casino theatres. There were men with deep voices singing, women with high voices singing, men and women dancing together, and men with powerful fists knocking people out.

At first it was just Resorts International hosting fights. Then, as new casinos opened, they decided to add boxing cards to their entertainment menu. Between press conferences announcing upcoming fights, visits to training camps to see fighters training for their matches, and the fights themselves on Saturdays and Sundays, a boxing writer could spend most of the week at one casino or another at the shore. The tolls on the Expressway began to mount up. And you always had to be careful that the deer, which gathered right next to the highway at dusk, didn't wander out in front of your car.

The most remarkable thing about Atlantic City jumping in with both feet was that it didn't even get in the way of Las Vegas. Vegas still held a monopoly on mega fights, the ones that demanded bigger seating capacities and millions of dollars more in purses to attract the one percent of the biggest names. Atlantic City sucked up the shows that Philadelphia used to stage at the Spectrum and the Blue Horizon and put the squeeze on regular club fights because casinos paid the fighters more. But when Larry Holmes was going to defend his World Boxing Council heavyweight championship, chances were that the bout was going to Las Vegas, or if by some quirk, another city if it outbid Vegas. Sugar Ray Leonard did not fight in Atlantic City. Neither did Thomas Hearns. Neither did Roberto Duran, with one exception (he had defended the lightweight title in Philadelphia in 1977, but that was a different lifetime for Mr. Hands of Stone).

The more Atlantic City became ingrained in the mindset as a regular big-fight venue, the more celebrity boxers appeared in town. Aaron "Hawk" Pryor fought in A.C., but what was even more unlikely, he began hanging out there as a boxing spectator. On any visit to town, one might bump into the future Hall of Famer wandering about a fight site. He seemed to wear either a sweatsuit or a three-piece suit. One was for comfort, the other was for style, and when someone noticed the slickness of his tailored suits, Pryor almost purred with pleasure. He wasn't just trying to show off his threads, he claimed, there was meaning behind dressing sharply for business occasions, even if they were the type of press conferences that other boxers might attend wearing T-shirts. According to Pryor, "It shows I'm serious about what I'm doing, to always wear a shirt and tie."

For most of his career, Aaron Pryor showed how serious he was by compiling a 39-1 all-time record. At 140 pounds and originally from Cincinnati, he was arguably the greatest junior welterweight of all time. Although Pryor's career ended badly when he ran into monumental trouble with drugs, and suffered from cataracts and a detached retina, he was inducted into the International Boxing Hall of Fame in 1996. It wasn't just three-piece suits that Pryor chose as a way to demonstrate class in his wardrobe. He had silk handkerchiefs tucked into his suit pockets and wore white golf gloves. That was less a fashion accessory than a winter accessory, he confided. "I wear them to keep my hands warm."

Mostly, Aaron came off as mischievous. He had a glint in his eye that made one wonder if he was just fooling no matter what he said. When Pryor entered a room, he shouted, "It's Hawk Time!" and usually it was. In the ring, he did attack like a hawk. He seemed to have no off switch except for the sound of the bell at the end of each round.

Pryor was at almost all times charming in public, except when he took time to beat up a challenger, as he did in one of his two Atlantic City experiences in 1982. At the peak of his game, he took on Miguel Montilla of the Dominican Republic. Montilla was a rough customer, and it took until the 11th round for Pryor to completely solve his defense when he fired off an estimated 30 unanswered punches. Still, the fight was not stopped until the next round. "His heart is as big as mine" was the compliment Pryor paid to the loser.

Other big names with big aspirations fought in Atlantic City during this era, men who had no ties to the neighborhood, but who were lured there because the shore offered the best exposure and the best paydays. Lightweight "Boom Boom" Mancini, heavyweight Greg Page, lightweight Sean O'Grady, featherweight Juan LaPorte, featherweight Eusebio Pedroza, and cruiserweights Marvin Camel and Carlos DeLeon all contested title fights in casinos in Atlantic City. The Miss America contest was held once a year. A world title fight was held once a week. Atlantic City hadn't been this popular since the horses dived off the Steel Pier.

Eusebio Pedroza, a Panamanian, was not especially well known in the United States, but had a well-deserved reputation as a great fighter. When

Pedroza stopped Juan LaPorte at the Sands Hotel & Casino in 1982, it was his 14th defense of the featherweight title. With that bout he made boxing history, breaking a 60-year-old record for most defenses at the weight class set by Abe Attel of Philadelphia. This was the kind of stuff a fight fan might run across every week in Atlantic City during this era.

"I feel very good about that," Pedroza remarked about grabbing the record. He spoke in Spanish through a translator. "I feel very good to be ranked the best of the fighters in the featherweight division." He retired with a record 19 defenses of the crown and held the title for seven years. Atlantic City was just a stopover for the accomplished champ.

It was still the early days of the cruiserweight division when Carlos DeLeon and Marvin Camel rumbled in A.C. Although he fought long beyond the time he should have retired (and accumulated eight unnecessary losses and two draws in his last dozen fights), in 1982, Camel was a pride of the cruiserweights. When the World Boxing Council invented the weight class of 176 to 190 pounds in 1979, Camel was the first champion. He defended the title twice against Mate Pavlov and then lost it to DeLeon. The Atlantic City bout was a rematch.

Camel was born on the Flathead Indian Reservation in Montana in 1951, and he wore a colorful Indian headdress into the ring when he fought. He was a game, tough fighter, but DeLeon was slicker, faster and more powerful, and he won the title at the Playboy Hotel & Casino. DeLeon dominated from the start and doctors would not permit Camel to come out for the eighth round.

Carlos DeLeon lost the title to S.T. Gordon in an upset in his next fight, but regained it and kept it until 1988 before losing to Evander Holyfield. DeLeon won the title back again after Holyfield moved up to heavyweight. Marvin Camel lost big in Atlantic City, but he bounced back and gained control of the International Boxing Federation belt.

The Sean O'Grady Show was splashier. O'Grady was from Oklahoma City, an unsophisticated boxing town with limited opportunity. Yet O'Grady was born into a boxing family and that gave him an advantage. His father, Pat, was a trainer and his mother, Jean, was a promoter. The family moved around a lot, almost like circus people, until O'Grady was 11 and Oklahoma City became the base of operations.

It was difficult at first for O'Grady to gain credibility in the boxing world outside of the Plains states. O'Grady had the quirky habit of chewing bubble gum and blowing bubbles in between knockout punches, and was called "The Bubblegum Bomber." He was a heartthrob and was probably the only boxer around who attracted young girls to the sport. They viewed him as another teen idol, only instead of crooning, O'Grady was punching.

That wasn't all to Sean O'Grady's story. He was attending college at Central State and he often wore all green. That was an Irish thing, but I remember referring to him as The Leprechaun. O'Grady wasn't all flash and color, though. He could fight. For a 135-pounder, he could pound. O'Grady didn't go to Toys R Us as a kid, he went to Knockouts R Us.

Because he was from the hinterlands, the boxing establishment demanded more from O'Grady. He had to keep winning and winning to get ranked and get a shot at the lightweight title. He traveled to Scotland to face Jim Watt, but a head butt got his forehead bleeding and he lost. O'Grady's next title opportunity was in Atlantic City against Hilmer Kenty of Texas. When Kenty won the World Boxing Association crown in 1980, he was living in Detroit. Kenty was famed trainer Emmanuel Steward's first pupil to win a world title, and he was Detroit's first world title-holder since Joe Louis more than 30 years before.

It was boxer Kenty versus puncher O'Grady, and O'Grady overwhelmed the champ with harder blows and knockdowns in the second and eighth rounds en route to a 15-round unanimous decision. Kenty carved up O'Grady pretty well, too, but the most telling impact came from a clash of heads, which scared him into believing he was going to lose a second title fight in a row because of a head butt. This time he didn't bleed as much as he did against Watt and the contact made him angry. While Kenty kept landing jabs, O'Grady bulled his way past them to score with the heavier blows.

The funny thing about O'Grady's reign as lightweight champ for all of his popularity was that it was so short. He never did defend the WBA title and had it stripped. Then he went on to other pursuits as a TV boxing commentator and a real estate businessman.

Ray "Boom Boom" Mancini, proudly connected with Youngstown, Ohio, was another extremely popular face in the boxing world at the time. Mancini was the son of Lenny Mancini, a promising lightweight of the 1940s who was deemed to be a future champion until being wounded during World War II. When Ray took up the profession, he became an extension of the old man. They shared the same dream, and Boom Boom made it come true when he captured the WBA lightweight title from Arturo Frias in Las Vegas in 1982.

Immediately before that victory for his family, Mancini fought three straight times in Atlantic City. In October 1981, he faced the great Alexis Arguello at Ballys Park Place Hotel Casino in a challenge for the World Boxing Council lightweight crown and suffered the first loss of his career in a 14th-round technical knockout. Arguello was a future Hall of Famer from Nicaragua, a multiple-weight-class champion, and later mayor of Managua, the Nicaraguan capital. A gentleman boxer who some felt might have been over the hill, he eventually took his own life. But Arguello had fought a skillful bout and had surprised Mancini.

The only thing for Mancini to do was rebuild. Two and a half months later, Boom Boom lived up to his nickname and used two molecule-altering left hooks to knock out Manuel Abedoy of Mexico at the same Atlantic City location. Mancini had been discovered by trainer Murphy Griffith in a national amateur tournament and for a manager he had the former sportswriter David Wolf. Boom Boom was trying to put Arguello in his rearview mirror and think ahead, but he had trouble doing so.

Mancini had a bit of a roguish look: wide forehead, unruly dark hair, and eyes that came off a little sad even when he laughed. It was an Old West, lived-in face that girls loved. Those looks, coupled with his aggressive style and punching power, contributed to his fan popularity. Ray was still only 20 when he took on Julio "Diablito" Valdez of the Dominican Republic in Atlantic City in late January 1982. This was a pivotal contest. If he lost, Mancini would drop out of the ratings and might never be able to swim his way back in. If he won, he was guaranteed a title fight.

The knockout power that Mancini was blessed with often prompted the playing of the rock song "Boom, Boom, Out Go the Lights" when he was in the house. It made more sense to play it after he had delivered in such fashion, but when Mancini met Valdez at the Sands Hotel & Casino, it was played over the loudspeaker as he bounded up the steps to the ring. Was this a foreshadowing? It didn't matter much because a minute into the 10th round of the scheduled 12-rounder, the lights went out for Valdez.

The victory meant that Mancini had done enough to satisfy the powers that be and qualify for a world title shot against Arturo Frias. Promoter Bob Arum said the fight would be in Las Vegas or Atlantic City. It would have been a coup for Atlantic City, but ultimately the August 5, 1982 fight was set for The Aladdin in Vegas.

It was the chance of a lifetime—really the chance of two lifetimes with dad thrown in. But no one could imagine that the scheduled 15-rounder would turn into the round of a lifetime. Mancini's entire life changed in one three-minute stanza. There was no feeling-out process when the bell sounded for the first round. The fighters charged forward and began throwing haymakers.

Frias almost immediately clocked Mancini with a right that sent ripples of pain through his body down to his toes. Somehow he stayed upright. While he was recovering, Frias unloaded a combination that cut Mancini. But rather than become demoralized and retreat, he clobbered Frias with a big punch in the middle of the ring and down went Arturo. The shot was such a hard one that although Frias beat the 10-count, he was still wobbly. He backpedaled into a corner and Mancini stalked him, throwing rights and lefts until Frias was ready to tumble. The fight was stopped and Boom Boom Mancini became world lightweight champion with a first-round technical knockout. Against Julio Valdez in Atlantic City, he had said, "The ring's no place to be a gentleman." In Las Vegas he proved it.

Mancini experienced a troubling and haunting incident in November 1982 when South Korean boxer Deuk-Koo Kim died five days after being pummeled by Ray's fists. From the elation of winning a championship to depression over the accidental death of a fellow fighter, Mancini's emotions were on a roller-coaster. Although he did defend his title twice more, he retired with a 29-5 record and went on to other things in life, including producing films. A biography, *The Good Son: The Life of Boom Boom Mancini*, was published in 2012.

Greg Page was from Louisville and in another era might never even have visited Atlantic City, but the big-bodied heavyweight with fast hands came into his prime just as A.C. was coming into its prime as a boxing destination. Page fought at the Philadelphia Convention Center in his fourth pro bout and for the first time in Atlantic City in his sixth pro bout. He was affiliated with promoter Butch Lewis, whose top client at the time was Michael Spinks. Spinks lived in Philadelphia and seemed to be fighting in Atlantic City every time he took a deep breath, so it was easy to find work for Page in the area as well.

Anyone who saw Greg Page early in his career came away convinced that he would one day become heavyweight champion. He was gifted with speed and at six-feet-two had good size. What Page seemed to lack was fire. He might show up in the ring with some flab around his waist, tipping the scale in the high 220s. He didn't exude aggressiveness, but he did get results. As an amateur, Page was 94-11. He stopped Frank Brown in three rounds in his Philadelphia fight. Page was only 20 at the time and being from Louisville, he said it was natural to idolize a noted predecessor from the city—that being Muhammad Ali. Since Ali was a stick-and-move guy, Page trained at his own speed to utilize the same type of moves. At the time, he was being billed as "The Louisville Rage," though that nickname seemed to evaporate before long.

Page made his first appearance in Atlantic City in February 1981 to fight Stan Ward with the United States Boxing Association belt at stake. It may not have made much sense, but employing the tried-and-true boxing philosophy that any publicity is good publicity, a couple of days before the 12-round bout, Page sparred with a six-year-old Siberian tiger named Bombay. Both the boxer and the tiger survived.

In the sanctioned fight, Page danced circles around Ward, peppering him with his hard, fast jab and finally stopping him on an eighth-round technical knockout. He fought twice more in Atlantic City and fans there probably thought one day they would be able to boast that they saw the great Greg Page when he was young and on the way up. Only it didn't work out that way.

Page did eventually win a piece of the heavyweight title by stopping South African Gerrie Coetzee, the WBA champ, in Sun City in Coetzee's homeland. But this time, he did not capture the crown while riding a big wave. Page lost his previous two fights before claiming the title. He lost it to Tony Tubbs in his first defense and then lost a fourth out of five fights. He also took some heat as a black man traveling to South Africa to face Coetzee. David Bey had been in line for the title fight, but he refused to meet Coetzee in a country that practiced apartheid. That opened the door for Page, who won convincingly, scoring two knockdowns.

It was almost inexplicable that Page lost to Tubbs in his next fight in Buffalo because he beat him six out of seven times in the amateurs. While busy losing his title in the ring, Page also lost his belt when someone broke into his hotel room and stole it, as well as other valuables.

Page stopped fighting for a while, began training boxers, and then after a long layoff, he resumed his own career and kept fighting until 2001 when he was severely injured in a bout in Kentucky. At the end of the fight, Page was knocked out and there was insufficient medical attention at ringside to rouse him. He was rushed to a hospital and lapsed into a coma in which he remained for a week. Even after being revived, Page suffered numerous side effects from the injury for the next eight years before he passed away at age 50. His boxing record was 58-17-1, and he never regained the title after losing it to Tubbs. When he was tragically and permanently injured in the ring, Page was fighting for only $1,500 a bout.

By the time Marvin Hagler got his first crack at the middleweight title in late November 1979, he was viewed as a sure thing against Vito Antuofermo. But Hagler was dismayed after Antuofermo hung on to the title at Caesars Palace with a 15-round draw. Disheartened and angry, Hagler won three more fights, including taking revenge on Bobby Watts in Portland, Maine of all locations. By then, Antuofermo was no longer champ. Alan Minter had taken the belts and if Hagler wanted them, he had to go to England, Minter's home, to get them.

Marvin Hagler at last became champion on September 27, 1980 at Wembley Arena in London when he scored a third-round technical knockout of Minter. After that he went on a rampage, cleaning out the 160-pound division with victories over Fulgencio Obelmejias, Antoufermo and Mustafa Hamsho before signing to fight William "Caveman" Lee in Atlantic City. For Hagler, it marked only the beginning of vindication and proof that he was the best middleweight in the world. Sporting a shaved head, Fu Manchu facial hair and a penetrating stare, he fought with the desperation of someone who was always trying to fend off a bully attempting to steal his lunch money.

That outlook and attitude had deep roots. While Hagler was closely identified with Brockton, Massachusetts, the same community south of Boston that spawned heavyweight champion Rocky Marciano, he was actually born in Newark, New Jersey. He was a kid trying to grow up when that city was going to hell because of decay and race riots.

Hagler was into his teens before escaping Newark. He grew up without a father, and during the 1968 riots after Dr. Martin Luther King Jr. was assassinated, Hagler hid under a bed to dodge bullets. Anger was burnt into his soul, and he did not trust white people. Hagler wore his hatred on his sleeve and in his scowl, and he expressed his inner savageness in the ring, channeling the bad stuff from his past through his fists into the opponent's face. It was not until he disposed of the unwanted description "the uncrowned middleweight champion of the world" and instead made it official that Hagler began to change. He would say, "I'm a lot meaner now than I was before," because everyone he fought was going after his title, but he seemed different, probably because he had reached the great goal of his life. It wasn't clear how changed Hagler was if the only difference was that he stopped talking about tearing challengers apart and just did it.

One day, I cornered Hagler for a chat on a patio outside a hotel in Houston where he was on assignment to do closed-circuit TV commentary for the upcoming Sugar Ray Leonard–Thomas Hearns bout. He displayed new levels of candor, revealing his inner feelings as he spoke about his past and his outlook after winning the middleweight crown. "I'm happy," he told me, "but I'm not satisfied. I'm meaner when I'm training for a fight. I'm happy the way things are for me. But if you get satisfied, you tend to relax."

Once he had eased into the rhythm of taking charge of the title and making the calls on who deserved a title shot, Hagler looked better and better in the ring, more formidable even than he had been on his way up. When he signed to fight Bill Lee, who listed his home as Detroit, the world was reminded that Lee was originally from Philadelphia—still another Philadelphia middleweight.

Lee's father, Bill Sr., is the one who got him into the gym in North Philadelphia when he was young, but he was nicknamed Caveman by his Philadelphia Boy Scout troop because he wore his sideburns long and was kind of hairy. Lee didn't like the moniker much at first, but as a fighter in a profession where he could knock people out, it kind of grew on him. When he checked into Ballys Park Place Casino Hotel for the Hagler fight, Lee was presented with an unusual but emblematic gift not routinely given to other guests. It was a brown plastic toy club. Whether Lee was going to wield it like a true caveman on Hagler or would resemble Bam-Bam from "The Flintstones" was open to question.

More into the flute than the club, Lee did not plan to wear leopard-design shorts into the ring, but going along with the club gag, he did wave the plastic toy at Hagler when they appeared at a pre-fight event. There were times in his life when an irritated Marvin might have grabbed the club and stuck it somewhere the sun don't shine, but on this occasion, he kind of chuckled. Lee was 8-1 as a pro when he departed Philadelphia for Detroit to become a sparring partner for Thomas Hearns at the Kronk Gym and stayed on, making himself into a world contender at 22-2 by the time he received this title chance.

Caveman fell under the sway of trainer Emmanuel Steward who looked him over and proclaimed, "You should be a contender yourself." Steward helped Lee to fill that bill, and he got to within one clubbing of the title. But Hagler was not particularly intimidated by someone calling himself "Caveman" and threatening his well-being with a plastic club. "I'm going to send Caveman back to the Stone Age" was Hagler's snappy comeback.

One thing that traditionally occurs at title fights is for the tuxedo-clad ring announcer to introduce celebrities at ringside. Typically, there are a number of former champions in attendance to watch how modern-day guys treat their old weight class, or current contenders to study the champion they someday wish to meet. Then there are show business types. On the afternoon that the Hagler and Lee fisticuffs were set, there was a rarely seen celebrity on hand.

Those who saw the Academy Award–winning movie *Raging Bull* about former champ Jake LaMotta will surely recall the gorgeous young blonde he fell for in real life and the film. Not long before the Hagler–Lee fight, Vicky LaMotta, considerably older but showing very little wear, posed nude in *Playboy* magazine. She was at ringside and if red-blooded American male inclinations could be counted on, she was going to be more the object of eyeball study in the single minute between rounds than all that happened in the fighters' corners. The only problem was that there were no breaks between rounds. Hagler knocked out Lee in the first round of a scheduled 15-round bout that lasted barely more than a minute. Since Vicky was seated right behind me, I would have had unobstructed staring time. As it was, glimpses of a clothed Ms. LaMotta were about as short as Caveman Lee's time as an official contender.

Lee charged out to face Hagler, but as a southpaw, Marvin immediately staggered Caveman with a right jab. The champ followed with a left and a right, and Lee hit the floor. Knockdown. He was up at an eight count and seemed coherent to referee Larry Hazzard. About 40 seconds later, Hagler trapped Lee against the ropes and was teeing off with right hand after right hand when Hazzard jumped in. Lee slipped down to the second rope before Hazzard caught him and carefully laid him flat on the canvas. That was that. Bye-bye, Caveman and bye-bye, Vicky.

This was also the last time Marvin Hagler fought in the Philadelphia area and the last time he fought a middleweight from Philadelphia. He defended the title eight more times before losing a controversial decision to Sugar Ray Leonard in 1987. Rumors of a rematch persisted for a long time, but Hagler never fought again. He retired with a 63-2-2 lifetime record and was inducted into the International Boxing Hall of Fame in 1993.

Hagler moved to Italy, where he began a new career making movies. He has rarely made public appearances in the United States in recent years, but he regularly attends the annual induction festivities at the Boxing Hall of Fame in Canastota, New York.

One of the most famous and accomplished fighters of his generation or any other, the great middleweight champion spends most of his time quietly being Marvin Hagler—far from the ring that made his reputation.

13

JOURNEYMEN, HOPEFULS AND DREAMERS

J immy Young was a heavyweight without a punch, but he was a skilled boxer who made opponents miss and look bad. Seemingly always laconic, Young convinced everyone who watched him that he had more talent than he used, that he wasn't hungry enough to become a world champion, but could have been if he applied himself. How much of that was true and how much was a bad rap is uncertain, but Young twice came close to winning a piece of the heavyweight title anyway because he was a brilliant defensive practitioner and at times seemed as light on his feet as Fred Astaire. The Philadelphia heavyweight could be compared to a professional sports team that was always good enough to make the playoffs, but never good enough to go all the way.

Young stood six-feet-two and did his best work when he weighed about 215 pounds. When he weighed in at 220, there was going to be some flab around his midsection, and that image was bad for public relations. Young was soft-spoken and a nice guy to be around, but he wasn't a glib talker and didn't make jokes during his pre-fight preparations. But he built a following anyway because he came from Philly and he showed people that at his very best, he was pretty darned good.

For those who didn't think he had a warrior's mentality, Jimmy Young demonstrated his guts by his willingness to take on anyone who had a name in the heavyweight division, anywhere, and at all points in his career. That pro career began in October 1969 when Young was 20 and continued (for too long) into 1988 when he retired with a record of 34-19-2 with one no-contest. In between, Young fought Earnie Shavers and Ron Lyle twice, as well as Muhammad Ali, George Foreman, Ken Norton, Greg Page, Tony Tubbs, Michael Dokes, Gerry

Cooney, Ossie Ocasio, Marvin Stinson, Jody Ballard and Tony Tucker. He drew with Shavers, beat Lyle both times, beat Foreman, Stinson and Ballard, and most importantly, almost beat Ali.

On April 3, 1976, Ali put his heavyweight crown at risk in Landover, Maryland, and Young nearly swiped it. The fight went all 15 rounds to a decision and although Ali won a unanimous verdict, it may have been Young's finest hour. Still, his 1977 bout with George Foreman was nearly its equal, even if no title was at stake. In a battle in Puerto Rico, Young knocked Foreman down in the 12th round to win the match. The fight was chosen as *The Ring* magazine's fight of the year, and Foreman retired after his defeat. In one of the more remarkable stories in boxing history, he returned to win the heavyweight title after 10 years in retirement.

Jimmy Young topped Foreman, beat Ballard, and then was matched against Ken Norton in a title elimination bout. Norton won a 15-round decision and then was awarded the vacant World Boxing Council crown because Leon Spinks refused to fight the winner. That sort of bad luck dogged Young. Yet he was the master of the bob and weave, part of the science of the sweet science. His facial expression ranged from stoical to blank in the ring, and he picked his spots with his punches. Among his 34 wins, Young scored just 11 knockouts. He out-pointed people more than he out-punched them. This didn't always play well with the crowds in the bombs-away division, but it was smart boxing.

The biggest problem Jimmy Young had was that in the late 1970s and early 1980s, he grew indifferent about boxing for a while, and although he still took fights for money, he didn't focus to get into first-rate condition. Soured by his close-call losses, Young became an opponent rather than someone to be feared, living more off of his name than his present reputation. In 1980, as Gerry Cooney was looking for a tune-up before his title fight with Larry Holmes, Young's name surfaced. He accepted the challenge, but the scene at his weigh-in was stunning. When Young stripped off a T-shirt before stepping on the scale, he looked fat. When the officials read his weight at 233, Young's trainer George Benton reacted with disbelief and unhappiness. "You weighed 224 pounds yesterday," he said to Young.

"I just ate," Young replied.

"What did you eat, a cow?" Benton quipped.

The day before the weigh-in, Young did not leave a big impression of readiness with me when we talked. I suggested that he didn't look all that interested in what was going on. "You can tell?" he asked.

The fight ended after the fourth round when Young was cut on the forehead above his right eye and was gushing blood in his corner. He made a trip to a hospital for nine stitches.

Late in 1981, Young took a fight that he hoped would jump-start his endeavors. He was 32 and weighed in at 221 pounds to face Tommy Franco Thomas in Pittsburgh. Before the fight, Young addressed about 200 interested listeners at a luncheon and his telling comment summed up his career to date: "I guess you've all been wondering what's happened to me in the last couple of years."

Young won that fight in a 10-round decision, his fifth victory in a row, but then the wondering really began. He promptly lost to Greg Page (no disgrace there), but he endured a six-bout losing streak that ended his career as a serious contender. Young kept fighting periodically well into 1988 and won the last fight of his career against Frank Lux.

The world was not very kind to Jimmy Young after his career ended. He ran into financial difficulties, battled a drug problem, and then his health went bad. In February 2005, he was in the hospital when he died of a heart attack. Young was 56.

There are many ways that boxing can be construed as an odd sport, but the strangest aspect of all is when friends fight friends for money. They may be guys who grew up together, went to school together, worked out together in the gym, but one day fate or circumstance put them together in the ring to whale on one another for real. They can decline to take the fight, but often enough men who say the other guy is a pal go through with it.

Jimmy Young was in one of those bouts with Marvin Stinson, another Philadelphia heavyweight of the era, in 1981 at the Sands Casino Hotel in Atlantic City. No one was more philosophical about this seeming contradiction than Stinson, who lost a 10-round decision to Young. Stinson was trying to advance his career by gaining more notoriety. Another easy-going guy outside the ring, he was the same height as Young but more firmly muscled. He had been a terrific amateur with 119 wins, won a national AAU championship, and represented the United States in Cuba in 1974 at the first world amateur championships. Stinson, known as a regular sparring partner for another friend, Larry Holmes, was 12-1-3 at the time he faced Young. "If the price is right, you get in the ring with him," he said of fighting friends as part of the job. "Money is the root of all evil, right? He's your friend when you get in and when you get out." A regular person on the street might hold a grudge if a friend beat him up, but that's professional boxing.

Young knocked down Stinson in the first round and captured an easy decision. Stinson fought only one more time. His next fight was stopped when he was bleeding from a head butt, and he sat in his corner and cried. Stinson remained active as an in-demand sparring partner, working with Holmes for 13 years. Their friendship was strong enough that despite exchanging all those blows, Stinson traveled to Canastota, New York for Holmes' induction into the International Boxing Hall of Fame in 2008.

Decades later, Stinson seemed well-preserved. He had a little pot belly, but mostly looked as if he was in shape, and while a bit more craggy-faced, he also looked younger than his age, which by 2012 was 60. He was also still in the game, working as a trainer.

When Marvin Stinson was a kid in Williamston, New Jersey, he was a magnet for trouble with the law. Not big stuff, but big enough for him to wonder where his life was taking him: "I sat in my cell and told myself that my daddy didn't raise me for this." Stinson got a job working construction and within two weeks went to work to become a boxer. After his shift ended, he hitchhiked to public transportation and took either a train or a bus to Philadelphia for 65 cents. He was successful and had some thrills as soon as he turned pro, fighting on the cards at the sold-out Blue Horizon. Stinson remembers the quality of the fighters being high because great Philadelphia trainers demanded that their guys take the sport seriously. "We had good trainers and if you quit on them, they wouldn't train you," said Stinson, who had moved into the business of training. He began training because a lot of guys told him he would be good at it. "I love it, man."

The difference between young guys now aspiring to become fighters and the fighters 40 years ago when Stinson started out is a massive gulf. Today's generation is hooked on electronics, and one rule that Stinson has to enforce is to get guys to forget about their cell phones for a couple of hours. He's developed a motto as part of his teacher-pupil lecture: "When you come to the gym, you come to train. If you aren't serious, find somebody else to train you."

One Philadelphia heavyweight who was able to reach the summit of the mountain was "Terrible Tim" Witherspoon. In a long and successful career, interrupted by some dips and a long-running court battle with promoter Don King over money, Witherspoon twice captured versions of the heavyweight championship. The catchy nickname was coined by Muhammad Ali when the Philadelphian worked for him as a sparring partner. It stuck.

Witherspoon's first fight was in 1979 and his last in 2003, and he finished with a record of 55-13-1. Tim combined good punching power and good boxing style to make a mark early, and he won numerous fights over name opponents. He set the tone when in just his eighth pro bout, he decisioned Marvin Stinson over 10 rounds in Atlantic City. "It was a real confidence builder," he admitted. A victory over Alonzo Ratliff left Witherspoon at 13-0 and facing a match against Leon Spinks. An intelligent, thoughtful boxer who enjoyed kidding around, he said that the older of the fighting Spinks brothers was his idol: "He was my idol because I liked his warlike type of fighting."

Spinks grabbed the heavyweight crown from Muhammad Ali in one of boxing's biggest upsets in 1978, but the Witherspoon–Spinks bout never came off. It didn't hurt Witherspoon's advancement, though. A win over Renaldo Snipes positioned him for his first title shot in 1983 against Larry Holmes. In what would have been a huge upset, Witherspoon lost a split decision. Rarely do losses in boxing enhance stature, but this defeat did improve his standing since he was in just his 16th pro fight after a short amateur career.

Wins over Floyd "Jumbo" Cummings and James Tillis set up Witherspoon for another title shot and he defeated Greg Page, Larry Holmes' WBC successor. Although he lost the belt in his first defense to Pinklon Thomas, Witherspoon bounced back and won the World Boxing Association title from Tony Tubbs in 1986. As he fought on into his forties, he lost more frequently before finally hanging up his gloves at 45. When he finally stopped throwing punches for pay, Witherspoon switched to training others to throw them, including his son Tim Jr.

One prominent fighter victimized by the saturation of the light-heavyweight marketplace was Philadelphia's Jerry "The Bull" Martin. In his prime he was surrounded, not only by top-rate talent in the 175-pound weight class from around the world, but also from around the area. Matthew Saad Muhammad of Philadelphia was the World Boxing Council champion, and he was succeeded by Dwight Muhammad Qawi from Camden. Michael Spinks moved to Philadelphia and won the World Boxing Association title. That was not long after Turnersville's Mike Rossman held the belt.

"Philadelphia is famous for middleweights," said Philadelphia boxing historian John DiSanto, "but Philadelphia has had more great light-heavyweights." Jerry Martin was originally from Antigua in the West Indies where cricket was the top sport and boxing ranked below checkers in the hierarchy of the most popular. Martin couldn't even find anyone to train him. "In Antigua, there's a boxing card about once every three years," he lamented.

Martin fled to New York, but he couldn't get hooked up with the right connections to advance his career. One day, he read about Joe Frazier's Gym and moved to Philadelphia. Promoter J. Russell Peltz worked to find Martin fights before he developed into a world-ranked prospect. To this day, Peltz says that one of his biggest thrills in boxing was in May 1980 when Martin went into Rahway State Prison as an unknown and emerged as a budding star because of the way he handled James Scott in a 10-round decision. "That was a big day," Peltz recalled. "He beat the crap out of him. Jerry had a bunch of friends from Antigua with him, 12 or 15 of them, and afterwards we all went out to dinner. It was just a wonderful experience."

Less than two months later, Jerry Martin was in a title fight for the WBA crown against Eddie Mustafa Muhammad. Martin's strength was his strength, hence his nickname. The Bull's style was to keep pressure on his opponents, not to box on the outside. He spoke English with a West Indies accent, and was never long-winded. When Martin discussed the scouting report on him, he said simply, "I want to slug."

Speaking of the title bout, Mustafa Muhammad declared "bring it on" because he was a counter-puncher who loved to fight guys like Martin. He turned out to be right, and Martin was stopped in the 10th round of the 15-round fight. Some fighters aim for a title shot as the culmination of their career and then if they lose, they also lose their drive and confidence. To some extent, that happened to Jerry Martin. "The title fight put me way down," he admitted. "I've got to come back up and get that security and confidence back."

Martin did so by winning his next three fights. That rebuilt his résumé and his outlook. Fourteen months after the loss to Eddie Mustapha Muhammad, he had a date with Matthew Saad Muhammad for a shot at the WBC crown at the Golden Nugget Casino in Atlantic City. Some wondered if Martin deserved the second title chance so soon because he had not been beating ranked contenders, but only second-tier opponents. Martin thought otherwise. "This is a brand-new day," he announced in the days leading up to the showdown with Saad Muhammad.

It was Matthew Saad Muhammad's eighth title defense and all of a sudden, he seemed to be channeling Muhammad Ali, who used verbal trickery and insults to discombobulate his opponents. "You're too ugly to be champion," Saad Muhammad informed Martin. The Bull could only laugh at that comment. Normally, boxers only make such "beauty contest" comparisons after fights when the various cuts, swellings and bruises are totaled to help determine who won.

Saad Muhammad knew enough about Martin's cavalry-charge approach to recognize that the issue was going to be protecting his cheekbones from his opponent's coiled right fist, not so much from his jabs. That was all Martin could do. Not that he worried about being labeled a puncher. "I've got fire-power," he insisted.

So did Matthew Saad Muhammad, as well as the ability to take a punch. Martin threw all he had at Saad Muhammad's head, but it bounced off. Saad Muhammad threw all he had at Martin, including some particularly lethal left hooks in the 11th inning, and The Bull was going down like a giant redwood tree when referee Larry Hazzard caught him and called him out. Martin's trainer Leon Tabbs was infuriated and rushed out of the corner at Hazzard. Tabbs screamed long and loud and even bumped into the referee, but the noise couldn't undo the decision. Tabbs was fined for his behavior.

Martin was so unhappy with the stopping of the fight that he almost cried in his corner. In his mind, he had done the equivalent of a field sobriety test when he clearly answered Hazzard that he was OK and counted to five. But for Hazzard that didn't cut it and he stopped the fight, saying that Martin's eyes had rolled up in his head. "He was hurt," the referee added. "He was a sitting duck for Saad Muhammad."

Three months later, Matthew Saad Muhammad no longer owned the crown. Dwight Muhammad Qawi staged a coup and became the new champ—still another Philadelphia area guy grabbing a light-heavyweight belt. Jerry Martin watched those proceedings with interest. Then, without taking another fight in between, he launched right back into title mode. Just six months after Martin fell to Saad Muhammad, he met Dwight Qawi in Las Vegas. It was Qawi's first title defense. Everyone agreed that a Martin–Qawi title fight should be held nowhere except the Philadelphia area (Atlantic City included). In a not-so-unusual development for boxing, logic did not prevail, and the host became the Showboat Hotel & Casino. The main reason was that there was a dispute over dates given out to rival promoters for another fight card in Atlantic City.

Martin, who is six-feet-one, may have thought his height would give him an advantage over Qawi at five-feet-seven, but it didn't help. It was as if Qawi had appropriated Martin's nickname for the night. He bulled his way in and clobbered him. Martin was done in the sixth round.

That was the third strike for Jerry Martin. He had three title tries, all against opponents good enough that he was not favored over any of them. When he retired in 1984, Martin was 25-7. The Bull was a major-league warrior, but he always ran into a matador who was a little bit slicker.

Those in boxing who are slick in the ring are called boxers. Those in boxing who are slick outside the ring are called businessmen. Actually, they are mostly promoters. But boxing is very much a political sport. Unlike Major League Baseball, the National Basketball Association or NASCAR, there is no one clear-cut boxing authority. There are international organizations that sanction title fights, but almost every state has its own athletic association that supervises the bouts within its borders.

During the late 1970s and early 1980s, Pennsylvania had one of the most important and active athletic associations, but with the proliferation of casinos in Atlantic City as hosts for numerous world championship fights, New Jersey was clearly ascendant. The commissioner of the New Jersey State Athletic Association at the time was former heavyweight champion Jersey Joe Walcott. He held one of the most important jobs in the world of boxing at the time. His deputy, Robert W. Lee, the details man in the hierarchy, also held significant power.

Not every state athletic association was sophisticated enough to deal with even the most basic safety issues. In New Jersey, fighters could count on ring doctors who knew their stuff and referees who were among the best in the world. They had more experience than similar officials in other states. Nevada, New York, Pennsylvania and California were probably the only other states as busy, though for a time Atlantic City pretty much led the universe in holding world title bouts with only Las Vegas contending in that ranking.

If you worked as a judge, referee, doctor or other type of official, it was an exciting time to be part of the sport in New Jersey. World champions and top challengers were dropping by your neighborhood every week, it seemed. Yet not all of the work was glamorous. Sometimes the boxing game was not on the up-and-up. Imagine that. There was the fight card in 1981 at the Playboy Hotel & Casino in Atlantic City when Robert Lee, the New Jersey deputy commissioner, played the role of investigator and the heavy in a mini-drama, and it was not the heavyweight class being discussed.

Lee got a tip that one fighter on the card was not who he claimed to be. The boxer competed on the undercard of the Matthew Saad Muhammad–Dwight Muhammad Qawi light-heavyweight title fight using the name Stan Tull. However, it was alleged that the same person fought in Brooklyn a day earlier under the name Ra'Sean Parker. That boxer was knocked out in the first round of the fight in New York and in the third round of his fight in New Jersey. For safety reasons, cooperating states required boxers who had been KO'd to lay off fighting for 30 days. There really was a Parker and there really was a Tull, and only two months earlier they had both appeared on the same card elsewhere in New Jersey. Robert Lee even had an eyewitness to the Brooklyn card in house who said he saw Parker get knocked out the night before.

Lee confronted the fighter listed as Tull, who admitted that he was really Parker, but denied that he had fought in Brooklyn the same weekend. In a classic explanation of why he used the name Tull in Atlantic City, the boxer said he was trying to hide his earnings of about $200 from his girlfriend who was the mother of his daughter because she was pressuring him for money: "If you went through as much agony as I have, you would do that, too."

Parker said he had never heard of Tull, even though they had fought on the same card together, and just happened to pick a name at random when he agreed to the Atlantic City fight. Although an angered Lee said Parker might be banned for life from fighting in New Jersey, that did not happen at the time. Ra'Sean Parker, who retired with a 1-10-1 record, fought six more times—three times in Philadelphia and three times in Atlantic City—before retiring. A glance at Parker's lifetime record does note that he fought two days in a row in Brooklyn and Atlantic City on December 18 and 19, 1981.

Only two weeks after the Parker fiasco came to light, the United States Boxing Association and its 28 member states agreed to implement a new identification system for boxers that required them to hold a passport license. At the time, Robert Lee was also president of the USBA. It was a step toward preventing boxers from using phony names or impersonating others in order to fight throughout most of the country.

Additional steps were implemented in New Jersey to protect boxers from themselves early in 1982 when the athletic commission for the first time banned 10 fighters from being licensed in the state again. A study was made of numerous cards and a notice was sent to 10 fighters to attend a hearing if they wanted to keep fighting in New Jersey. None of the fighters showed up and then all were banned. The boxers had a combined record of 5-56-2 and had been knocked out 40 times as a group. "I saw every one of them fight and every one of them should be stopped because they don't have the overall ability to protect themselves in the ring," Robert Lee maintained.

There were definitely some horrible records listed alongside the men's names, most of them from New Jersey, a couple from Philadelphia and a few from outside the region. The best two records among those banned were 3-11 and 2-10-2. The other eight boxers had never won a fight. The decision to limit their boxing involvement to watching Rocky movies was for their own good.

One thing lovers of baseball say about their sport is that any time they go to the ballpark, they are liable to see something happen that they have never witnessed before. Neither basketball nor football lovers make that same claim. But followers of boxers must be on the alert for the distinctive, the remarkable and the unprecedented.

One day in late 1981 at the Playboy Hotel & Casino, activity took place in a bout that no one involved could recall ever seeing. Welterweights Mike Picciotti of Upper Darby in the Philadelphia suburbs was fighting Johnny Cooper of Blackwood, New Jersey on the neutral territory of Atlantic City in a scheduled 10-round bout.

In the fourth round, referee Joe O'Neill asked the ringside physician Dr. Michael Sabia to examine a cut near the corner of Picciotti's right eye. Blood was flowing like a river, and Sabia told O'Neill to stop the bout. The referee waved off the action at two minutes and 25 seconds of the round. He then raised Cooper's arm, signifying him as the winner.

Up until then, things were pretty routine. But chief ring physician Frank Doggett and New Jersey State Athletic Commissioner Jersey Joe Walcott happened to be ringside and disagreed with the move. Picciotti was re-examined and cleared to go after Walcott ruled. The arguments that ensued were almost as violent as the fighting. After a 10-minute delay, Cooper's gloves were laced up again and the boxers continued. When the bell sounded to end the event, the judges' scoring went for Picciotti by a split decision.

Johnny Cooper was hot. The phrase "We wuz robbed" was coined by boxing manager Joe Jacobs in 1932 when his client Max Schmeling apparently defeated Jack Sharkey, but the decision went the other way. Cooper echoed it and said that winning and losing the same fight didn't seem fair to him. But fairness is just what Walcott invoked when he explained his decision: "I insisted the fight continue in fairness to both fighters."

It was interesting that Jersey Joe Walcott admitted he had no memory of seeing anything like this in a ring before. And judge Harold Lederman chimed in with a similar comment: "I haven't seen this before." If anyone has seen such a decision since that time, it's been kept pretty quiet.

Another one of those you-can't-believe-it-if-you-don't-see-it fights occurred on a 1981 Philadelphia card at Martin Luther King Arena. Jimmy Clark, the 1977 National Golden Gloves heavyweight champion (he beat Greg Page in the final), met Robert Colay of Pleasantville, New Jersey in a six-rounder. Hailing from Coatesville, Pennsylvania, Clark attended West Chester State and became a lawyer after a 17-1-1 pro career. This was his fifth pro fight.

The card attracted nearly 1,800 live witnesses and was shown on ESPN. Colay received more exposure than he bargained for when his trunks split right up the back in the second round. Because he didn't listen to his mother to make sure he wore clean underwear in case of an automobile accident, the world learned that Colay was butt-naked under the shorts. There was considerable laughter as his bottom was advertised to the spectators. To his credit, Colay did not cease firing punches. He overcame his embarrassment by splitting Clark's lip open with a punch.

Keenly aware of their man's unfortunate predicament, Robert Colay's corner assistants scrambled to fix the situation and stuffed white towels down the back of his shorts. But because the shorts were too tight to begin with, the towels served less as a patch than an imitation of the kind of cottontail Playboy bunnies wore. The insult already incurred, Colay suffered the injury of being stopped by Clark's punches in the fifth round.

When Philadelphia boxers of the late 1970s and early 1980s think back to that era, one thing they feel they had in common, and one thing they believe the gyms had in common, was good teachers. The trainers of the time all seemed like old wise men. But 30 years later, most of them have passed away, those legendary gym rats for whom the smell of liniment was as intoxicating as the smell of coffee.

Willie Reddish died at age 75 in 2008. He became a heavyweight contender (41-12-4) while working full-time as a stevedore on the Philadelphia docks. Later, he ran a barbershop and a grocery store and drove a dump truck. Then he became a trainer and guided Sonny Liston to the heavyweight championship.

Sam Solomon was roly-poly and bald in his later years, but he was a strong athlete in his youth as a catcher in the Negro Leagues and an amateur fighter with 300 bouts. He was known for training Leon Spinks when he upset Muhammad Ali for the heavyweight championship and for training Ernie Terrell,

Matthew Saad Muhammad and Frank Fletcher. Born in Savannah, Georgia, Solomon's family moved to Philadelphia when he was a child. The trainer was retired when he died at age 83 in 1998.

Joe Gramby, manager of Philadelphia lightweight champion Bob Montgomery and heavyweight contender Randall "Tex" Cobb, died at age 78 in 1991. Gramby, who had been both an amateur and professional fighter after moving north to Philadelphia from Norfolk, Virginia when he was 10, was nicknamed "The Fox" because he was a wily businessman. Philadelphia promoter J. Russell Peltz said Gramby, who wore Italian custom-made suits and silk ties, was an honest man whose word was golden: "He was a man of his word. If he told me the fight was in, it was in. He had a little bit more class than the average fight manager."

One of the classiest of boxers and trainers was George Benton. He was an extraordinary middleweight who, between 1949 and 1970, compiled a record of 62-13-1, but never got to fight for the title. He became a renowned trainer known for improving his disciples' defense, and at various times he coached champions Leon Spinks, Pernell Whitaker, Mike McCallum, Rocky Lockridge, Johnny Bumphus, Evander Holyfield and Meldrick Taylor. Benton was 78 when he died in 2011; he was already a member of the Pennsylvania Boxing Hall of Fame and the World Boxing Hall of Fame.

The biggest tragedy among Philadelphia boxing figures from the days of the special bygone era was the death in a motorcycle crash of middleweight James Shuler. That's because Shuler was still a young man, still seeking to fulfill his potential. He should have been looking forward to decades more of life, just like other Philadelphia icons.

Jimmy Shuler was a good kid, a good man, and was showing signs of becoming a great boxer, but he could not escape the streets of Philadelphia. They could have played the Billy Joel song "Only the Good Die Young" for him when he perished in a collision with a tractor-trailer in March 1986. The thing that made it all especially sad was that so many other young men could not escape the worst of the inner city—the drugs and crime, the pressure to conform and break the law—but Shuler was on his way; he had put that behind him.

James Shuler, whose younger brother Marty also fought, won two national amateur boxing championships, a Pan American Games silver medal, and qualified for the 1980 U.S. Olympic team. Much of that team was killed in plane crash in Poland, but Shuler was not on the flight because he was injured. Similarly, another Philadelphia area fighter who should have been on the plane but was also injured was heavyweight Jimmy Clark.

Turning pro late in 1980, Shuler won his first 22 fights. Although he lost his next, and last, fight to Thomas Hearns by knockout in the first round, everyone believed his future was bright and that he would become the middleweight champion soon enough. The accident that killed Shuler occurred a week after the Hearns bout when he was riding his new, red Kawasaki motorcycle and hit the stalled truck. Evidence indicated that Shuler had skidded 50 feet into and under the truck and died at the scene.

Open, chatty, intelligent and usually showing a big, gleaming smile, Shuler was devoted to his family. The first time I interviewed him as an amateur at Joe Frazier's Gym, he brought his mother along. You don't see that every day. When Shuler collected a $250,000 purse for fighting Hearns, he gave gifts to his parents and his brothers and sisters.

A graduate of Benjamin Franklin High School, where he appeared at a school assembly only a few months before the accident, Jimmy Shuler was not yet 27 when he died. In some ways, he represented the end of the succession of talented middleweights who helped make Philadelphia boxing famous. None of them won the title, but that was Shuler's job. He was going to make up for all of their disappointments. Fight fans told him that on the street all the time as he was moved up through the rankings. Although he was disappointed by the loss to Thomas Hearns, falling to such a great champion was no disgrace. Shuler believed that other chances would beckon and that someday he would be on top of the world—king of the middleweights.

Shuler died too soon to make good on his plan, but Philadelphia always remembered him. In 1994, the James Shuler Memorial Gym opened in the city to nurture the dreams of other young men trying to fight their way to the top.

14

JOE FRAZIER, FATHER; MARVIS FRAZIER, SON

One reason that Joe Frazier gave for not continuing his boxing career after his comeback draw with Floyd "Jumbo" Cummings was that he was going to spend more time passing it forward. He was going to be more involved in making sure that his son Marvis one day succeeded him as heavyweight champ. Joe was very excited by the idea, and what father wouldn't be? It's been an American tradition for sons to follow fathers in the family business, whether it was taking over the farm, running the corner store, or as an executive in the family financial institution. Boxing was the Frazier family sport, even if it wasn't exactly a wholly owned subsidiary of Joe Frazier Inc.

Frazier also spent a fair amount of time singing his lungs out with Joe Frazier and The Knockouts. He belted out tunes instead of belting out fighters. There were a few differences between Marvis and Joe that were apparent to anyone. Joe was born into poverty in South Carolina and was an unknown when he broke into the fight game with his first pro bout in 1965. Frazier was one of 13 children growing up in Beaufort, South Carolina, and he dropped out of school in the sixth grade to help support the family. By age 16, he was living in Philadelphia.

Marvis was the son of a champion, one of the most famous men in Philadelphia, who had made millions in the ring and could afford to raise his family under the best circumstances. Marvis, who called his father "Pop," was an accomplished amateur, which made him somewhat of a known quantity before he turned pro. That was in addition to having a famous last name in the sport. The younger Frazier was closer to six-feet-two than his dad's five-feet-eleven.

Some suspected that Joe pushed Marvis into boxing, but Joe insisted: "I tried to talk him out of it day and night. Every father in this world would like to have a son follow in his footsteps. Now I just want to help him to be a fine man. As long as he wants to fight, I'm going to be there to give him my know-how."

Marvis Frazier won an Amateur Athletic Union national championship and a Golden Gloves national championship. His overall record was 56-2. When still an amateur, Marvis told a boxing magazine that it hadn't always been sunshine and roses growing up as Joe Frazier's kid. Other kids at school picked fights with him and thought it was some kind of feather in their cap if they bullied the former heavyweight champ's son. "I used to get beat up on the street a lot," Marvis said in a 1979 article. "They took my lunch money away. They picked on me."

Soon enough, Marvis was big enough to pick on anybody who was willing to tie on those fat red gloves. His brother Hector also fought, and so did his sister Jackie, who later became a Philadelphia judge. Marvis' goal was to make the 1980 U.S. Olympic team, but he lost in the final rounds. The U.S. boycotted the Moscow Games, anyway, and he turned pro later that year. Joe Frazier won Olympic gold in 1964, filling in for injured Buster Mathis as an alternate while nursing his own broken thumb, showing the kind of boldness and determination that defined his boxing career.

Just before the younger Frazier made the leap to the pros, *The Ring* magazine wrote a story headlined, "Will He Become Part of the First Father-Son Champion Act in History? Marvis Frazier: A Chip Off the Old Blockbuster." It was a heck of a thought, and Joe was working to make it happen.

The younger Frazier made his pro debut at the Felt Forum in New York on his 20th birthday on September 12, 1980, and it was a very happy birthday indeed. More than 2500 fans sang "Happy Birthday" to Frazier, and then he blew out the candles for Roger Troupe at two minutes, eight seconds in the third round. And that was before Madison Square Garden management presented Frazier with a cake.

Marvis halfway grunted, halfway yelled with the delivery of each punch, sort of like the young women of tennis as they slug their backhands. But he was caught off guard in the first round and was staggered by a punch to the jaw. That's what he remembered most clearly from the Troupe fight. "I'm a little disappointed," he remarked. "I knew I was hit, but I wasn't really concerned."

Marvis moved to 2-0 with another fight a month later, but in a disturbing incident in the gym when felled in sparring, he felt a tingling sensation in his neck. That was a replay of what happened when James Broad stopped him in their Olympic Trials bout. Doctors said Frazier had a pinched nerve in his neck, and the issue was raised about whether he could continue in the ring.

Frazier went on hiatus and had an operation on his neck that left him with a six-inch scar and temporarily derailed his career. The diagnosis was that a ligament was pressing against a nerve in his neck. During a six-month break, Marvis was ordained as a deacon in the Greater Harvest Baptist Church of Philadelphia, and he focused more on healing the sick than busting up the aggressive. The deacon healed himself, too, and in April 1981, he returned to the ring. Back in New York, Marvis earned a six-round unanimous decision over Melvin Epps to move to 3-0 and prove that he was healthy.

The Epps fight was about shedding rust. Marvis' next fight was about moving ahead. Against 22-2 Steve Zouski, Frazier dealt with a much more experienced opponent, and one with a fair amount of power. This bout was like the old days when father Joe was in the ring, closing in on guys who couldn't hold him off in tight. Marvis and Zouski spent their entire night inches apart, and young Frazier did the more damage, winning when the fight was stopped in the sixth round. It was a good display of solid power. He also turned the neck story into an old story. "I felt him, but I wasn't hurt," Marvis stated. "I think I proved myself. I guess we can leave that alone about the neck."

After his recuperation and return, Frazier was on the fast track. In his ninth pro fight, he avenged his Olympic Trials loss to Broad in Atlantic City with a 10-round decision. He followed that up with another Atlantic City 10-round decision over Joe Bugner, who eight years earlier met Muhammad Ali for the heavyweight title. Improbably, with a 10-0 mark, Frazier fought Larry Holmes for the heavyweight title in late November 1983. Holmes won his 45th straight fight with a one-round stoppage that was a mismatch.

Although the timing of such a bout was wrong for Frazier's advancement, he compartmentalized the loss and bettered several top fighters over the next few years, defeating six men in a row, including Bernard Benton, James "Quick" Tillis, José Ribalta and James "Bonecrusher" Smith. That positioned Marvis for a title fight against Mike Tyson in 1986, but hauntingly for him, that bout also ended with a one-round knockout. Marvis fought a few more times and retired in 1988 with a 19-2 record.

While the younger Frazier left the fight game, he did not leave religion behind, and in 1994, he was ordained as a minister at the Faith Temple Church of God in North Philadelphia. It was a promotion from deacon. Appropriately enough, the *Philadelphia Inquirer* sent a boxing writer to cover the ceremony when Frazier was ordained. And just as appropriately, when asked if he was nervous when he woke up that morning, Marvis answered with a boxing analogy:

"I was a little bit nervous beforehand. But I figured preaching couldn't be as hard as facing Larry Holmes and Mike Tyson. Then again, now I'm fighting the devil and those two can't be badder than the devil, can they? So I wasn't that nervous."

Marvis got out of the boxing business young. His father kept his famous gym going for years, but in 2008, he lost it for failure to pay back taxes.

Joe Frazier had been a fixture on the north side of the city and was always viewed as one of Philadelphia's sporting icons, so it was shocking when it leaked out in early November 2011 that Smokin' Joe was in hospice care with liver cancer and had only a short time to live.

Offers came in from potential liver donors, but the diagnosis of Frazier's illness came very late. Muhammad Ali, Frazier's foil in possibly the greatest sporting rivalry of the 20th century, said he was praying for Joe to rebound. But by the time everyone learned what was happening, it was too late. Only a couple of days after news of his illness became public, he died at age 67.

Acknowledgment of Joe Frazier's greatness poured in not only from the boxing world, but from many civic leaders and citizens of Philadelphia who viewed him as a local treasure. He passed away on November 7, 2011, and his magnificent career was revisited in many newspaper, magazine and broadcast stories.

Frazier won the world heavyweight championship while Muhammad Ali was in exile, banned from boxing for three and a half years after refusing induction into the Army during the Vietnam War because he was a conscientious objector. When Ali resumed his career after his enforced vacation, he and Frazier engaged in the greatest trilogy of contests in the sport's history.

Their first battle in 1971 at Madison Square Garden was called "The Fight of the Century," and Frazier won a 15-round unanimous decision. The victory further legitimized his hold on the title. Their second fight was a 12-round decision for Ali, also at Madison Square Garden, in 1974, but it was not a heavyweight title fight. In the interim, Frazier lost the crown to George Foreman, who brutalized him in two rounds of the scheduled 15-rounder in Jamaica. The third Ali–Frazier war was "The Thrilla in Manila" in 1975. Ali had regained the title by besting Foreman, and he risked the belt against Frazier in the Philippines. Ali gained the upper hand in the slugfest, and Frazier's trainer Eddie Futch famously ended Joe's quest for the crown in the 14th round for his own good. Both men were so exhausted and battered that the winner and loser went to the hospital.

Any relationship between Ali and Frazier remained cool following the trio of bouts because Ali went overboard in his attempts at humor to distract Frazier and became insulting. Joe never forgave Ali the nastiness of his comments, even though attempts were made by others to bring about a reconciliation. The best that could be said was that things had thawed sufficiently that icicles did not automatically form when the men stood on the same block. The warmth between them may have reached room temperature by the time of Frazier's death.

Joe Frazier's career record was 32-4-1, and there could be no analysis of his career without the trio of bouts with Ali. Frazier was very much admired on his own merits as a symbol of the blue-collar fighter the public loved from his days of wading in and dispensing destruction to any fool willing to stand in front of him. Among Frazier's other name victims as a pro were Billy Daniels, Oscar Bonavena, Eddie Machen, Doug Jones, George Chuvalo, Buster Mathis, Jerry Quarry, Jimmy Ellis, Bob Foster, Joe Bugner, and some of them twice.

Smokin' Joe was so nicknamed because his big punches were like six-guns, and when he shot them off, his opponents fell. Frazier won the heavyweight title in 1970, raising his record to 25-0 with a five-round knockout of Ellis. The once poor boy from South Carolina made it big that day, February 16, with the championship belt as a symbol of leaving his youth in poverty behind. It was the beginning of a great run that made Joe Frazier a household name in the 1970s.

That was the vigorous, energetic, overpowering Joe. During his last years on the planet, he wasn't as spry. Frazier suffered from diabetes and high blood pressure, he had vision problems and occasionally had difficulty walking as the result of a car accident early in the new century. There were times when Frazier seemed more jovial than ever, and times when he seemed embittered and wanted to sue anyone around him for a perceived slight. There were rumors that Joe was hurting financially. There was no telling where such talk began, and Frazier didn't admit it.

Joe Frazier's Gym didn't become a special place for training until Frazier retired. His name attracted a big league clientele. At his gym, the sparring was hot, the training was sharp, and Philadelphia boxing stars prepared there for title bouts. In later years, when the frequency of fights in the area dropped off and the talent was thinner, Frazier said he kept the doors open so that neighborhood kids would have a place to go. He didn't charge them dues.

Joe Frazier was one of the greats of his time and of all time. When he died, the words and memories came pouring forth from other great fighters. While Larry Holmes, whose reign as heavyweight champ lasted seven years and 20 defenses, had more publicized workouts as Ali's sparring partner, he said he got to know Frazier well when the hopeful from Easton, Pennsylvania was still finding his way in the fight game.

Holmes worked as a sparring partner for Frazier, too, and said the hard-hitting champ frightened him. Larry had a wonderful jab, so it made sense for him to stick and move and then follow up with a big right. Because he stayed light on his feet, Frazier called him "Rover." One of the reasons for his roving, besides the fact that it was his natural style, was the fear that Frazier would clock him. "I was afraid," Holmes admitted. "Smokin' Joe—that name scared you. The left hook scared you. He caught me with the left hook and broke three of my ribs. After that I ran even faster."

Several days after Joe Frazier's death on November 7, 2011, there was a two-day public viewing at the Philadelphia Wells Fargo Center and then a five-hour memorial service conducted at the Enon Tabernacle Baptist Church in Cheltenham. It was estimated that more than 3,500 people attended, including such luminaries as Muhammad Ali, promoter Don King, Larry Holmes, Michael and Leon Spinks, Gerry Cooney, and older fighters such as Willie Monroe and Stanley "Kitten" Hayward.

At the memorial service, Frazier was referred to as a man of the people and a sterling representative of the city of Philadelphia. Until his final days, Frazier lived in the heart of town and regularly frequented Con Murphy's bar as just another neighborhood customer. Of course, Joe Frazier was never just that. He was a celebrity who mingled with people and signed autographs when asked. When he died, the *Inquirer* sent a writer to the bar to talk about Frazier's connection to the place and learned that the bartender poured a farewell drink to the former heavyweight champ—Courvoisier brandy and ginger ale on the rocks—and left it on the bar as a tribute. Certainly others toasted Joe Frazier, but this farewell glass served as the ultimate symbol.

It was telling that at the Frazier memorial service there was not only wide representation from the boxing world, but large numbers of people who wished to pay respects even though they had never met Joe. Frazier's career was famous. He knew a great many people in Philadelphia, but his image for those who never met him was solid. He seemed truly accessible—a hard-working man who gave his all in pursuit of a dream and lived it well.

Any boxer that climbed into the ring with Frazier knew he was not a man to trifle with. If you weren't ready, you were going to pay. For that matter, even if you were ready, you were going to pay, because for a period of time, he was the best heavyweight boxer on earth.

Joe Frazier's funeral was called "a joyful celebration" rather than an occasion to mourn, and the Reverend Jesse Jackson presided. Few probably realized that Jackson had presided at the funeral of Joe Louis, one of Frazier's predecessors as heavyweight champion. Although Frazier had 11 children, 22 grandchildren and 21 great-grandchildren, attention among the mourners inevitably focused on Muhammad Ali, Joe's great nemesis in life. It was an ordeal for Ali, suffering from Parkinson's disease, to make the trip, and he was unable to speak publicly. But when Jackson asked those in attendance to "rise and show your love" for Frazier, Ali did so and vigorously applauded.

The death of Joe Frazier and the physical decline of Muhammad Ali could be read as a symbol of the general decline of boxing as a great American sport. In their own way, through their three magnificent fights, the duo represented the best of the sport when they were in their prime. Jesse Jackson, himself a walking symbol of civil rights, was eloquent in summing up the real achievement Joe

After the late heavyweight champion Joe Frazier gave up his gym on North Broad Street, it became a discount furniture store. (Photo by Lew Freedman)

Frazier's life, calling him a person who "came from segregation, degradation and disgrace to amazing grace."

During the service, a championship belt and a pair of gloves were draped over Frazier's casket. Often after the passing of a boxing figure, tribute is paid at ringside before a fight with a 10-bell salute accompanying a moment of silence. For Joe Frazier, the bells rang at the church, the echoing sounds indicating that he was down for the count. Philadelphia's sendoff showed how much its people cared about the former champ. Frazier did not begin life in Philly, but he lived it to the fullest in the city of brotherly love. Those brothers showered him with love when he passed away.

There was one discordant element in the passing of Joe Frazier. It concerned the brick-and-mortar place where he would be best remembered: the gym where he presided and helped train others while on their own quests for boxing greatness. After Frazier lost the gym, the North Broad Street site became a discount furniture store. There always seemed to be a sign advertising a sale on mattresses. On one side of the building, the faded lettering that identified "Joe Frazier's Gym" was barely readable. After Frazier died and was no longer connected to the building, some fans made pilgrimages to leave flowers and stuffed animals at In and Out Furniture and Bedding. For a brief time, the store became just like one of those roadside memorials that sprout up when someone perishes in an automobile accident.

This kind of change in a building's use happens all the time in big cities. Leases run out, businesses fail, and real estate developers speculate. Sometimes history is lost. Almost as soon as Joe Frazier died, Philadelphians began talking about how best to preserve his connection to the city. They talked among themselves and they spoke publicly. Many thought that there should be a statue of Joe Frazier to honor him. His family thought so. Friends thought so. Government officials thought so.

There was no agreement over how or when to erect the statue, but the sentiment was strong. No matter who funded it or how long it took, everyone agreed that creating a lasting monument to Smokin' Joe Frazier was imperative.

15

FISTS STILL FLY

O n a Saturday night in mid-May 2012, the function room at Ballys Atlantic City was filled with fight fans taking respite from the gaming tables and downing cocktails as they roared at the rumbles playing out in front of them. It was a seven-bout show promoted by J. Russell Peltz. There were no famous names. In fact, there wasn't even a 10-rounder on the card. But of the 14 young men who strapped on gloves that night, 10 of them could be construed as Philly fighters. They were either from the city or the immediate New Jersey suburbs.

These were the kind of guys who used to fill out the lineup at the Blue Horizon, only that famous institution had a padlock on its front door at the time. Peltz was in his 42nd year of promoting fights, and one thing he never lost was his own connection to the sport as a fan. Probably more than anyone else in the game, Russell Peltz had the reputation of a promoter who put together even matches. He always made matches that he wanted to see.

Ideally, although it never works out that way, every bout would be action-packed and close. The room had a low ceiling and bright lights, and it held a few hundred seats. Most of the fighters on the card had less experience than some of the guys walking down the streets of South Philadelphia. Some were making their pro debut—always a nerve-wracking venture that might lead to one-and-done careers or the start of something big.

The first bout pitted junior welterweight Korey Pritchett of Camden with his 2-1 record against David Gonzales of Philadelphia, who was 0-0, over four rounds. Gonzales won a unanimous decision. "I was nervous," he admitted of his first bout for pay. "I was wondering what was going to happen. I would have been very mad [if I'd lost]. My first one. That's where you start. It was nothing like I thought it would be. I thought it would be easier."

Gonzales, who said his favorite Philadelphia fighter was former Olympic gold-medal winner, junior welterweight and welterweight champion Meldrick Taylor, brought 20 friends and family members to see him fight. "I'm going to remember that win," he predicted. He would, too. It was like a first at-bat in the majors. A career began with this quiet, four-round victory. No one could know what it held. But for one special night, David Gonzales was 1-0.

Atlantic City still offered opportunities to young fighters. There weren't title fights every week, but there were fights. For this night of fighting, one judge had a definite link to the era of 30 years earlier. Julie Lederman, daughter of Harold, the longtime New York judge and HBO figure, was one of the three score-keepers working the fights just like dad. Julie started going to the fights when she was five, and Harold taught her how to score the way fathers used to teach sons how to keep their own box scores at baseball games. Her other early role model was Carol Polis, who in 1980 was the only woman judge in New Jersey.

Harold Lederman's territory was pretty much New York, Atlantic City and Philadelphia. While HBO gave him an audience as its house official, making

While the legendary Blue Horizon arena on North Broad Street is shuttered and scheduled for a makeover into another business, the boxing mural on the side of the building lives on. (Photo by Lew Freedman)

him better known than any other boxing judge, Lederman always kept his day job as a pharmacist. Casinos and Atlantic City, he believed, had completely altered the boxing landscape in the region: "What it boils down to was the hotels were paying decent fees to promoters. Certainly, it was convenient for the networks. Those were the economics of boxing. You had the economics change."

The dynamics of boxing have changed over the last few decades since Atlantic City pushed its way into the sport and partially shoved Philadelphia aside. Through the 1950s, boxing was a bigger sport in the United States than anything else except baseball. Everything from pro football to college basketball to NASCAR has superseded it since. Athletes from tough neighborhoods became boxers as the way out of poverty. Now they play other sports.

New York City and Madison Square Garden ruled the sport of boxing, but because of its very large number of skilled fighters forming a feeder pool, Philadelphia grew in stature. There were Spectrum fights and Blue Horizon fights, and with gyms in every part of the city, it seemed as if boxing would last forever. When casino gambling was approved in New Jersey, no one imagined that the byproduct of the hotel-casino industry would create an entirely new outlet and focal point for the sport.

When Atlantic City shoved Philadelphia aside, boxing fell on hard times in general and the golden years receded. But boxing is far from dead in Philadelphia. More than almost any other major city, boxing is rooted in the community, and gyms still exist and thrive. Atlantic City still has its shows, and Russell Peltz, having outlasted several big-name promoters who retired or died, is still at the heart of the action.

"Philadelphia has always been one of the big fight locations," said writer Jack Obermeyer, who has covered the sport since 1970. "You had a lot of guys in the city who wanted to be fighters. There were fighters who wanted to fight and arenas to be had. With the society we have today, people tend to look for the easier way out. Boxing is a tough sport." Obermeyer believes that Peltz deserves credit for persevering and keeping boxing alive in Philadelphia: "Russell wanted to make fights for the fans. He wanted to make matches. He was a boxing fan who was a matchmaker. He was able to survive all that."

Nigel Collins grew up in a family that loved boxing. His father and his grandfather were big fans and they influenced him. Collins, who became the longtime editor of *The Ring* magazine, the bible of the sport, remembers sitting on his grandpa's knee as a five-year-old, listening to stories about Gentleman Jim Corbett and Bob Fitzsimmons. That's going back a ways. Collins began following fights in the 1950s, before his 35-year run with *The Ring*. Between the fights he saw in person and the fights he watched on TV, as well as those he heard about from the older males in the clan, Nigel Collins has most of the 20th century covered. "Joe Louis, Sugar Ray Robinson and Archie Moore, they were like family in my family," he recalled.

Later, Collins' extended family became the Philadelphia boxing scene—the fighters and the trainers, all mixed together to create a vibrant atmosphere. "Boxing was part of the culture," Collins noted. "It still is to a degree. It's a place where good fighters come from now, not where they fight. That period [the late 1970s and early 1980s] was the last golden era of Philadelphia boxing."

You can't tell that to someone who is 21 years old and just starting out with stars in his eyes. Those 14 fighters on the Peltz card at Ballys have their own dreams and they are looking to the future, not back at the record books.

Todd Unthank-May of Philadelphia was a light heavyweight in for four rounds against Louis Robinson, another Philadelphia fighter, and Unthank-May, who wore advertising on the seat of his trunks, upped his record to 4-0. It was an action-packed fight, but Unthank-May won an easy decision. He delivered the bigger blows. He also knew the history of his sport, and knew about his elders. He wasn't fighting in a vacuum.

"My favorite fighter is Sugar Ray Robinson," said Unthank-May, who was 23 at the time. "Just a beautiful fighter. I used to watch boxing all the time

On the sidewalk in front of the Blue Horizon there is a marker explaining the historical significance of the famous old fight venue that once hosted fisticuffs by 50 boxers who went on to win world championships. (Photo by Lew Freedman)

instead of playing tag with the other kids. I like Floyd Meriweather, Thomas Hearns and Tyrell Biggs. I like the old George Foreman."

Todd Unthank-May was sweaty and he bled under his lip from a cut, but he was ebullient. He had done some showy things in the ring, and said he hoped that people would remember him for it: "I see a world championship in the future. I'm patient. It's going to take a lot of time, sacrifice, hard work and dedication."

There was one familiar listing on the card, but it was because this boxer had inherited his name. Twenty-five-year-old Fred Jenkins Jr. of Philadelphia took a 5-0 record into his super-middleweight bout against Roberto Yong (4-4-1) of Phoenix. Fred Jr. was trained by his father, Fred Sr., who has been around Philadelphia boxing for more than 40 years. Fred Jr. got more applause than anyone else when he was introduced. But that was before the fight. Roberto Yong was all over Jenkins, his long arms creating all sorts of problems. Yong scored a fourth-round TKO in the scheduled six-rounder, and Jenkins left the ring disconsolate. Russell Peltz tends to get attached to some of his Philadelphia fighters, and he had known this family for four decades: "Fred Sr. fought for me. I didn't want to see him [Fred Jr.] get hurt. This is devastating."

Sitting behind a curtained-off area that served as a dressing cubicle, Fred Jr. got a long talking to from his father. It was as quiet as a library, and the first sound that was uttered loudly enough to travel a dozen feet beyond the curtain was, "It's what we do to come back." That's always the truth when a fighter absorbs a loss, and it is especially so when it is his first loss.

Fred Sr., 56, began boxing in 1971, and after a brief pro career low-lighted by a broken hand that never healed right, he turned to training in 1973. He helped David Reid and Charlie "Choo Choo" Brown win world championships, and he now works at the ABC Recreation Center in Philly. The gym is open to a lot of youths that Jenkins hopes he can keep off the streets and out of trouble. His theme is getting them into a sport instead of getting into trouble. "It's a hard career," he admitted. "You've got to love it. There's good, bad, and ugly. You raise a lot of fighters and other promoters come and take them away. You've got to stay strong for the next guy." Jenkins feels that he is carrying on a tradition by training new generations of local fighters. Being a Philadelphia fighter "meant a lot because everyone knew that Philadelphia always put out great fighters."

There may never have been a better period for legendary Philadelphia fighters than 30 years ago, and boxing historian John DiSanto loved it. He was then a student at Rutgers–Camden, and while he didn't exactly major in boxing, you might say he minored in it. "It was an exciting time," DiSanto recalled. "It was so exciting. There was great boxing. I would leave school and go watch them train in the gyms and then watch them in Philadelphia. I loved the Spectrum days, but was thrilled by Atlantic City because there were so many big fights."

Closed-circuit TV for big fights was popular, and Joe Hand Sr., a onetime police officer, invested $250 (when that was a lot of money to him) to help Joe Frazier's pro career get off the ground with the Cloverlay, Inc. group. Hand was the man who ran the closed-circuit scene in Philadelphia. He is in charge of Joe Hand Promotions, and he started a gym as well. "There were quality fights that people wanted to see," Hand said recently. "The fighters all wanted to fight and it was just a lot of fun."

White-haired with a white mustache and a small beard, Joe Hand at 75 was inducted into the Pennsylvania Boxing Hall of Fame in 2012, and he gave an emotional acceptance speech. "It meant a lot to me," he later recalled, "because I never thought I would be inducted. I guess I didn't think I deserved it." In a sport generally bulging with major-league egos, Hand's humility was touching. Many others did believe that he deserved to be inducted.

John DiSanto was one of them, and talking about the era when he became a boxing fan brought out a smile. Some of his favorites were Jeff Chandler, Matthew Saad Muhammad and Curtis Parker. "You can put Chandler up against the best bantamweights, and you can put him up there with the best Philadelphia fighters of all time. Jeff Chandler's legacy is solid."

DiSanto, whose hair, mustache and beard first showed signs of gray as he moved into his fifties, is passionate about keeping the spotlight on Philadelphia boxing and not letting its history recede in fans' minds. That's why he lobbies on behalf of certain fighters for acceptance into the Pennsylvania Boxing Hall of Fame. He doesn't want to see them overlooked or forgotten. Those efforts and his boxing website make John DiSanto a keeper of the flame for Philadelphia boxing history. "It's a history I love," he freely admitted. "And it's a history I want to keep alive."

LEW FREEDMAN is a veteran sportswriter who covered the boxing scene for the *Philadelphia Inquirer* in the late 1970s and early 1980s. He also wrote for *The Ring* magazine and *Boxing Illustrated*. In addition, he worked for the *Chicago Tribune* and the *Anchorage Daily News*. Freedman is the author of more than 70 books, mostly about sports but also reflecting a longtime interest in Alaska. His numerous sports books include *African American Pioneers of Baseball*, *LeBron James: A Biography, Peyton Manning: A Biography* and most recently, *The 50 Greatest Players in Boston Red Sox History* (Camino Books, 2013). Freedman and his wife Debra live in Indiana.